AF334103

The Careers of British Musicians, 1750–1850
A Profession of Artisans

The study of the social context of music must consider the day-to-day experiences of its practitioners; their economic, social, professional, and artistic goals; and the material and cultural conditions under which these goals were pursued.

This book traces the daily working life and aspirations of British musicians during the sweeping social and economic transformation of Britain from 1750 to 1850. It features working musicians of all types and at all levels – organists, singers, instrumentalists, teachers, composers, and entrepreneurs – and explores their educational background, their conditions of employment, their wages; the systems of patronage that supported them; and their individual perceptions. Deborah Rohr focuses not only on social and economic pressures but also on a range of negative cultural beliefs faced by the musicians. Also considered are the implications of such conditions for their social and professional status, and for their musical aspirations.

DEBORAH ROHR is Associate Professor of Music at Skidmore College in Saratoga Springs, New York. Her research interests include the social history of music, music and gender, and rhythm in tonal music, and she has published in the *Journal of Musicological Research*.

The Careers of British Musicians, 1750–1850

A Profession of Artisans

Deborah Rohr

CAMBRIDGE
UNIVERSITY PRESS

PUBLISHED BY THE PRESS SYNDICATE OF THE UNIVERSITY OF CAMBRIDGE
The Pitt Building, Trumpington Street, Cambridge, United Kingdom

CAMBRIDGE UNIVERSITY PRESS
The Edinburgh Building, Cambridge CB2 2RU, UK
40 West 20th Street, New York NY 10011–4211, USA
10 Stamford Road, Oakleigh, VIC 3166, Australia
Ruiz de Alarcón 13, 28014 Madrid, Spain
Dock House, The Waterfront, Cape Town 8001, South Africa

http://www.cambridge.org

First published 2001

Printed in the United Kingdom at the University Press, Cambridge

Typeface Times 10/12pt   *System* Poltype® [VN]

A catalogue record for this book is available from the British Library

Library of Congress Cataloguing in Publication data

Rohr, Deborah Adams.
The careers and social status of British musicians, 1750–1850: a profession of
artisans / Deborah Rohr.
     p.   cm.
Includes bibliographical references and index.
ISBN 0 521 58095 1
1. Music – Great Britain – 18th century – History and criticism.   2. Music –
Great Britain – 19th century – History and criticism.   3. Music – Social aspects
– Great Britain.   4. Musicians – Great Britain.   I. Title.
ML285.3.R65 2001   305.9'78'094109033–dc21   2001018413

ISBN 0 521 58095 1 hardback

To the memory of my mother,
Frances Adams Rohr

Contents

Tables

Acknowledgments

Many individuals and institutions have contributed generously over the years to the evolution of this book. My research in England was supported by a grant from the University of Pennsylvania History Department. Many years later, a generous sabbatical from Skidmore College and a fellowship from the National Endowment of the Humanities to attend the 1997 Aston Magna Foundation summer institute contributed significantly to the process of revision.

I am grateful to many libraries and archives for access to their manuscript collections, including the library of the Royal Academy of Music, the Parry Room of the Royal College of Music, the British Library Manuscripts Division, the London Public Record Office, the Norwich Public Record Office, and the archives of Westminster Abbey. Special thanks are due to the Royal Society of Musicians, and in particular to the late Marjorie Gleed for her constant helpfulness and kindness.

Thanks are owed also to the Music Department of Skidmore College for much assistance, but especially for its atmosphere of great warmth and creativity. A few other people provided superb technical support: Joshua Clayton contributed his talents to configure the tables; Laura Davey provided astute and meticulous copy-editing; Catherine Fox created the index; and Marilyn Sheffer deserves thanks for her heroic inter-library loan achievements.

The material on p. 177 regarding the RSM is taken from my article "Women and the Music Profession in Victorian England: The Royal Society of Female Musicians, 1839–1866" © 1999 Overseas Publishers Association N.V., published in the *Journal of Musicological Research* 18, 307–46, and is reprinted with permission from Gordon and Breach Publishers.

Several people have provided great assistance as readers and advisors. Thanks are still due to Cary Mazer, who helped in many ways with the original study, and to Lynn Lees, who guided the early research. The updating and revision of the work would not have occurred without Ralph Locke's unflagging encouragement; his belief in the project as well as his wise comments on the draft have been invaluable. Thomas Denny provided insightful critiques of each chapter's organization as well as innumerable other helpful suggestions. Charles Joseph kept me mindful of how editors might react and raised my spirits with his talent for appreciation. Richard Troeger was the guardian angel of the final revisions; his enthusiasm, meticulous reading and comments, alternately questioning and cheering me on, ensured the successful completion of the book. To all of my other friends and colleagues who have watched and waited patiently, offering encouragement all along the way, you have my deepest gratitude.

Abbreviations

BL   British Library
B&S   Brown, James Duff, and Stephen S. Stratton, *British Musical Biography*, Birmingham, 1897.
Grove   Grove, Sir George, *Dictionary of Music and Musicians*, London, 1879 (and subsequent editions).
JAMS   *Journal of the American Musicological Society*
QMMR   *Quarterly Musical Magazine and Review*
RAM   Royal Academy of Music
RSM   Royal Society of Musicians
Sainsbury   Sainsbury, John, *Dictionary of Musicians*; refers to 1825 edition unless otherwise indicated.

Introduction

When I began this study many years ago the social history of music was still a fledgling discipline, and the few works in that field tended to focus primarily on sources of financial support such as patrons and audiences.[1] Although patronage is certainly very important, from the perspectives of a social historian it is only one part of the story and neglects the lives, perceptions, and values of the musicians themselves. The present study was influenced by a number of approaches – the themes and methods of labor history, Marx's assertions that consciousness evolved from human interactions in pursuit of material subsistence,[2] and the French *Annales* historians' rich interweaving of social and intellectual history.[3] Inspired by such sources, it proceeds from the assumption that in order to study the social context of music it is necessary first to consider the musicians who created music and made decisions about musical life – their economic, social, professional, and artistic goals, and the material and cultural conditions under which these goals were pursued. Recreating the landscape of musicians' careers and perceptions from 1750 to 1850 is the central task of this book.

It soon became clear to me that during the social and economic transformation of eighteenth- and nineteenth-century Britain, professional musicians occupied a complex and ambiguous social status that did not fit neatly into existing social categories. Their low social origins and severe financial hardships might have made them sympathetic subjects for labor historians, but the same musicians' glaringly middle-class social values and aspirations would certainly have tempered those sympathies. Their professional claims and values might have inspired the interest of historians of the professions, but such scholars have tended to focus on occupations that either already enjoyed or eventually achieved professional status. But even well after the mid-nineteenth century the social and professional status of musicians remained equivocal. Of course it was just such ambiguities, interacting as they did with the musical life of the time, that made musicians' careers so intriguing a field of inquiry.

I also thought it possible that investigating the social ambiguities and economic struggles of musicians might shed light on a larger musical conundrum. The apparent lack of great native composers in England in the eighteenth and early nineteenth centuries has led some to describe it as the "land without music."[4] Finding explanations for the relative dearth of musical creativity during this period has been an ongoing challenge for historians of British music.[5] I suspected that the preoccupation of musicians with day-to-day social and economic concerns may have led them to place relatively less emphasis on musical and artistic values, with potentially serious implications for the development of British music during those years. This suspicion was confirmed; indeed, musicians' preoccupations extended beyond social and economic struggles to include a range of negative cultural beliefs which thwarted their social, professional, and artistic aspirations.

The focus on the struggles and aspirations of individual musicians led my research away from a more conventional study of musical institutions and patronage and toward a study of career patterns and perceptions. This meant not only the sequence of events in individual careers, but the minutiae of musicians' daily professional lives: choice of career, training, employment, wages, job security, hard times, relationships with colleagues and employers, and perceptions of social and professional status. Methods and concepts that proved useful for answering these questions included the empirical resources of social history, the richness of the *Annales* school's concept of *mentalités*,[6] and the technique of prosopography (collective biography), especially as it was developed by historians of science. The latter were experimenting with this technique as a way of deriving cultural meaning from the social identity of certain groups.[7]

Toward accomplishing the task of reconstructing the daily realities of musicians' careers, I compiled a biographical catalogue of almost 6,600 professional musicians who worked between 1750 and 1850 in all branches and levels of musical activity: church organists and singers, secular singers and instrumentalists, teachers, composers, and entrepreneurs. The catalogue drew from a wide range of sources, some of them previously unexplored: manuscript letters and account books, contemporary musical directories, periodicals, books and pamphlets. One of the richest was the manuscript archive of the Royal Society of Musicians, which includes membership applications for 696 musicians during this period. These applications indicate the musicians' age, marital status, number of children, musical training received and the name of the master (if the applicant had served an apprenticeship), current sources of employment, and current income. In the cases of musicians who requested financial assistance, the files contain letters filled with insights into the conditions of musical employment, the extent of musicians' financial resources, and, in many cases, the values and perceptions of musicians struggling to endure illness, old age, unemployment, and even debtors' prisons. Occasionally the files include indenture agreements to apprentice the children of musicians who had become claimants on the Society. A number of other manuscript sources – including the Treasury Account Book of the Philharmonic Society and the choir records of Westminster Abbey – provide useful information on wages.

Viewed through the same conceptual lens – the professional lives of musicians – even the printed sources yield up new treasures. Biographical dictionaries play an important role. John Sainsbury's *Dictionary of Musicians*, compiled in the early 1820s, incorporates autobiographical letters that Sainsbury solicited from professional musicians throughout Britain. In some cases he seems to have incorporated parts of the responses verbatim, resulting in entries which are both uneven and rich, frequently offering colorful insights into the values and perceptions of contemporary musicians. Early editions of Sir George Grove's *Dictionary of Music and Musicians* as well as a later source, James Duff Brown and Stephen Stratton's *British Musical Biography*, provide additional information. Inspired by a patriotic wish to preserve the memory of British musicians, Brown and Stratton's late nineteenth-century professional ideals caused them to list professional memberships and awards while tending to omit evidence of the sorts of traditional patronage relationships that had been proudly included in the same musicians' accounts in the Sainsbury dictionary.

Other contemporary printed sources supply much biographical information as well as glimpses of values and perceptions. Musical periodicals provide evidence of the history and contemporary character of musical institutions, membership lists of orchestras and concerts, and heated editorials on issues of concern to professional musicians. Books and pamphlets by musicians are a particularly rich source of values and perceptions. Among the most valuable are works by H. J. Banister, William Hayes, Michael Kelly, W. T. Parke, John Potter, R. J. S. Stevens, S. S. Wesley, and T. D. Worgan.

The resulting catalogue (referred to as 'the catalogue' throughout this study) is more representative of some decades than others. Table 1 indicates the number of musicians in the catalogue who were present in each decade, the total number of names in musical directories, and the number of musicians counted in census years. The two directories – Doane's 1794 directory and the Musical Directory of 1855 – provide many names as well as brief biographical information. The catalogue is probably most representative in the period from 1790 to 1830 and in the 1850s, because the sources were particularly complete for these decades.

Since I compiled the catalogue and first wrote about it several years ago,

Table 1. *Number of musicians in the catalogue, by decade*
n = 6,587

Date	Catalogue	Directories	Census	
			London	Britain
1750–59	368			
1760–69	421			
1770–79	569			
1780–89	681			
1790–99	1,821	1794: 1,271		
1800–09	906			
1810–19	1,162			
1820–29	1,456			
1830–39	1,440			
1840–49	1,727		1841: 1,168	3,992
1850–59	3,117	1855: 2,246	1851: 3,686	11,203

both musicology and social history have traveled far. In the past two decades British musicology has flourished, producing much valuable analysis of the institutional, biographical, and musical landscape.[8] The field of social history has also been transformed profoundly: late twentieth-century political developments challenged some of Marx's interpretations of class and history;[9] linguistic studies have alerted historians to the role of language and ideas in social history;[10] and the evolution of gender studies and feminist history have offered new perspectives on all aspects of society and culture.[11]

Several of these developments have enriched the conceptual framework of the present work. My earlier, gently Marxist assumption that musicians' careers and concerns represent an essential link between musical life and its social context still seems to be on target. But this is far from a narrowly materialist view. Perceptions of music and musicians, the attitudes and ideals of musicians themselves, and the intersections among gender, class, and nationality – all play central roles. The social and economic conditions of musical careers presented one set of challenges to musicians as they collectively struggled to define and enhance their professional status; the complex networks of values and perceptions that were interwoven with musical experience presented another. A synthesis of approaches to both these groups of issues is essential if we are to understand musicians who focused simultaneously on sometimes desperate economic struggles, complex social interactions, and the creation and production of music. We need to take all these elements into account in order to reconstruct the *mentalités* of professional musical life.[12]

Chapter 1 of this study sets the stage for musicians in the eighteenth century, in the early days of the social, economic, and political transformation of Britain, just as British musical life started to expand dramatically.[13] The chapter also introduces the central issues for musicians throughout this period: their relative lack of professional status, organization, and autonomy; foreign competition; and a network of cultural values about music, nationality, gender, and class – values that English musicians navigated with great difficulty. Chapter 2 considers musicians' social and geographical origins and circumstances. Since the financial support for music and the range of patronage relationships are very important for understanding both careers and perceptions, chapter 3 examines the system of patronage and how it evolved. Chapter 4 describes the evolution of institutions for musical education, proposals to reform the system, and implications for musicians' professional autonomy. Chapters 5–8 present the career characteristics of various branches of the profession. Although wages are discussed throughout, chapter 9 specifically addresses the economic conditions of musical careers and the institutions that were founded to assist impoverished musicians. Finally, chapter 10 focuses primarily on the nineteenth-century context, particularly the solutions proposed by musicians as they attempted to redefine their social and professional identity. By the 1840s, after a century of social, political, and cultural transformation, we can discern new and pragmatic compromises in musicians' professional identity, careers, and aspirations at a time when musicians had not yet attained an unequivocal social and professional status.

The place of women in the profession was important and increased significantly in the nineteenth century, but to insert a separate chapter seemed an inadequate treatment, for the careers and struggles of women musicians were intricately connected with the careers of their male colleagues, and the evolving gender values and perceptions of the time presented professional and artistic challenges to male and female musicians alike. In a separate study I have traced one influential attempt by women musicians to organize themselves into an effective professional group, the Royal Society of Female Musicians.[14] For the purposes of this book, however, the findings of that study (as well as other information about women musicians) have been incorporated where relevant throughout.

I   The social and professional status of musicians in the eighteenth century

Like many other eighteenth-century professionals, musicians belonged to the large, socially and economically fluid group that historians term the "middling sort."[1] The economic pressures and occupational reconfigurations of the late eighteenth and early nineteenth centuries presented them – both individually and collectively – with significant challenges. As a result, their social identities evolved in a variety of possible directions. The historian John Seed has argued convincingly that focusing solely on the "rise of the middle class" during the late eighteenth and early nineteenth centuries neglects the history of the "middle ranks" from which it emerged. It is essential to perceive "the way in which as a social category 'the middling sort' were splintering into a number of quite different strata and quite divergent individual fates."[2] Many members of the middle ranks experienced downward social mobility. Others rose to the level of small employers, although perhaps not entirely partaking of the new cultural definition of "middle-class." Still others stayed more or less in the same place but with some loss of social status and stability, evolving into what has been termed the "middling class" of the early nineteenth century.[3] And some moved into "quite new and distinctive middle-class groups: new professions, white-collar groupings, specialised functionaries within commerce and so on."[4]

A close study of musicians has revealed the full range of outcomes just described, with important implications for the evolution of the profession. The nature of the struggle of musicians to maintain or raise their social and professional status will be a central theme of this book. This chapter will first consider "profession" as a general category in the eighteenth century and the musical profession in particular,[5] including the minimal but growing presence of women in the profession. It will then examine two of the major obstacles facing the musical profession's autonomy and status: foreign competition, and a variety of negative cultural perceptions about music and musicians.

Professional status

"Profession" was not a new concept or occupational category in the eighteenth century. While the rise of the professions has often been linked with the development of a middle class in the early nineteenth century, the professions in England had had a long history.[6] The three traditional professions were divinity, medicine, and law, although other occupations increasingly shared their social status and professional ideals. Music had at one time enjoyed some of the trappings of an elite profession, and in the eighteenth century still retained vestiges of its former status.

The traditional professions were characterized primarily by their suitability as careers for gentlemen: they involved no manual labor, were based on a liberal (classical) education, and were protected by church, state, and university from undue competition. There were two educational routes to membership in a profession. The historian W. J. Reader describes the elite route: "the essential qualification for entry into any of these three occupations, which were sometimes called the 'learned' professions, was a liberal education: that is, the education of a gentleman, not of a trader or an artisan."[7] It was assumed that individuals with a sound classical education and general erudition would be entirely capable of learning whatever else they needed to know through independent study. At the same time, part of the claim to independent and exclusive professional status depended on access to specialized knowledge: "it was the type of learning which professionals possessed, rather than social status or institutional forms of organisation, which set them apart from other groups."[8] The status of the old elite professions was guaranteed by their presumed theoretical bases, classical educations, and links with church, state, and university.

Alongside the old elite professions, there were lower branches – especially in law and medicine. Sometimes viewed as specifically eighteenth-century upstarts, the professional status of attorneys (later called solicitors), surgeons, and apothecaries in fact began much earlier. They were distinguished from the elite branches of the professions by the social origins of their members, who generally emerged from a lower, artisanal, social stratum of the "middling sort," and by their educations, which were largely practical and obtained through apprenticeship. In the eighteenth and early nineteenth centuries, such groups organized and attempted to gain increased legitimacy as professions. At the same time, newer aspiring professions (veterinary surgeons, civil engineers, architects, surveyors), which did not have high-status counterparts, were also organizing to achieve middle-class professional status and independence. The attempts by these occupations to assert their own professional importance posed a threat to the traditional professions. W. J. Reader points out the tendency of the higher-status branches, especially in medicine, to try to obstruct the process of professionalization in the lower ranks: "The physicians were fighting a determined defensive action, not at all to their own credit or ultimate advantage."[9]

How did the lower branches of both the old professions and the new, aspiring ones achieve their goals? The main strategy was to assert control over entrance, training, and certification. For example, the Apothecaries Act of 1815 granted the London Society of Apothecaries the legal right to forbid anyone to use the title "apothecary" who had not fulfilled the minimum qualifications set by the Society. The new professions thus established minimum educational standards, formed qualifying associations that gave examinations and granted licenses, and established professional training institutions that replaced the traditional apprenticeship route.[10] In this way, aspiring professions formulated a theoretical basis for their work that put them on a level with the established professions, and protected their credibility, while also asserting the importance of more practical kinds of expertise to justify their ability to complement or compete with the traditional professions.

Professional status was inextricably linked with social status, and the professionalizing impetus was largely about raising or preserving a particular social position. As a result of the redrawing of social categories, members of the middle ranks experienced heightened pressure to achieve and to consolidate their middle-class status, both as an end in itself and to safeguard access to a middle-class clientele. M. S. Larson has argued convincingly that the "market control" achieved by professional self-regulation was closely harnessed to the goal of collective social mobility.[11] The Society of Gentlemen Practitioners (attorneys), founded in the first half of the eighteenth century, was concerned primarily with raising the notoriously low public image of attorneys. Wilfrid Prest identifies this organization as "a precursor of the Victorian 'qualifying associations' which eventually came to control most professional and would-be professional occupations."[12] It tried to exclude members whose low social origins and/or unscrupulous business practices contributed to the popular prejudices against attorneys.[13] Such measures also gave the professions power to assure conformity with the emerging middle-class standards of decorum and respectability. Another example was the founding of the Royal Academy in 1768. Jeremy Black explains that it was founded to elevate the fine arts, and that "engravers were excluded from the ranks of the Academy for many years because they were regarded as artisanal."[14]

It is particularly important to note the character of the social aspirations shared by both traditional and aspiring professions. According to Harold Perkin, the ideals of the professional middle class were at first closely related to those of entrepreneurs, but diverged increasingly into a discrete ideal by the mid-nineteenth century.[15] The professional ideal, obsessed with social status, eager to dissociate itself from trade, and focused on formal education and high standards of moral conduct, in some ways aimed even higher than a middle-class ideal. As Reader expresses it, "Their idea of social standing was to get as close as they could to the pattern set by the landed gentry, or what they imagined the pattern to be";[16] "the new professional man brought one scale of values – the gentleman's – to bear upon the other – the tradesman's."[17] The uneasy combination of such ideals is particularly characteristic of musicians, whose careers often combined both relatively low social and economic conditions with direct dealings with wealthy patrons.

Unlike emerging professions such as apothecaries, architects, engineers, and the artistic professions of painting or acting, music could claim a long history of association with the requisite characteristics of a traditional profession: a high-status career track securely linked to church and universities; a foundation of theoretical knowledge; recognition as a liberal art by the universities (which had been granting degrees in music since 1463); and essential social value due to its role in the cathedral services of the Anglican Church. The formal education of musicians, which included classical languages, had been provided for in the centuries-old royal endowments attached to the cathedrals.

Music also had a lower-status, artisanal branch made up primarily of secular musicians such as stage singers and orchestral instrumentalists. These musicians benefited as the increasingly prosperous middle classes eagerly adopted the practices of a cultured elite – attending concerts, purchasing instruments and sheet music, and taking private lessons.[18] As one periodical reported in 1821, "There are ... the strongest proofs that it [music] is becoming the ornament and the solace of other classes beside the most affluent ... The proofs to which we allude are, the increasing manufacture of instruments, the vast augmentation of musical publications, and the number of professors and instructors."[19]

It would seem that musicians were in a good position to enjoy both the advantages of traditional professional status and the growth in demand for secular musicians. However, even in the mid-eighteenth century the high-status branch of the musical profession no longer commanded its former prestige, the financial and social advantages of careers in church music and of university degrees in music had declined considerably, and the old profession with its church and university ties became much less significant in the profession as a whole. No successful attempt to reverse this trend occurred until at least the middle of the nineteenth century. This decline weakened the theoretical, intellectual component of the profession, and with it music's identity as one of the liberal arts. Since the intellectual component, recognition by the universities, and an essential role in the church were the primary legitimizing characteristics for the musical profession, the decline in church music careers in the eighteenth century struck at the foundation of musicians' traditional claims for professional status.

By the late eighteenth century, music was no longer viewed primarily as a liberal art or a liberal profession, but rather as an artisanal craft with links to the theatres and pleasure gardens, financial insecurity, and poor long-term economic or social prospects. Partly as a result of the growing demand, the urban, secular branch had in the eighteenth century already started to become the most significant branch of the profession, both musically and economically. This occupational classification is accurately reflected in Patrick Colquhoun's tables of national income distribution for 1806.[20] In the more detailed of his two tables, he defined the liberal arts and sciences as medicine, literature, and the fine arts. In the more general table the term "liberal professions" includes the same items as well as law. Musicians, however, whose estimated incomes were somewhat lower than those in the professional category, were labeled as "Persons employed in theatrical pursuits, and attached to theatres and concerts, as musicians, etc."

In order to withstand the loss of prestige of its higher branch, as well as the social and economic pressures building toward the end of the century, musicians needed to organize in some way. As Reader explains, "An occupation's rise to professional standing can be pretty accurately charted by reference to the progress of its professional institute or association."[21] At first such associations were usually informal, without recognition outside the profession; the more important next step was incorporation, usually by means of a royal charter, "which may be said to confer official recognition by the State that the occupation has achieved professional standing."[22]

The musical profession included a number of organizations, and individual musicians proposed others, but only one – the Royal Society of Musicians, founded in 1738 – had any of the characteristics of a professional association.[23] Application for membership in the Society usually required a statement of the nature and extent of the musicians' training, employment, and income, and this information was verified by the signatures of other musicians. A royal charter was granted in 1790.[24] However, the RSM had none of the powers normally granted by royal charter such as control over examinations and licensing, or the authority to take legal action against unqualified practitioners. Although composed of the leading London musicians, it had been founded to provide charitable assistance to its members, and this remained its primary function. The RSM's royal recognition and incorporation could conceivably have formed the basis for more characteristic professional innovations, but the Society remained committed to charity, and this, with its unfortunate implications for the economic prospects of musical careers, did little to further the professional status of musicians.

Without the institutions essential for professional autonomy, advancement in musical careers depended on an uneven mix of merit and patronage. In many cases, however, musical merit was still determined by patrons rather than professionals, and was defined solely as expertise without consideration of such social criteria as education, manners, and respectability. As a result, musicians of low social origins, narrow educational backgrounds, and limited social skills might advance in their careers. (Similar challenges to professional control characterized the other performance occupations, as well as that of writing.[25]) Little, therefore, could be accomplished to raise the social and professional status of the musical profession as a whole.

The status and organizational issues facing the musical profession were largely debated with male musicians in mind. Even though growing numbers of women pursued music as an amateur accomplishment in the second half of the eighteenth century, most branches of the profession were closed to them. Furthermore, the traditional association of music with immorality (see below) could take on even more virulent forms once women crossed unambiguously into the public sphere. In this context, it is not surprising that relatively few women succeeded in pursuing music as a profession. In the eighteenth century, the notable exceptions were the female singers in the Italian Opera, English theatres, pleasure gardens, and oratorio performances. A few women also held employment as church organists, especially in the last decade of the century, and there were a few who became harpists and even composers.

The singers, however, were by far the most public and well-known female professionals. Those who sang in theatres suffered the same personal and, in the case of the Italian singers, xenophobic attacks as their male colleagues. For most of the century actresses were assumed to be sexually disreputable and of the lowest moral level,[26] and similar assumptions were often applied to female theatre singers. Even the most renowned, such as the opera singer Mrs. Billington, were vulnerable to scurrilous attacks on their conduct and morals.

Consistent with the heightened early nineteenth-century emphasis on respectability in general, the potential loss of reputation was an even more compelling reason for discouraging women from professional activity. One music periodical in 1820 described "those to whom it would be almost annihilation to witness the performance of a daughter, a sister, or a mistress [wife] in public."[27] There were also numerous cautionary tales about the fates of young women whose families were unable to prevent them from pursuing careers as singers in the theatres, with disastrous results. And of course there was a general ambivalence about women being in the professions at all. The editor of the *Musical World*, showing more diplomacy than logic, commented, "We hold music to be altogether too *laborious* a profession for women ... it is, however, much followed by them, and finds among the sex some of its most distinguished ornaments."[28]

Although the ideology of separate spheres asserted that women's place was in the home, where they could nurture the moral and civic development of society, evidence suggests that new intensity was lent to this ideology in response to the growing visibility and activity of women outside the home.[29] In any case, by the early nineteenth century there were several loopholes for women who aspired both to musical careers and to the middle-class status valued by their male colleagues. Since music was a completely acceptable amateur accomplishment for women, it was considered understandable and even laudable if a woman who found herself in difficult economic circumstances supported herself by teaching or even by performing music (see chapter 4). Furthermore, the female English singer – one who fulfilled the requisite ideals both of femininity and cultural nationalism – could offer an important alternative to the much more threatening voices and deportment of the Italian opera singers. (The complex interaction of gender, nationalist, and vocal ideals will be discussed in chapter 6.)

In the nineteenth century, several developments opened more doors for women as professional musicians. One of these was the founding in 1822 of the Royal Academy of Music; another was the evolution of concert life, offering performance venues where women could sidestep both the primarily male tradition of the church and the social stigma of the stage. In addition to singers, women were often pianists – performers as well as teachers – and a number became composers. All, however, had to navigate cultural prejudices about music and musicians, restrictions on women's musical education, prejudices about women appearing in public, and some resistance among their male colleagues in the profession.

Foreign competition

From early in the eighteenth century, foreign musicians traveled to England to take advantage of the opportunities there.[30] Since entry to the profession was determined solely by free competition and musicians could travel to London and move directly into remunerative and prestigious musical employment without any regulation, they presented serious competition to native musicians, and also weakened the potential for native musicians to achieve the market control that was essential to professional status.

At least as early as 1720, with the founding of the Italian Opera in London, English musicians and observers of the music scene frowned upon the number of foreign musicians employed in England and the extremely high fees they commanded. Many of these musicians were connected with the Opera as singers, orchestral instrumentalists, composers, and librettists; other sources of income included music copying, accompanying, teaching, and even managing singers' careers.[31] In 1728, Daniel Defoe observed that London was oversupplied with "heaps of Foreign Musicians"[32] who were attracted to London because of the higher wages available there. The foreign presence continued throughout the century. G. F. A. Wendeborn, a German pastor residing in London, remarked in 1791 that "Many foreign singers, fidlers, and dancers, are extravagantly paid; and, if they are the least frugal, they are enabled to retire to their own country where they may live in affluence, enriched by English money."[33] Another observed that these musicians often had little incentive to return to their native countries: "The greatest part of the foreign musicians who visit London remain there: for as that great city is actually a PERU to them, they do not choose to deprive themselves of the lucrative monopoly which they there enjoy, in regard to their own profession."[34]

Through the second half of the century, Italians continued to dominate at the Opera; German musicians held a distinct advantage at court, and were also among the leaders of London's concert life. From the 1790s, however, with the military and social upheavals and reduced opportunities in much of Europe, Italians and Germans in English musical life were joined by musicians from France and other European countries. The tone of competition became more focused, with the most acute resentments still reserved for the Italians, whose cliques were thought to exert undue influence on musical life. In 1811 the *Dramatic Censor* applauded one singer for choosing a Mozart opera for her benefit concert, explaining that "such a choice affords a decided proof of her good taste, and of her contempt for that bitter jealousy and vicious prejudice against the German composers, which has so long actuated the Italian musicians, and so long been successful in withholding from the public the noble performances of Bach, Mozart, and Winter."[35]

In the early decades of the nineteenth century, the social and economic pressures on musicians intensified. Competition, especially for private patronage, was at its height. In this atmosphere, the resentment of British musicians was deepened further by the apparent advantages some foreign musicians enjoyed in obtaining aristocratic patronage. Each year during the 1820s, the musical press reported unprecedented gains by foreign musicians. In 1821, one musician wrote of the "influence foreign music is gradually gaining in this country, and which threatens the almost total oblivion and expulsion of English composition."[36] An account of the 1822 London season reported that

the capital circumstance that has lately marked the study and practise of music in England is, unquestionably, the increasing notice and estimation which foreign compositions, foreign execution, and foreign professors, have attracted... The influx of foreign musicians – the substitution of Italian songs, duets, and concerted pieces for the compositions of our own countrymen ... afford abundant demonstration.[37]

The composer G. H. B. Rodwell, writing in 1833, claimed that 1824 had been the year when "the flood-gates of foreign music were thrown open."[38] The distinguishing feature of each ensuing year seems to have been the same, however, together with the recognition of increasing competition from German musicians:

The phenomena ... of the season were then – the immense influx of foreign performers, and the almost entire diversion of the patronage of the leaders of fashion and the public from the English to the foreign style and to foreign artists ... A double source is now opening upon us – Germany as well as Italy. It has been pronounced by one very competently informed, both by experience and by knowledge, that in fifteen years the German will bear away the palm.[39]

Why were foreign musicians perceived as such a threat? Patrons often seem to have preferred hiring foreign musicians, especially for private concerts (see chapter 3); foreign musicians were sometimes more highly trained and skilled than their British counterparts. Proposals to reform the system of musical training, as well as to provide some mechanism for certification, almost always gave as a rationale the need to offer more effective competition against foreign musicians (see chapter 4).

Objections to the foreign presence also expressed larger, pervasive cultural attitudes. Xenophobia had a long tradition in England, and one which was closely intertwined with the development of a national identity in the eighteenth century. A growing cultural nationalism fueled native developments in many of the arts, especially theatre and the visual arts. In music the cult of Handel and the development of an English vernacular opera illustrate the trend.[40] As will be discussed below, the perceived foreign intrusions were viewed increasingly in terms of xenophobic anxieties about class, morality, and especially gender identity and roles. Cultural anxieties of this sort continued to compound the real social and economic obstacles faced by musicians.

Cultural perceptions

Musicians labored under a number of negative attitudes, some of which derived from the real structural problems in the competition for social and professional status: economic hardships, social and educational limitations, membership in an unstable social stratum during a period of sweeping change, and competition from foreign musicians. For example, it was frequently assumed that musicians came from relatively low social origins, that they were poorly educated, socially unskilled and inferior individuals. Other negative perceptions were due to prejudices and fears about music and musicians, whose activities inadvertently tapped deep cultural anxieties.[41] These included notions that music was frivolous and had no essential social value; that music and musicians were associated with immorality; and that music – especially in its connections with the world of the theatre – posed a threat to Britishness, to existing power relationships, and to accepted definitions of gender. Such beliefs significantly undermined musicians' chances for achieving middle-class social and professional status and respectability.

A number of mid-eighteenth-century musicians wrote about the problems of social status and of widespread contempt for professional musicians. The image of the musician as "mere fiddler" was a recurrent theme. William Hayes, a well-established church musician and theorist, complained in 1753 that

Not only in *Italy* but in most Countries abroad, a thoroughly accomplished Musician is at least upon the Footing of a Scholar in any other Science; and is treated with equal Respect: whereas in *England* we are often too apt to despise the Professors of Music, and to treat them indiscriminately with Contempt: But although every Fidler may have the Vanity to look upon himself as a Musician, yet we ought not to regard every Musician, only as a Fidler.[42]

Another contemporary musician, John Potter, who composed songs for Vauxhall Gardens, wrote a book about the state of the musical profession in 1762. Like Hayes, he addressed the widespread contempt for musicians: "The elegant art of music, when consider'd as an occupation, is by some thought to have little dignity."[43] He suggests several reasons for this attitude:

The contempt thrown on music, arises from two objections: The one, representing it as not being in general so profitable and reputable as many other professions, as having for its object nothing better than pleasure and entertainment. The other, that it not only requires a particular genius to excel in it, but also a great deal of time to make any progress, and by this means hinders and disqualifies a person for anything else.[44]

In other words, music as a profession lacked essential social value, and left so little time for broader education that it risked producing nothing but "mere fiddlers."

Such objections carried little weight with Potter, who believed anyone who achieved a high level of skill should be respected for that alone: "Great excellency in any profession, is sufficient to recommend and entitle us to honour and reputation."[45] Although he did not rank music "before the sciences of divinity, physic, law, or the study of languages," he thought that "it certainly must be allow'd to be next in dignity."[46] Furthermore, he reminded the reader of the role of music in the church: "the great use of church music in the worship of our Creator, is ... a circumstance of greater weight and value than those two ascrib'd to music, of pleasure and entertainment."[47] Potter further argues that if an individual loved music enough to spend many years of study in exchange for meagre financial rewards, why should anyone complain?

[I]f [musicians] can be pleased with a moderate fortune, that they may be more at leisure to study and improve the science of music, for the benefit of the rising generation; they may hope for a pardon from those, who are engag'd in the plunder of the world; as leaving them the more room, and easing them of rivals, who by their performances shew, they did not want either capacity, or application (if they had thought fit) to shine in courts, or camps, in the pulpit, or at the bar. If therefore men conspicuous for their love and close attachment to music, have preferr'd the desire of an innocent fame from their works, to the love of wealth and grandeur; let this singularity of theirs, be at least excus'd since it is [to] themselves most delightful, advantageous to many, and hurtful to none.[48]

However, disdain for the person whose artistic aspirations outweighed financial motives continued to be cited as a reason for the low status of musicians. G. F. A. Wendeborn wrote in 1791:

No wonder ... if the greatest part of the English, whose *summum bonum* is money, are tasteless in the arts, and treat them with neglect, or even look upon them with a kind of disdain; no wonder if a tradesman or merchant, favoured by liberty, regards the accumulation of money above all, and considers a man of talents and learning, or an artist endowed with excellent genius, as beings far below him.[49]

Potter and Hayes viewed themselves as the equals of other professionals, and enjoyed a higher sense of self-esteem and social status than existed for many later musicians. That even these distinguished professionals found themselves on the defensive illustrates the degree to which the high-status career track had declined.

By the early nineteenth century, musicians were becoming even more defensive about their social value, morality, and respectability. The image of musicians as poor artisans degraded by association with other musicians and theatre employees, late working hours, and low earnings, continued to oppress professional musicians in their quest for higher status. One musician wrote a long article in 1818, "Letter on the Character of Musicians," in which he attempted to point out the strengths of musicians' attainments and morality. He emphasized the degree to which a decline in respectability was merely a product of poverty, and did not necessarily represent basic flaws of character or family background: "The early character of the musician is liable to be tinged by opposites; by an overweening opinion of his own accomplishments and by vulgar and dissolute habits acquired during the season of obscurity."[50] He went on to explain how this hurt the musicians' relationships with patrons, and he reiterated the common theme of the musician as "mere fiddler" whose intensive musical studies rendered him inadequate for social contact with his employers:

The labour of practice can scarcely ever be relieved, except by some coarse or dissolute species of dissipation. The poor musicians can find no better associates than those of his own condition, and while his sensibility is sharpened by his art, his taste occasionally awakened, and his manners improved by the good company into which that art casually introduces him, it is most probable he is only made to feel the more acutely those deficiencies which he has not the means to repair. The polite and the informed who are induced to enter into conversation with him discover at once that his recommendations are confined to his fiddle or his voice, and they quit him in that hopeless conviction.[51]

The same author went on to note that there were, in fact, many exceptions who suffered for the failings of a few, since "there exists a great confusion relative to the several orders of musicians."[52] He described the exceptional cases as "men educated under the intelligent care of parents or friends, whose previous success in the profession or in life, has enabled them to find the easier path to greatness." However, he argued that the exceptions "give a contrast but not a contradiction to our more universal description. Were they perhaps to trace back even a single generation, they would arrive at the original of our portraiture."[53] Throughout the 1820s, in the context of an evolving ethos of middle-class respectability, contributors to musical journals addressed the contempt and disdain for musicians that resulted from perceptions of musicians' social uselessness, narrow education, unrefined manners, and immorality.

The complex network of prejudices about music and musicians added layers of cultural meanings and associations to the more obvious economic and occupational challenges faced by musicians. These attitudes included the long history of suspicion towards music, specifically the notion that it was fundamentally a feminine art; xenophobia, with its corollary anxieties about cultural intrusion and effeminacy; and the reorientation of cultural beliefs about gender and sexuality, accompanied by an ongoing discourse

about the new ideals of masculinity and femininity.[54] While a full discussion of these changes lies outside the scope of the present study, several
aspects are pertinent to our understanding of music and the musical
profession in eighteenth-century British culture.

Well before the eighteenth century, music was associated with the feminine. As Linda Austern has convincingly demonstrated, music and women
in early modern England were thought to share many characteristics, most
of them negative, or at least potentially dangerous. "Feminine nature" was
defined "as especially disordered, convoluted, deceptive, changeable and
uncontrolled, a literal inversion of the positive, direct qualities associated
with the era's masculine ideals."[55] And it was believed that "all sounding
music ... potentially invites the physical senses of the listener to useless,
base, sensory pleasure and therefore reduces the mind to a simpler, more
passive and ultimately more feminine state"; in other words, music was
"an emasculator and destroyer of manly virtue."[56] Although it was argued
by some that military marches could have appropriate effects for men, love
songs and other sweet sounds would have "a feminizing effect."[57] These
categories were even applied to the craft and rhetoric of music, with
chromaticism, ornamentation, and the falsetto voice being considered to
have feminine attributes.[58] The underlying assumption that music was
feminine, and even feminizing to men, appears in various guises throughout the eighteenth and nineteenth centuries, with important implications
for music as a profession.[59]

During the eighteenth century the evolution of new gender roles and
beliefs found expression in misogyny, homophobia, xenophobia, and more
restrictive definitions of masculinity and femininity. An obvious focal
point for such anxieties about otherness was provided early in the century
by the full-scale importation of music and musicians for the Italian Opera.
Thomas McGeary has identified the intricate and pervasive cultural, national, and gender anxieties that were stirred by the Opera, including the
persistent notion that the enterprise was intrinsically feminine.[60] The cas-
trato singers presented especially complex gender ambiguities. English
fears of opera in general, and the castrati in particular, included the
possible femininizing effect on listeners; beliefs that homosexuality had
been imported from Italy along with the Opera and that the practice would
spread;[61] and fears of the attractiveness of castrati to women. The high fees
paid to the singers were described by one critic as the Italians "cuckolding"
the nation.[62] In sum, the effeminate Opera threatened the masculine basis
of British culture, and "questioned and threatened the stability of those
gender distinctions essential to maintaining stable social institutions."[63] In
fact, such fears encompassed an entire complex of class, gender, national
identity, religious, and cultural associations. An aristocracy spending large

sums of English money to import homosexuality, castrati, Catholicism, and music into London threatened masculine, Protestant "British sense, reason, wit, and virtue."[64]

Ideals of masculinity and femininity – frequently linked with and used as metaphors for developments in commerce, politics, and art – were discussed and debated throughout the eighteenth century. Effeminacy was perceived as a perennial threat and was thought to result from many causes: increased wealth and "luxury," consumerism, foreign influences, overly refined manners and sensibility, and the cultivation of arts, especially music.[65] Unchecked effeminacy, it was feared, could lead to the dismantling of society, defeat by foreign invaders, or even national decline analogous to that of the Roman Empire. As Richard Leppert argues, "The appetite for music was great; the fear of satisfying that appetite was still greater."[66] "Music's impact on the body was characterized as a moral question, which in truth operated as a smoke screen for anxieties about identities grounded in nation, class, and gender."[67] Throughout the eighteenth century, music and musicians were powerful symbols in the ongoing renegotiation of gender, national and social identities, and roles.

The view of music as a feminine art was further reinforced by the cultivation of music as an amateur accomplishment for women. The growing wealth of the middle ranks and the avid consumption of musical instruments, printed music, and private music lessons fueled the trend.[68] Music as an amateur pursuit for men, however, was viewed quite differently.[69] The widely quoted Lord Chesterfield argued "that performance upon an instrument is derogatory to character, both as becomes a man and a gentleman."[70] Such attitudes persisted throughout the period under study. In 1820 an article entitled "Music as a Pursuit for Men" tried to refute such prejudices.[71] The author credited this attitude partly to the influence of Chesterfield, and partly to "the not absolutely unfounded opinion that the cultivation of music leads to dissolute habits *and association with dissolute companions.*"[72] Once again, the moral question thinly veiled the underlying concern that "the musical gentleman ... potentially threatened ... the definition of gender upon which both the society and the culture ultimately depended."[73]

Despite the virtual disappearance of the abhorred castrati from England late in the eighteenth century, cultural anxieties about music, and especially opera, only intensified in the 1790s. The primary reason was the French Revolution and subsequent wars, which further fueled both xenophobia and misogyny. In addition to the political and military threat, the upheavals on the Continent resulted in even larger numbers of foreign musicians competing for employment in London. And, as Barker-Benfield has shown, from the onset of war in 1793 there was also a swift reaction against sensibility, women writers, and any challenge to the "natural ordering of the sexes."[74] Political and social pressures encouraged the evolution of strict definitions of gender roles and the further development of an ideology of separate spheres – respectively public and domestic – for men and women.[75] As Linda Colley describes,

There was a sense at this time . . . in which the British conceived of themselves as an essentially "masculine" culture – bluff, forthright, rational, down-to-earth to the extent of being philistine – caught up in an eternal rivalry with an essentially "effeminate" France – subtle, intellectually devious, preoccupied with high fashion, fine cuisine and etiquette, and so obsessed with sex that boudoir politics were bound to direct it.[76]

In combating these challenges, early nineteenth-century musicians attempted to prove that they were respectable members of society by echoing middle-class fears of music-related dissipation. Cyril Ehrlich aptly describes this phase in the history of the music profession as "the transition period from rakishness to sobriety."[77] It is possible that no group expressed a more delicate sense of propriety and morality in these years than the defensive professional musicians. For example, in the following passage the author distinguished between the love and appreciation of music, and the music-making that occurred in all-male tavern singing-clubs:

Music, as it is understood by persons who thus associate its pleasures with a love of the joys of the table, is neither more nor less than the faculty of singing a Bacchanalian song, or trolling a merry catch, or joining in a boisterous glee . . . It must soon be seen that the species of vanity which is pampered and fed by the praises of tavern-friends half mad, half maudlin, is a low, depraved, and contemptible passion: and I contend, that the mind which is once capable of turning itself towards the contemplation of music, and aiming at the acquisition of any tolerable share of practical skill, will nauseate and reject such applauses as garbage fit only for the most vulgar animal appetites.[78]

This kind of moralistic writing is characteristic of the early nineteenth-century besieged professional musician, and is very different from the defensive but still professionally minded commentary of the mid-eighteenth-century musician, John Potter. Music, not morals, was Potter's main concern. Early nineteenth-century musicians could no longer enjoy the luxury of primarily musical priorities.

Music's identification as a feminine form of expression, one linked with women and with male effeminacy, automatically put male practitioners of the art on the defensive about their masculinity, their morality and respectability, and even their Britishness. In fact, the evolution during these years of a specific definition of British masculinity – one characterized by sobriety, simplicity, and virtue – can be viewed as part of the larger struggle for middle-class political power and legitimacy.[79] The link between gender definitions and class identity was pervasive. As Catherine Hall explains,

Definitions of masculinity and femininity played an important part in marking out the middle class, separating it off from other classes and creating strong links between disparate groups within that class – Nonconformists and Anglicans, Radicals and conservatives, the richer bourgeoisie and the petite bourgeoisie. The separation between the sexes was marked out at every level within the society – in manufacturing, the retail trades and the professions, in public life of all kinds, in the churches, in the press and in the home.[80]

In sum, achieving and consolidating middle-class professional status required conformity with a wide range of cultural beliefs about Englishness, gender, morality. Professional musicians, with their varied social and educational backgrounds, and their pursuit of an activity tainted with femininity and foreignness, faced an uphill battle. As one mid-eighteenth-century writer explained, he would "think it more respectable to bring up my son a Blacksmith ... than find him Apprentice to the best Master of Music in England ... I love my country so well, that I hate everything that administers to Luxury and Effeminacy."[81] To be identified with the "other," especially in a time of sweeping social and cultural change, was not a strong platform from which to launch a bid for professional autonomy or middle-class respectability.

Musicians struggled against perceptions that they were artisans, "mere fiddlers" from low social origins, in regular contact with foreigners and even more disreputable elements of society. Was there any truth to such ideas? If so, the ideal of middle-class professional status would remain elusive. This chapter will consider where professional musicians fit in the social and geographical landscape. It will then be possible to ascertain the scope of the obstacles to musicians' social and professional aspirations, and to what extent they would have to change not only the perceptions but also the realities of their social identity in order to emerge as nineteenth-century professionals.

Social origins and mobility

The social origins of professional musicians can be gleaned from the occupations of their relatives (table 2). Information on the occupations of female relatives, particularly their mothers, is relatively scarce, although the musical families represented in the table undoubtedly included women musicians. Such information appears more frequently toward the mid-nineteenth century, when more women were entering the profession. The information in the table confirms that the vast majority of musicians in Britain from 1750 to 1850 came from the middle ranks of society. The higher ranks represented here are almost all foreigners whose children or grandchildren became successful musicians in England. This is one of the many indications of the musical profession's comparatively low social status in England. Whereas the children of wealthy or high-ranking Europeans were sometimes free to pursue musical careers, their English counterparts virtually never made such a choice. Sometimes the parents of musicians worked in the realms of literature, art, and the theatre as well as the professions. The musical children of clergy frequently became church organists. Also represented in the table are independent artisans and artisans/laborers. The most striking feature is the large proportion of

Table 2. *Occupations of musicians' relatives*

	Fathers n = 721	Grandfathers n = 100	Spouses n = 332	Children n = 763
I. Aristocracy	6	2	14	—
II. Middle ranks				
1. Agriculture				
Farmers	1	—	—	—
2. Industry and commerce				
Eminent merchants	3	1	1	—
Lesser merchants	8	—	—	—
Manufacturers	4	1	—	—
Shipbuilders	1	—	—	—
Surveyors, engineers	3	—	—	4
Independent artisans	32	4	1	11
Shopkeepers	14	2	—	7
Clerks, shopmen	3	—	—	—
3. Professions				
Civil offices (1)	3	—	1	1
Civil offices (2)	6	2	1	—
Law	4	1	2	—
Clergy	22	4	—	5
Education	12	—	1	4
Army and naval officers	7	—	3	—
Medicine	4	3	1	—
Visual arts	8	—	2	3
Literature and letters	6	—	5	7
Music	577 (80%)	71 (71%)	287 (86%)	668 (88%)
Theatre	6	1	7	—
III. Lower orders				
Artisans/laborers	26	6	6	37
Seamen	—	—	—	—
Soldiers	8	—	—	2
Laborers	8	1	—	1
Domestic servants	5	1	—	2

For the specific occupations subsumed within each of the occupational categories listed above, see table 21 in the appendix.

musicians (about 80 percent) whose fathers were also professional musicians.

A number of musicians were originally schooled for other work, and sometimes pursued other careers before turning to music as a profession (tables 3a and 3b). Usually these were higher-status professions such as law, medicine, or the church (and, in later years, engineering), although some musicians were first apprenticed to crafts such as boat-building,

Table 3a. *Musicians intended and/or trained for non-musical occupations*

n = 39

	Before 1800	After 1800
Law	7	4
Medicine	2	3
Clergy	3	7
Business/accountancy	I	I
Apprenticed to:		
boat-builder	I	—
cabinet-maker	I	—
paviour (?)	I	—
silk-weaver	I	—
printing trade	—	2
Classical education	I	I
Studied theology at Cambridge	—	I
Engineering	—	2

Table 3b. *Occupations held before becoming professional musicians*

n = 37

Before 1800	After 1800
army officer	accountant (2)
bookbinder	army
cabin-boy, then actor	business
carpenter	bookbinder
carver and gilder	bookseller
clerk in merchant's counting-house	clerk in Broadwood's, then surgeon
coach-builder	civil servant
cooper	civil servant, then private secretary
factory worker (in Halifax)	farmer
law-stationer, then actor	music seller
lawyer	post in Treasury
music copyist	reader in printing office
ran a brewery and distillery	soldier
shoemaker	solicitor
soldier (2)	tallow-chandler
stonemason	weaver
surgeon	wood-carver
officer in the Austrian army	

cabinet-making, silk-weaving, and printing. Those who pursued non-musical occupations before embarking on their musical careers include lawyers, surgeons, civil servants, and soldiers, as well as skilled artisans: bookbinders, coopers, shoemakers, stonemasons, tallow-chandlers, weavers, and wood-carvers.

Given the unpredictable social and economic status of the music profession, what motivated individuals to choose musical careers? The evidence suggests that the choice came from a combination of factors including family influence and training, strong interest and/or talent, and the hope of financial rewards.

The high proportion of musicians with one or more parents in the profession has been noted. Sometimes the parent directed the child's training and choice of profession, as in the case of Charles James Griesbach, whose father was part of an extended family of German musicians employed in the royal household: "It was my Fathers determination that I should be brought up to Music."[1] People were rarely forced to pursue music as a profession, however. (The reverse – being forbidden to pursue music – was much more common.[2]) In general, it seems that the sons and daughters of professional musicians were the most likely of any group to choose music as an occupation, in part because of the advantages which musicians' children enjoyed in obtaining musical training and professional connections.

Early signs of ability in music could of course lead to musical careers. The talent of a prodigy coming from a family of limited means was often viewed as an unexpected advantage toward significantly expanding the child's future horizons. Such children were taken to perform for aristocrats, other wealthy persons, and professional musicians who might foster their careers. Examples include the cellist Robert Lindley; the pianists George Aspull, William Crotch, and Elizabeth Randles; the violinist Joseph Bottomley; and many others.

In the absence of early and prodigious talent, a driving interest in music often prevailed, even against parental objections. The organist J. Whitehead Smith (born *circa* 1827) discovered his love for music when hearing the Wells Cathedral choristers at practice while he sat in the schoolroom of the grammar school. This led him to ask for music lessons as a young child. However,

My father was averse to my choosing music as a profession, so my lessons ceased, and my playing too (at age 10); but some time after I took up the violin, in order to join a musical society; when taken from school, I was kept at home as my father's accountant; but my love of music gained ground, and after much discussion, it was decided that I was to go to London, and I entered the Royal Academy as a pupil.[3]

A better-known example is the English opera composer, Thomas Arne (1710–78). His father intended him to study law, but

Being obliged to conceal his love of music from his father, he privately took lessons from Michael Festing, the violinist, and practised on a spinet with muffled strings. He at the same time studied harmony and composition, and attended the opera in the disguise of a servant's livery. His father accidentally discovered him leading a band of amateurs, and, after his first wrath was over, allowed him to give up the career of a lawyer . . . and devote himself entirely to music.[4]

The financial motive for choosing a musical career was less clear-cut than talent or driving interest. Among artisans and laborers, music could be viewed as a means of social advancement. One observer noted such a motivation in 1818:

The rewards which music promises are perhaps as frequently the motive to adopting it for a profession, as any real or supposed aptitude, and of the hundreds of persons now annually trained to the science, perhaps there is a pretty equal portion of those who follow it from mere necessity or from some casual facility . . . and of those who take to it by descent as it were.[5]

John Stevenson (1761/2–1833), son of a Glasgow coach-builder and himself trained in that work,

continued to follow it [coach-building] in his youth, until he began to think that he could do better for himself in the world by scraping the strings of a fiddle than by performing the less harmonious and interesting operation on the spokes of coach-wheels.[6]

Stevenson became an itinerant fiddler, eventually settling in Dublin as a teacher and orchestral player; his son, trained in a Dublin cathedral, became a famous choir singer and composer of church music. Michael Kelly (1762–1826), the successful London concert and theatre singer, was the son of a prosperous Dublin wine merchant. Kelly wrote in his reminiscences that as a boy he had observed his Italian music teacher (who he later realized had become wealthy by marriage) feasting on expensive fruits in a Dublin shop. He assured the reader that "trifling as this little anecdote may appear, I firmly believe it was the chief cause of my serious resolution to follow up music as a profession."[7]

When sons or daughters of bourgeois families chose music for financial reasons, it was usually due to unexpected economic reversals. Originally intended for businesses or professions that were distinctly more respectable than music, they sometimes fell back on music when the family fortunes declined. One 1822 observer who described the reasons for the choice of a musical career mentioned only the financial motive, not the dreams of riches that inspired others. Such individuals are well educated persons who take up an art, cultivated for other purposes than emolument, from the decay of their connections or circumstances. Delicacy forbids me to cite the names of those who have been impelled by such motives to so honourable an exertion of talent, but there are many.[8]

For example, John Feltham Danneley (1786–1836) was born into a prosperous family in Berkshire, his grandfather having been a successful solicitor with much property in Windsor. After his grandfather died, however, the family experienced financial difficulties; his father became a choir singer in Windsor, and John trained for a career in music. He later became an organist, composer, and author of a number of books including an *Introduction to Thorough Bass* (1820).[9] Another instance was Catherine Bisset (*circa* 1790–1864), whose father had written books on Edmund Burke and George III. She was a promising music student, so that

in consequence of the death of her father, when she was quite a child, she was advised by many friends to study, as a profession, that art which she had previously cultivated as an accomplishment; and notwithstanding the high rank of several of her nearest relatives, at twelve years of age she was giving lessons to assist in supporting her family.[10]

She went on to receive free lessons from the pianist J. B. Cramer, and became a successful performer. (Her sister also became a performer, on the harp.) Charlotte Sainton-Dolby, one of the most successful English concert singers of the nineteenth century, originally studied music only as an accomplishment but came to regard it as a profession after her father died, when she enrolled in the Royal Academy of Music.[11] And Antonio Sapio, born in London of an Italian singer father, was first given a classical education and then joined the army, but subsequently pursued a musical career as a tenor singer "in consequence of family circumstances, that led him to prefer a profession offering speedier and more certain emoluments."[12]

In short, musicians had varied social and occupational origins but came, for the most part, from the lower-middle ranks having the least to lose from association with music: artisans of greater or less independence and members of the lower levels of the professions. The four reasons for choosing a musical career were (1) following in the family tradition, (2) the socially neutral circumstance of talent (an advantage for a person of relatively low social origins and a potential source of conflict for someone from a more middle-class family), (3) the hope of becoming rich, and (4) unanticipated economic hardships.

The social and occupational identities of musicians' spouses offer additional perspectives on the social milieu in which musicians lived. Many of them married other professional musicians, although of course the records are biased toward this conclusion since both spouses are generally included in the tally, and because it is more likely that these individuals are mentioned in the records. Since records are less complete for the wives of musicians, most (89 percent) of the non-musical spouses in the table are men.

Marriage patterns suggest some degree of upward social mobility. For instance, English musicians were much more likely to marry wealthy or titled persons than to be descended from them. It should be noted, however, that in no instance was marriage the only source of upward mobility; all the musicians who married aristocrats had achieved substantial financial and professional success before their marriages. In other words, aristocrats do not seem to have formed such alliances with poor or even moderately successful musicians. Such marriages almost always entailed the discontinuation of professional musical employment. All but three of these musicians were women, and most of them and their spouses were British (although one foreign musician, J. S. Schroeter, married his English pupil, and an English musician, Clara Novello, married an Italian count). In two cases, the marriages were clandestine. In consequence of his marriage, Schroeter had to agree to stop performing in public, and later surrendered all rights to his wife's property in exchange for an annuity of £500.[13] The Earl of Peterborough did not avow his thirteen-year marriage to the stage singer Anastasia Robinson until just before his death in 1735.[14]

The remaining numbers of non-musician spouses are too few to support many generalizations. Musicians seemed less likely to marry into families of artisans, shopkeepers, and small manufacturers than they were to have fathers in those categories. They were more likely, if they did not marry musicians, to marry members of other relatively low-status and/or artistic professions.

Most of the musicians' children for whom records exist became professional musicians. However, the number of musicians in this group is undoubtedly overrepresented. Most of the children known to be in the artisan/laborer and independent artisan categories had been apprenticed to various trades by benefit societies as part of the benefits due to their destitute fathers. Since there are no records for the children of impoverished musicians who never even gained admission to a benefit society, the number whose occupations represented downward mobility is undoubtedly much greater than the figures reveal.

Geographical origins and mobility

The geographical distribution of musicians' origins and careers provides another view of the social milieu in which they lived. Table 4 illustrates the

Table 4. *Geographical origins of musicians in Britain*
n = 1,821

	Number	%		Cathedral towns
England[a]				
London and Middlesex	558	30.6		
South	162	8.7		47
South Central	93	5.1		28
East Anglia	58	3.1		31
Midlands	98	5.4		12
West	28	1.5		9
Devon and Cornwall	43	2.4		18
North	157	8.6		65
Unknown	3	0.2		
Wales	22	1.5		14
Scotland	144	7.9	Edinburgh	46
Ireland	74	4.0	Dublin	42
Italy	156	8.6		
Germany	133	7.3		
France	45	2.5		
Other Western Europe	15	0.8		
Central/Eastern Europe	17	0.9		
Colonies	6	0.3		
Foreign but unspecified	9	0.5		

[a] The geographical areas listed represent the following counties:

SOUTH: Kent, Sussex, Surrey, Hants, Wilts., Dorset, Somerset
SOUTH CENTRAL: Herts., Essex, Beds., Berks., Bucks., Oxon., Worcs.
EAST ANGLIA: Norfolk, Suffolk, Cambs.
MIDLANDS: Hunts., Northants, War., Derby., Notts., Lincs., Staffs., Rutland, Leics.
WEST: Salop, Ches., Herefordshire
NORTH: Lancs., Yorks., Durham, Northumberland, Cumberland, Westmorland

geographical origins of musicians during this period. Although the table may overrepresent London relative to the provinces, almost one-third of Britain's professional musicians were born in London, and an even greater proportion settled there. The substantial foreign presence may have been even larger, because only those who actually settled in England are included. The large numbers of professional musicians who made seasonal or occasional visits from other countries do not appear in the table. The table also illustrates that many professional musicians continued to emerge from the cathedral towns. Despite the economic decline experienced by towns such as York and Norwich during the eighteenth century, they continued to supply small but significant numbers of professional musicians as a result of the chorister training that went on at the cathedrals.

Table 5. *Locations of musicians' careers*
n = 5,456

	Number	%	Cathedral towns
England			
London and Middlesex	3066	56.1	
South	367	6.7	83
South Central	201	3.7	74 (Oxford: 46)
East Anglia	116	2.1	20
Midlands	303	5.5	41
West	169	3.0	118
Devon and Cornwall	88	1.6	25
North	468	8.6	61
Provinces (unspecified)	57	1.0	
Wales	109	2.0	70
Scotland	275	5.0	127
Ireland	135	2.5	46
Italy	10	0.2	
Germany	7	0.1	
France	11	0.2	
Other Western Europe	3	0.5	
Central/Eastern Europe	6	0.1	
America/Canada	72	1.3	
Australia/New Zealand	15	0.3	
Other colonies	20	0.4	
Itinerant/international	58	1.1	

Table 5 presents the geographical locations of musicians' careers. London was the unchallenged center of British musical life. Other significant musical centers included Liverpool and Manchester with 194 musicians during this period, Edinburgh with 127, and Dublin with 46. Cathedral towns also had a somewhat higher proportion of musicians, particularly in the western provinces, where 118 (69.8 percent) lived in cathedral towns, and in Wales, where 70 (64 percent) did. The relatively limited opportunities for musical employment at cathedrals cannot account for all these musicians; an added factor was probably the social structure of these towns, which included enough middle-class families to support a small community of performers and, especially, teachers. Most of the other musical employment in the provinces, even in the relatively larger musical centers, was in private teaching. Other opportunities included church and cathedral organist work, membership of cathedral choirs, and orchestral or singing work in provincial theatres. Private employment in the homes of noble patrons was rare. When there were private concerts for the nobility, and when large provincial oratorio festivals occurred, the professional instrumentalists and singers (especially the solo and first-chair players) were almost always imported from London.

The number of British musicians who established careers on the Continent was very small; the flow of musicians was much greater in the other direction. But England did export musicians to two geographical regions: America/Canada and Australia/New Zealand. In the same way that German and Italian musicians in England derived status from their national origins, English musicians seem to have enjoyed relative prestige in America or Australia and to have been preferred for important organist jobs and private teaching. For example, Frederic Archer emigrated to America, becoming first organist at H. Ward Beecher's church in Brooklyn, then moving on to a church in Pittsburgh for £800 a year.[15] Most of these musicians emigrated in the nineteenth century, although there was an early wave of emigration to America in the 1790s, particularly to Philadelphia, where musicians were being recruited for new orchestral and theatrical ventures.[16]

Table 6 illustrates the relationship between musicians' geographical origins and their eventual locations. Although most London-born musicians remained in that city, they accounted for only 40 percent of London's working musicians. Many musicians in London came from European countries (26 percent), notably Germany and Italy. The remaining third came from the English provinces and from Ireland, Scotland, and Wales; most of the musicians born in other regions of Britain left their homes and went to London or, less often, to other provinces. The only real exception is Scotland: 70 percent (96) of Scotland's native musicians remained there, with a much smaller proportion moving to London or other regions. (Many emigrated from other parts of Scotland to Edinburgh.) In fact, other than London, Scotland was the only place that imported more musicians than it exported.

The distribution of musicians in London offers clues to the social niche they inhabited. The neighborhoods well west of the City were more fashionable, while those to the east were more closely built, inhabited primarily by the lower classes. Between these extremes were the commercial City and, just to the west, a number of socially mixed neighborhoods. Roy Porter describes the landscape vividly:

Between the lords and the labourers . . . between Westminster and Whitechapel, lay Holborn, Hoxton and Hackney, the large metropolitan midriff inhabited by a couple of hundred thousand solid citizens: master craftsmen, genteel merchants, tutors, apothecaries, clothiers, skinners, brewers, ironmongers, salters, drapers, haberdashers, vintners, confectioners, chandlers, coalmen, joiners, cutlers, candle-makers, hatters and tailors – professional men, established artisans, journeymen and their families, apprentices and servants: thrifty, cautious, but comfortable.[17]

Table 6. *Cross-tabulation of geographical origins and locations of careers*
n = 1,766

	Locations of careers										
Geographical Origins	London and Middlesex	South	South Central	East Anglia	Midlands	West	Devon and Cornwall	North	Provinces (unspecified)	Wales	Scotland
London and Middlesex	100	11	6	4	4	2	6	16	7	1	14
South	49	19	—	3	1	1	1	6	1	2	4
South Central	17	4	26	2	6	7	1	1	—	—	—
East Anglia	21	2	2	16	—	1	1	2	—	—	2
Midlands	34	2	2	1	12	—	1	8	2	1	3
West	17	—	—	—	2	1	—	5	3	—	1
Devon and Cornwall	18	—	4	—	1	—	6	2	1	—	1
North	44	7	2	5	3	2	2	51	1	—	9
Unknown	9	—	—	—	—	—	—	—	—	1	—
Wales	5	—	1	—	—	—	—	2	—	9	1
Scotland	24	—	1	—	—	—	—	2	2	—	96
Ireland	23	1	—	—	—	—	—	—	2	—	2
Italy	114	2	—	—	2	—	1	—	—	—	4
Germany	115	4	2	—	1	—	—	1	—	—	1
France	10	1	1	—	—	—	—	1	—	—	1
Other Western Europe	11	—	—	—	—	—	—	—	—	—	—
Central/Eastern Europe	12	—	1	—	—	—	—	1	—	—	—
Colonies	4	—	—	—	—	—	—	—	—	—	—

Locations of careers

Ireland	Italy	Germany	France	Other Western Europe	Central/Eastern Europe	America/Canada	Australia/New Zealand	Other colonies	Itinerant/international
8	1	2	4	—	—	27	5	4	11
1	—	—	—	—	—	4	3	—	4
1	—	1	—	—	—	3	—	1	—
1	—	—	—	—	—	—	—	—	3
2	—	—	—	—	—	2	—	1	1
—	—	—	—	—	—	1	—	—	—
—	—	—	—	—	—	2	—	—	2
2	—	1	—	—	1	7	—	1	2
—	—	1	—	—	—	—	—	—	—
—	—	—	—	—	—	1	—	—	1
2	—	—	—	—	—	6	—	—	4
26	—	—	—	—	1	3	3	1	4
2	7	—	1	—	—	—	—	—	17
1	—	2	1	—	—	—	—	—	3
2	—	—	1	1	—	—	—	—	4
—	—	—	—	—	—	—	—	—	3
—	—	—	1	—	—	—	—	—	2
—	—	—	—	—	—	—	—	1	—

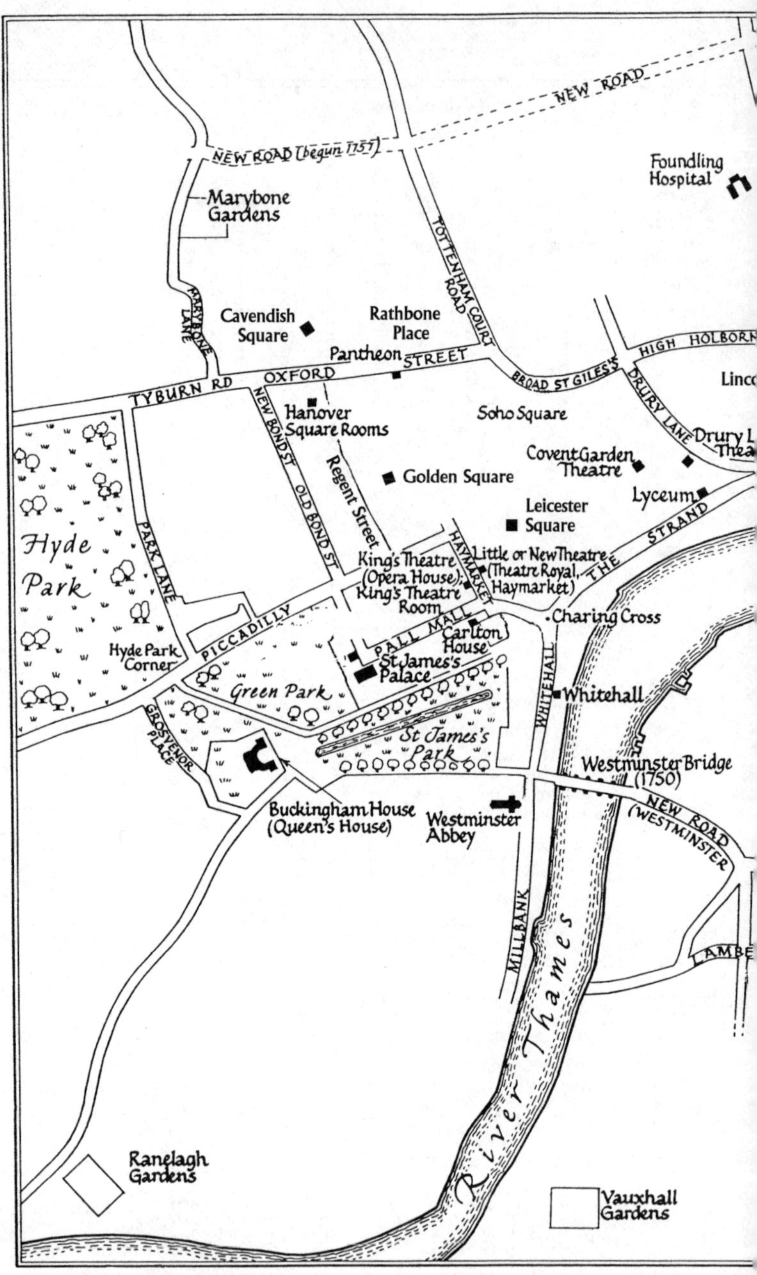

Map of London in the second half of the eighteenth century, showing the principal concert venues

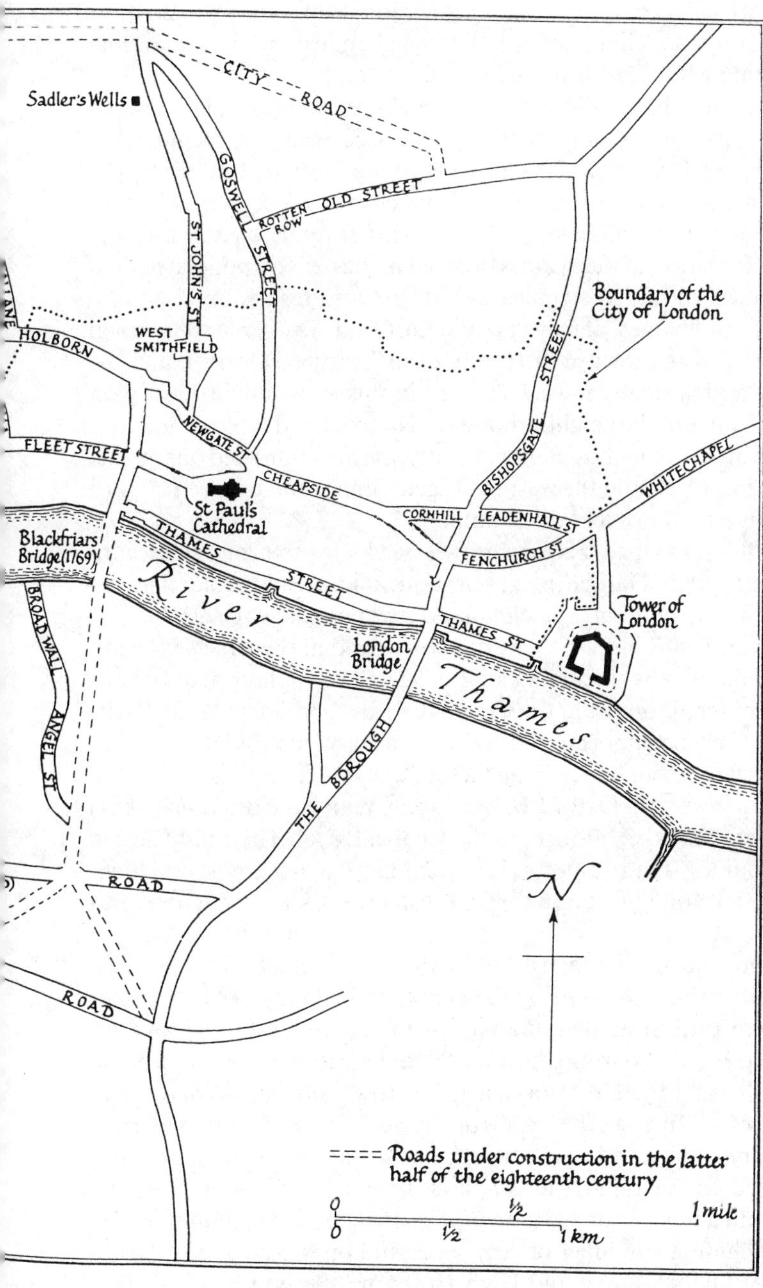

Sadler's Wells
CITY ROAD
GOSWELL STREET
ST JOHN'S ST
ROTTEN ROW
OLD STREET
Boundary of the City of London
HOLBORN
WEST SMITHFIELD
NEWGATE ST
BISHOPSGATE STREET
FLEET STREET
CHEAPSIDE
WHITECHAPEL
St Paul's Cathedral
CORNHILL
LEADENHALL ST
Blackfriars Bridge (1769)
THAMES STREET
FENCHURCH ST
River
Tower of London
BROAD WALL
ANGEL ST
London Bridge
THAMES ST
Thames
THE BOROUGH
N
ROAD
ROAD
Roads under construction in the latter half of the eighteenth century
0   ½   1 mile
0   ½   1 km

The mix of artisans, tradesman, and professionals of varying degrees of wealth and property characterized the social milieu of the "middling classes," among whom musicians lived and worked.

Documents providing a glimpse of the neighborhoods of London musicians include the 1794 Doane directory of musicians,[18] the membership records of the Philharmonic Society when it was founded in 1813, and mid-nineteenth-century census data and directories. Since the Doane directory included street addresses we can ascertain quite clearly that the greatest concentration of musicians occurred in the densely populated area Porter described, although significant numbers also resided in Westminster, south of the Thames, and even in the East End. The center of musical life, however, was the theatre district (Covent Garden, Drury Lane, the Haymarket); a great many musicians lived in this area and also just west into Soho and on into the neighborhoods of Hanover and Golden Squares. One hundred and twenty musicians resided in the area bounded on the east by Lincoln's Inn Fields, on the west by Regent Street, and between Oxford Street and High Holborn and the Strand.

Much of this area had become rather seedy by the late eighteenth century. The Covent Garden neighborhood, once fashionable, had become "raffish, disreputable, pockmarked by taverns and brothels."[19] Twenty-one musicians in the Doane directory lived in the streets immediately around the theatre, including stage singers and orchestral musicians such as the first-chair oboist in the Covent Garden orchestra, W. T. Parke (1761–1847). The neighborhood also housed very successful and well-known musicians from other branches of the profession, such as the composer, organist, and Oxford B.Mus. John Wall Callcott (1766–1821) and Israel Gore (b. 1759), a singer in the Chapel Royal. Their residence in the colorful but less-than-respectable Covent Garden neighborhood highlights the social ambiguities of the musical profession throughout this period.

Soho became the home of artists and writers early in the 1700s, but had lost some of its former panache by the period under study. As Roy Porter points out, Gerrard Street became known for coffeehouses and taverns, and Greek Street for boarding houses. "The Leicester Square and Soho precinct ... became the haunt of artists, writers, bohemians, rakes, and revolutionaries."[20] In 1794 the area from Soho Square to Charing Cross, between Drury Lane and Regent Street, housed about eighty musicians. These included orchestral instrumentalists, singers in choirs and theatres, composers, and a notable proportion of foreigners. Significant numbers of musicians, including a number of very successful ones, also lived immediately north of Oxford Street and High Holborn.[21] Seven musicians lived around Oxford Market and Titchfield Street, including J. B. Cramer and also G. B. Viotti, the violinist at Salomon's concerts (and, some years later, leader of the King's Theatre orchestra). A cluster of twenty musicians lived on Rathbone and Upper Rathbone Place; one of these was the opera composer Stephen Storace.

Some of the most financially successful musicians lived in more fashionable neighborhoods west of these central districts. Continuing west from Oxford Market and Rathbone Place and crossing into Marylebone, we find musicians such as Muzio Clementi, and the highly successful cellist, John Crosdill (1755–1825). Originally a chorister at Westminster Abbey, Crosdill later became a cellist in the King's Band and Chapel Royal. Largely because of his marriage to a very wealthy woman, by 1794 he was living on Upper Harley Street; when he died in 1825 he left £1,000 to the Royal Society of Musicians.[22] A surprising number (sixty-five) lived in the posh area extending westwards from Regent Street to the neighborhoods around the parks. This is partially explained by the twenty-eight musicians who were employed in the royal and aristocratic households (eighteen in Buckingham House), virtually all of whom were foreign musicians. The foreign musicians' near-monopoly of such patronage explains much of the antipathy felt toward them by their English colleagues. The Hanover Square neighborhood, which bordered Mayfair to the west and housed a number of important concert series over the years, also housed a number of renowned foreign musicians, including the violinist and concert impresario J. P. Salomon and the violinist Felice Giardini.[23] Even fewer musicians (sixteen) lived further west in Kensington and Chelsea, among them the ultimate "gentleman-musician," Charles Burney.

Musicians, not surprisingly, clustered around the cathedrals. Many of the nearly eighty musicians living in the City were within a few streets of St. Paul's, and proximity to the Abbey was probably also a consideration for the fifty-nine living in Westminster. A significant number also lived just over Westminster Bridge in Lambeth; in fact, fifteen musicians inhabited Stangate Street, and twenty-five others lived between Westminster Bridge and Vauxhall Gardens. Somewhat surprising, given the distance from most of the places of work for musicians, thirty-three lived east of the City, in working-class Spitalfields, Whitechapel, and Bethnal Green. They were not among the best-employed musicians of course, and probably combined music with other occupations.

The geographical distribution, then, mirrors the broad range of social and economic status among musicians. In 1794 only a very few musicians had the income to live in the western sections of the city, and most were servants of royal and noble households. A number lived east of the City in districts populated by weavers and other poor workers. Many inhabited the narrow streets surrounding the cathedrals, and most crowded into the seedy, central districts populated by artisans, shopkeepers, and theatre life.

The records of the Philharmonic Society, founded in 1813, include the addresses of some forty founding members.[24] Since these were among the elite of London musicians, it is interesting to compare their addresses to those of the broader sample of musicians from twenty years earlier. As might be expected, many lived in fairly central districts in and around the main theatres, just off the Strand, near Leicester Square, or in Soho. About as many lived in the more fashionable Marylebone, however, near Portland Place and Cavendish Square. Eighteen of the founders, who had been included in the Doane directory twenty years earlier, had moved within the same general area, but a few had moved to locations that suggest a social rise. The pianist J. B. Cramer had moved from Titchfield Street near Oxford Market to Sloane Street, and his brother, the violinist François Cramer, left the same neighborhood for Cavendish Square. Although the numbers are small, the larger proportion who lived in Marylebone probably reflects the relatively high status of the Philharmonic Society founders as well as some degree of upward social mobility for the most successful members of the profession.

A closer look at the neighborhood of Golden Square may further illustrate the subtle shifts in the character and musical inhabitants of the more central districts. Between Soho to the east and Mayfair to the west, the streets in and around Golden Square housed twelve musicians from the Doane directory. A mixture of natives and foreigners, they included two members of the Royal Society of Musicians and four from the New Musical Fund. Eight were string players: Clark and Slezack, violinists at the aristocratic Academy of Ancient Music; Scola who played cello in the King's Band and the Professional Concert; and Corfe, a double bassist at the Drury Lane theatre. The sole wind player in the neighborhood, William Windsor, played oboe, bassoon, and clarinet. Two singers resided in and around the square: one, J. Cooke, sang at Drury Lane, and another, "Signor Morrigi," was a bass singer at the Italian Opera. Finally, listed as composer and pianoforte player at the Professional Concert, the Opera, and Salomon's concerts, was "Dr. Joseph Haydn." A few years later, from 1799 to 1802, Golden Square was the home of the renowned double bass virtuoso, Domenico Dragonetti.[25]

The mix of native and foreign musicians was characteristic of such neighborhoods. However, the social character of Golden Square, like other such neighborhoods, may have shifted downward in the early nineteenth century. In his 1839 novel *Nicholas Nickleby*, Charles Dickens provides a glimpse both of Golden Square's decline and of English perceptions that music, foreigners, and seediness were inextricably linked:

Although a few members of the graver professions live about Golden Square, it is not exactly in anybody's way to or from anywhere. It is one of the squares that have been; a quarter of the town that has gone down in the world, and taken to letting lodgings. Many of its first and second floors are let furnished to single gentlemen, and it takes boarders besides. It is a great resort of foreigners... Two or three violins and a wind instrument from the Opera band reside within its precincts. Its boarding-houses are musical, and the notes of pianos and harps float in the evening time round the head of the mournful statue ... in the centre of the square. On a summer's night, windows are thrown open, and groups of swarthy mustachioed men are seen by the passer-by lounging at the casements, and smoking fearfully. Sounds of gruff voices practising vocal music invade the evening's silence, and the fumes of choice tobacco scent the air. There, snuff and cigars, and German pipes and flutes, and violins, and violoncellos, divide the supremacy between them. It is the region of song and smoke.[26]

The census of 1851 reveals that at that time the highest concentrations of professional musicians were still to be found near the theatres in the inner districts of London bordered by the Thames to the south and the City to the east: Holborn, the Strand, St. Giles, St. Martin in the Fields, St. James Westminster, St. George Hanover Square, and St. Pancras.[27] By the 1850s, a neighborhood such as St. Anne Soho, with several large lodging houses, was populated by poor professionals, foreigners, drapers' assistants, musical instrument makers, professional musicians (native and foreign), and an assortment of artisans.[28] Some of the most successful London musicians moved further west to less crowded, more respectable neighborhoods, perhaps a way of distancing themselves socially from the urban artisan as they sought a different image of the respectable, professional musician.

The social and geographical milieu of professional musicians encompassed wide variations, and the mixed and motley world they inhabited offers important insights into the struggle of the profession for a clear identity and status. Musicians were generally literate and highly skilled. Many can be classified as moderately independent artisans, although individual careers could range well beyond a narrow artisanal world.[29] Like other members of the "middling classes," musicians interacted with and occupied more than one social class at a time.[30] The profession included not only elite composers, performers, and concert impresarios who associated with aristocratic patrons, but also performers who sank into the lowest levels of the urban poor. Yet even destitute musicians might have a level of education, skills, cultural experience, and perceptions that clearly distinguished them from others at the same economic level. The variations of status within the profession and throughout this period will be clarified in subsequent chapters. First, however, it will be useful to examine the most tangible expression of musicians' social and economic status, and one that distinguished them from their counterparts in most other aspiring professions – the system of patronage.

3   Patronage

The period from the late eighteenth through mid-nineteenth century is often characterized as a time when individual patronage waned and was replaced by more anonymous and collective market forces. As Harold Perkin explains, traditional patronage relationships represented "the middle term between feudal homage and capitalist cash nexus,"[1] and were replaced, ostensibly, by more or less open forms of competition which relied on different criteria of merit: "Patronage . . . contained an element of selection by merit, measured by the judgment and importance of the patron. Competition, on the other hand, appealed to a far more impartial judge, 'fortune,' 'market forces,' or material success."[2] This alleged dichotomy between personal aristocratic patronage and competition for a middle-class audience appears frequently in the accounts of music history concerning this period. For example, Donald Grout writes that "Patronage was on the wane and the modern musical public was coming into being."[3] Longyear describes the early nineteenth-century musician as "no longer under patronage."[4]

There are several problems with this view. First, contemporaries used the term "patronage" to refer to any and all sources of financial support for music and musicians. The narrower definition – personal, aristocratic patronage – came to be expressed by the words "connection" and "interest." Secondly, the polarization between personal patronage and market competition is overdrawn. Musicians' careers reveal a much more subtle and complex range of personal, professional, and financial arrangements than can be subsumed under these two categories. For example, the competition that characterized free-lance careers often continued to be dependent on traditional determinations of merit by patrons. Furthermore, the shift from personal patronage to market competition was gradual and musicians combined many different types of patronage throughout the eighteenth and nineteenth centuries.

In Continental Europe, the dichotomy between traditional and market patronage was probably greater, and the rate of change swifter.[5] As Henry Raynor explains, European courts provided much more support for music and musicians than did the English royal household. There were also many more courts and aristocratic households on the Continent maintaining musical establishments on a grand scale. However, these traditional patrons of music were adversely affected by the French Revolution, subsequent wars, and post-war social and economic conditions: "As the huge aristocratic fortunes evaporated, a savage inflation and post-war depression after 1815 made the support of a paying audience essential to satisfactorily performing opera and large-scale orchestral music."[6]

Even on the Continent the shift from private aristocratic to public middle-class patronage was far from complete by the nineteenth century. As Raynor points out,

Court patronage did not end in the lifetime of Beethoven, as a result of the Napoleonic Wars or for any reason. From Weber, through Spohr and Wagner to Brahms, Richard Strauss and, as late as 1913, Reger, important composers were in court service. The customary simplification, that the courts were no longer able to support music, is really untenable. The lesser aristocracy lost their power of patronage; the greater did not.[7]

Of course, there was only one court in England, and it did not support music and musicians on the scale of some European courts. Nevertheless, Raynor's point is just as true for Britain. Aristocratic patronage continued to be an important and prestigious source of support for musical institutions well into the nineteenth century.

These differences are especially important given the number of foreign musicians emigrating to England. The shift to more open competition for various types of employment began much earlier in Britain. Foreign musicians suddenly encountered the possibility of free-lance careers, varied employment opportunities and extraordinarily high earnings – as well as greater insecurity.

Descriptions based on a simple dichotomy between personal aristocratic and anonymous middle-class patronage overlook the wide variety of patronage relationships which were important in musical careers. I have identified seven distinct types of patronage in this period: royal, aristocratic, middle-class, professional, church, military, and municipal. The last two became significant only in the mid-nineteenth century, and will be addressed in specific career areas in subsequent chapters.

The other categories require two other distinctions: private versus public (or collective) patronage, and direct versus indirect (or mediated) patronage. Private patronage refers to the personal connection between patron and musician. An aristocrat who hired a musician to perform at a private concert, or a middle-class parent who engaged a private teacher, both exerted private patronage. Since this involved a more intimate association between patron and musician, non-musical qualities such as respectable appearance and manners were often of primary importance for employment. Public – or collective – patronage, on the other hand, required collaboration with other patrons. Aristocrats might plan as a group to finance a new concert series or allow their names to be listed as subscribers, thereby enhancing the concert's prestige. Middle-class audiences engaged in public patronage when they purchased tickets or subscriptions to concert series.

It is equally important to distinguish between direct and indirect patronage, particularly with regard to the evolution of professional independence and authority. Individual patrons planning private concerts, and who had full control over the selection of musicians, exerted direct patronage. In many instances, however, the route from patron to musician was less direct, as when a patron engaged a musician to hire the rest of the musicians for a private concert. Similarly, public audiences bought tickets, but had no say in the hiring of the performers; such decisions – like most indirect patronage – were usually in professional hands.

The opportunity to provide patronage of all varieties allowed women to participate in musical life.[8] Royal and aristocratic women especially played important roles throughout this period, sometimes sponsoring their own concert series. Women of the middle classes employed music teachers, and bought concert tickets and printed music. This chapter addresses the different sources of patronage and their evolving role and importance during this period; their characteristics as private or public, direct or indirect; and the implications – for musicians' social and professional status – of each type of patronage relationship.

Royal patronage

Public royal patronage usually occurred in cooperation with aristocratic patronage. Private royal patronage took the following forms: the Chapels Royal – one each in London and Windsor; the private bands (orchestras) of the King and Queen; and the appointment of individual musicians as performers or instructors.[9] Such patronage conferred enormous social and professional prestige, which translated into other engagements as performers and teachers. The extent and character of private royal patronage varied with the musical tastes of individual monarchs, but some degree of royal participation in musical life can be observed throughout most of this period.

The Chapels Royal employed singers, choristers, organists, a choirmaster and, at least in London, a composer. The royal household paid for the salaries, surplices, and expenses such as food and transportation for the choristers. (Apparently it did not pay for the purchase or copying of music, which had to be copied out at the composer's expense.[10]) The musicians who obtained employment in the Chapels Royal were already elite professionals either as singers or organists, and some of them (including William Boyce, Thomas Attwood, and S. S. Wesley) were well known as composers of English church music.

The King's Band employed a Master of the Music and a band of musicians-in-ordinary. They performed at court balls and other occasions, and dressed in livery. In addition, royal appointments included a sergeant trumpeter as well as other trumpeters and drummers. Some of these positions may have been honorary gifts to non-musicians, and foreigners were not eligible for these appointments. In mid-century, Queen Charlotte founded an eight-person wind band, called the Queen's Band. The history and chronology of this group is reported differently in a number of sources,[11] but it seems to have been intended originally as a military wind band made up of native musicians only. But the Queen had also formed a Chamber Band with leading foreign musicians: J. C. Bach, C. F. Abel, Wilhelm Cramer, and J. C. Fischer. In 1783 the original Queen's Band was expanded by inviting twelve German musicians to come to England, including several members of the Griesbach and Kellner families.[12] This band performed nightly wherever the King was in residence at London, Windsor, and later Brighton. They wore uniforms, "a scarlet frock, white waistcoat and breeches, a cocked hat and sword. On Sundays they wore full dress coats very much ornamented with gold lace."[13]

It seems that during the reign of George III, the King himself supervised the choice of music in the programs. His preference for the music of Handel amounted to a prejudice, if not an obsession, limiting the variety of his own concerts as well as some public concerts. Michael Kelly's musical reminiscences suggest the influence that the King had even at large-scale performances such as the Handel Commemoration Festival of 1784:

The fine chorus of "Lift up your heads, o ye gates," was always given in full chorus, and indeed intended to be so given by Handel. The King suggested that the first part of it should be made a semi-chorus and sung only by the principal singers; but when it came to the passage, "He is the King of Glory!" he commanded that the whole orchestra, with the full chorus, should, with a tremendous force, burst out; the effect produced by the alteration was awful and sublime.[14]

Kelly thought the King an excellent judge of Handel's music, affirming the King's role as artistic advisor in this instance. Other professional musicians, however, suggested that since the King's narrow musical tastes were emulated by most other patrons, the musical life of the country was unduly restricted. "His court and country adopted not alone his general but his peculiar taste [Handel])."[15]

A third manifestation of royal musical patronage was the appointment of individual musicians as performers or teachers in the royal family. The oboist John Parke was appointed chamber musician to the Prince of Wales in 1783; Charles Wesley was organist-in-ordinary to George IV; T. Latour, a composer of popular piano music, was pianist to the King from 1824; Angus Mackay was piper to Queen Victoria in the 1830s and 1840s; William Ross, a military musician in Scotland, was appointed piper to the Queen in 1854; Ellis Roberts was harpist to the Prince of Wales in the mid-nineteenth century; John Balsir Chatterton was harpist to the Queen; John Thomas (Pencerdd Gwalia, Chief Bard of Wales) succeeded Chatterton in 1871; and there were many others. Such appointments probably involved occasional performances at court, but were primarily honors which undoubtedly furthered these musicians' careers.

Many musicians also enjoyed appointments as instructors to members of the royal family. Queen Charlotte employed a succession of eminent music masters: before 1782, Joseph Kelway, and afterward J. Schroeter, a German composer. Carl Friedrich Horn was appointed as music master to the royal princesses in 1782. The composer Joseph Mazzinghi was hired to instruct the Princess of Wales in the late eighteenth century. Later, Queen Victoria employed the singer J. B. Sale, who taught many royal pupils, Lucy Anderson as piano instructor, and Luigi Lablache, the internationally known opera singer, as her singing instructor.

In addition to the benefits conferred by actual employment in the royal household, the privilege of playing for the King or Queen, especially as a child "prodigy," could be helpful in obtaining further patronage. But royal patrons rarely supervised musical careers. One exception was Henry Gamble Blagrove (1811–72), a violinist appointed to Queen Adelaide's Private Band in 1830, toward the end of his studies at the Royal Academy of Music. The Queen gave him a temporary leave from the band and continued to pay his salary while he continued his studies in Germany.[16] Typically, however, private royal patronage of music was limited to employment in the Chapels Royal, in private ensembles, as solo performers with honorary titles, and as instructors.

Aristocratic patronage

Private aristocratic patronage on the scale of royal patronage had ceased to exist in England by the early eighteenth century. The latest example of an aristocratic household supporting music on a royal scale is provided by the private chapel of the Duke of Chandos in the 1720s. Even then, however, the Duke's musical establishment was considered to be exceptionally grand.[17] But more modest forms of private aristocratic patronage existed throughout this period and remained highly valued by professional musicians.

Aristocrats occasionally fostered the careers of young musicians. In the mid-eighteenth century Sir Watkins W. Wynn, a Welsh baronet and avid musical patron, discovered Edward Meredith singing as he worked in a cooper's shop. Wynn paid for Meredith's formal training and helped launch his career.[18] In other instances, aristocratic recommendations seemed helpful in obtaining admission to the Royal Academy of Music. Aristocratic support for study in Germany was rare, although two mid-nineteenth-century examples are flutist Robert S. Pratten and the bass singer Aynsley Cook.[19]

Aristocratic patrons routinely employed individual musicians, a practice that continued throughout the nineteenth century. Benjamin Milgrove directed the Countess of Huntingdon's chapel in Bath in the mid-eighteenth century; Joseph Hart was organist to the Earl of Uxbridge around 1820; other examples include Charles Moss Coote, pianist to the Duke of Devonshire in the 1830s; Edmund Bryan Harper, pianist to the Marquis of Downshire from the 1840s; Robert Sloman, organist to Earl Powis in 1852; William Ridley, organist to the Earl of Oxford in the 1870s; and Thomas Smith, organist at Hozzinger, the seat of the Marquis of Bristol, in the 1880s.[20]

Household musicians sometimes managed private concerts and instructed family members. Andrew Ashe, a flutist, was family musician to Lord Torrington in Brussels in the 1770s. William Tibet, a violin and viola player, reported in 1782 that he lived with "His Grace the Duke of Malbrough [Marlborough] as private Musician." In the 1790s, James Hyde was trumpeter to the Duke of York. John White, an organist and composer, was employed by the Earl of Harewood as leader and director of his private concerts and family instructor in piano and singing. Henry Lazarus (clarinetist) and George Macfarlane (cornetist and bandmaster) were members of the Duke of Devonshire's private band in the mid-nineteenth century. Sometimes the musician seemed almost a family member. Thomas Greatorex was reportedly "adopted" by the Earl of Sandwich in the 1770s, and George Baker "entered the family" of the Earl of Uxbridge in the 1780s. In neither case is legal adoption implied, but rather an intimate patronage relationship well suited to furthering the musicians' careers.[21]

Private aristocratic patronage also took the form of engaging private teachers, whose professional success was defined in part by the number of aristocratic pupils they instructed. For example, after the abovementioned

John White was employed as the Earl of Harewood's music director and teacher, he continued teaching in the Leeds area in the early 1800s and was "said to have had the patronage of nearly all the noblemen's and gentlemen's families within the space of twenty miles."[22]

In the eighteenth century, aristocrats pooled their resources (often in collaboration with royal patrons) to support musical institutions on a grander scale than would have been possible for individual households. This public, collective patronage involved varying levels of financial and personal commitment, from purchasing concert subscriptions to participating in a collective effort to finance and manage a musical institution. Such activities were largely responsible for the dramatic emergence of public concert life in the second half of the eighteenth century.[23]

Two of the leading musical institutions of this period exemplify the system of public (collective) aristocratic patronage: the Italian Opera and the Concert of Ancient Music. The management board of the Italian Opera was entirely aristocratic, but the artistic decisions were mediated by Italian singer/managers as well as by many of the more influential singers. One critic wrote in 1822, "the Opera is not to be considered as an entertainment for the British public. It has rather been taken as a place of fashionable resort for the elevated ranks of society – for the dilettante and the profession – and for the foreign residents. Of such are the constant audiences composed."[24] In fact, as Jennifer Hall has carefully demonstrated, the audiences for the Italian Opera were filled with aristocratic and middle-class elites jockeying for social status.[25] Still, it represented the most lavish and long-lived of aristocratically supported musical institutions during these years.

The Concert of Ancient Music (also known as the King's Concert), founded in 1776, was both culturally and socially even more exclusive than the Italian Opera. Only music written more than twenty years earlier could be performed. Perhaps this was a capitulation to George III's predilection for Handel, but William Weber has convincingly shown that the Concert also represents one expression of an evolving musical canon.[26] The performers were both native and foreign; they included the season's opera stars, the leading singers from the royal chapels and the London cathedral choirs, and the best English female stage singers. Certainly, the programs included more English music than was typical for concerts of this time.[27]

The aristocratic directors of the Concert hired singers and instrumentalists and planned the programs, often in collaboration with the King. As Percy Young explains,

The King was no passive patron. He was ready to express his views and to exert his influence. Thus he sent a memorandum to Lord Carmarthen regarding a programme submitted to him from the Ancient Concerts: "Lord Carmarthen's List of Musick for next Wednesday is very excellent and meets with the Approbation of those whose opinion on the Subject He wished to know; His introducing Mrs. Billington if He can get Her to sing pathetik Songs and not to overgrace them will be doing an essential service to the Concert."[28]

Later monarchs do not seem to have taken so active an interest, but the concerts continued to be managed entirely by aristocratic directors and to feature the works of Handel more than any other composer. By the 1820s, the concerts had earned a reputation for stodginess, at least from a musical point of view. Even then, however, the presence of the very best English and foreign performers maintained unrivaled performance standards.

A number of concerts combined aristocratic patronage with professional direction. Notable examples include those managed by Bach and Abel from the mid-1760s, Salomon in the 1780s and 1790s, and the Professional Concert of the same period. The high artistic standards of these London performances reflected a new and more distinct demarcation between amateurs and professionals, itself significant for the development of the profession. As McVeigh points out, the flourishing of such concerts was not in any way an indication of a growing middle-class audience: "The reins of taste were firmly in the hands of the higher aristocracy," and great pains were taken by selling subscriptions (not individual tickets), controlling the subscription lists, and by keeping the prices high to exclude attendance by members of the middle ranks.[29] As will be shown, this social exclusivity reached a peak in the 1820s, but gradually had to give way to the growing cultural role of middle-class patrons and consumers of music.[30]

The role of women in planning and supporting concerts in the last decades of the eighteenth century is remarkable. Excluded from administrative roles (and even from subscriptions) in some concerts, they managed to support many others, while organizing their own private concerts. A list of weekly concerts in a 1792 issue of the *Morning Chronicle* included seventeen concerts, of which eight were organized by royal and aristocratic women.[31] For several years around 1790 there was even a private concert series known as the Ladies Concert.[32] Of course, women were also the primary consumers of music lessons, instruments, and sheet music. Clearly, women of means were active patrons of music during these years.

The conflict between public patronage of concerts and the desire for social exclusivity resulted in a proliferation of private aristocratic concerts in the last decades of the eighteenth century.[33] This might be viewed as a deliberate rearguard action against both the growing power of middle-class consumers of music and the increasing transfer of artistic control to professional musicians. Both public and private aristocratic concerts, however, dwindled under the social and economic pressures of the war years. By the time London's concert life showed signs of renewal, the political and social challenge offered by the middle classes was more apparent – as were initiatives toward professional independence. Aristocratic patrons seemed much less willing to support concert series. Their retreat to private concerts, especially in the 1820s, alarmed observers of London's musical scene, who noted "the increase and predominance of private over public concerts" as "the most important musical phenomena of the times."

There are several causes which have no reference to music itself, that are working this revolution. In the first place, the passion of persons of condition is the exclusion of all but those of their own caste from their society and amusements. The same feeling (or the desire of imitating it) afflicts those of the next degrees to a lower gradation than is suspected. Hence every thing which is really open to the public at large, not only affords little temptation to rank and wealth, but is absolutely held in contempt by the possessors of these distinctions. To sit in the pit at the Opera, or in the body of the Argyll Rooms, is somewhat allied to a sense of degradation.[34]

Another article, in 1825, gave the same explanation, that the "exclusive spirit ... is perhaps the strongest impulse to private concerts. The equality of a public room instantly sinks those who affect supremacy to the common level. Were it not for the distinction which boxes bestow, the Opera would not continue three years."[35] Others suggested that the retreat of the wealthiest patrons to their own private concerts was due to the conflict between the hours of public concerts and the current fashionable late hours for dining; in private concerts, the music was timed to fit the convenience of the guests. It was also argued that the private concerts were more relaxed and personal than the public ones: "Private concerts have less formality, less observation in them than public. The guests approach the instruments or the singer – lounge from room to room or on the staircases – converse, and come or go at pleasure, and with far more ease than can be accomplished in public rooms."[36]

The flight of aristocratic patrons from public concerts, with the subsequent rumors that the best music could only be heard in private circles,[37] was thought to be the reason some public concerts foundered in the 1820s: "the public ruin is to a certain degree the private exaltation of Music."[38] One observer noted the spread of musical activity and appreciation in society, and hoped that the increase in general support would make up for the loss of aristocratic patrons who preferred concerts in their homes: "Since the love of its [music's] enjoyment has taken deep root in the nation, and since its shoots are spread throughout the whole population, it can never be eradicated, and perhaps it makes a part and not a very inconsiderable part of the question, whether universality of support will not compensate the partial defection of the more affluent patrons?"[39] Although this hope was realistic for the long run, the growth of a middle-class audience does not seem to have made up for the aristocratic defection from public concerts in the 1820s. One observer wrote in 1825: "From the rapid growth of wealth, and consequently of an affluent population, it is not possible to compute what the effects may be, but it is not difficult to perceive the highest classes are fast gliding away from the support of public concerts."[40]

Perhaps the major objection by professional musicians was the overwhelming preference given to foreign musicians in these private concerts, thereby conferring on foreign musicians the most socially and professionally prestigious forms of patronage. In 1823, it was reported that

[private parties] are becoming more numerous and extensive in their arrangements. It forms a curious feature of the enquiry into this department of music, that if you ask some of the English professors, they assure you private parties were never less frequent; if you address the question to the foreign artist, he says they never were so general. This strongly corroborates the ascendancy of foreign music.[41]

And in 1829, "there has been much private music in town during the season, at which however foreign musicians have been the principal attractions."[42] Not only the musicians but the music itself was foreign; there was apparently no English music at all on the programs: "when such facts are producible, the empire of foreign music is all but established."[43]

Neglect by aristocratic patrons was blamed for the general weakness of the native musical profession:

Our noble and opulent patrons of music ... close the avenues to the English professor – they hold out no encouragement to English talent – and in their admiration of all that is foreign, they forget that it is [due] to ... their own cold indifference to the natives of their own country that that country has not produced more Billingtons and Brahams... They forget that while they nurse and applaud foreign ability, the sun of noble patronage shines only in the narrow region of the antient concert upon English merit.[44]

Why did aristocrats prefer to employ foreign musicians at their private concerts? In some instances they were the best musicians available. But more than musical merit led to their successful competition for employment at private concerts. Foreign musicians rarely had any real extramusical educational or social advantages over English musicians. They did, however, have an apparent cosmopolitanism, sometimes a familiarity with several languages, and ingratiating manners developed in the service of European royal and noble patrons. In contrast, the relatively low social origins of English musicians were more difficult to disguise in their own country and language.

The Italian singer or the German violinist is a cosmopolite ... foreign artists find themselves equally at home at Vienna and at Paris, at London, or at

St. Petersburgh ... Not so the English professor. He very rarely indeed quits his highly valued country – and still more rarely rises to notice when he does ... it is clear that the English professor lacks advantages that have no small share in recommending the artist of the Continent ... there are technical varieties, to be gained by collision and competition among those who see men and cities[,] that confer a superiority, which to envy is not to emulate – to complain of is not to abate.[45]

The pleasing manners of foreign musicians took an even more endearing form for aristocratic patrons: a willingness to perform without pay. As one writer commented in 1821,

If we examine the materials of private concerts in London, we shall also, I fear, find that English talent is nearly excluded, and that the English profession is discouraged, principally because, as *it is said*, Italian performers are content to accept invitations in the hope of patronage at their benefits, while our native singers expect the reward which is to be the support of their existence.[46]

Another observer responded to the comments of one professional musician by agreeing that he "was not far from the truth, when he assigned the gratuitous assistance of foreigners at private concerts of the metropolis, as one of the causes of their predominance over our less insinuating, less politic English professors."[47] One English musician who learned to cultivate connections in this way testified in a lawsuit (in which a young Frenchwoman attempted to obtain payment for her harp performance at a private concert) that he "was not paid [for his services at private concerts] because he generally mixed with the company."[48] As long as musicians were dependent upon aristocratic patrons and were vulnerable to the competition from foreign musicians who did not appear to share their professional values and ideals, their social and professional status would remain low.

Despite these perceived problems, aristocratic patrons continued to support native musicians in several ways, including donations to charities such as the musicians' benefit societies. The Royal Society of Musicians gained its royal charter in 1790, but always attracted aristocratic patrons for the society, and for the annual benefit concert. And when the Society of Female Musicians was organized in 1839 it swiftly gained the sponsorship of Queen Victoria and a number of aristocratic women. Aristocratic patronage was entirely responsible for the founding and directing of the Royal Academy of Music in 1822.

This period cannot be described simply as one in which aristocratic patronage of music was supplanted by middle-class audiences. Aristocratic patrons continued to be extremely influential in furthering musical careers both by providing employment and also by conferring the social prestige of association with wealthy, high-class patrons. They were, moreover, central to the extraordinary flowering of concert life in the second half of the eighteenth century. However, aristocratic patrons tended, first in the 1780s and 1790s and then again in the 1820s, to retreat from socially mixed public audiences to the exclusiveness of private concerts. They did not disappear from public concert patronage, but their role grew more limited. In part, this retreat reflects an aristocratic response to the challenges from below about political legitimacy and leadership. They had to compete with the middle classes for identification with virtue and patriotism. As McVeigh explains, there was "a redefinition of the public image of the threatened aristocracy, from profligate pleasure-seekers to responsible servants of the country... Respectability, marked by seriousness of purpose and simplicity of taste, became the fashion."[49] They retreated not only to a more elite setting and audience, but to a relationship with musicians that, at least in England, was a social and professional anachronism. They were able to turn the clock back, at least temporarily, by employing the more ingratiating, less independent musicians recently emigrated from Continental Europe where the traditional patronage system was only then being dismantled. This more traditional, less professionalized patronage relationship continued to appeal to patrons, as well as to many professional musicians, well into the nineteenth century.

Middle-class patronage

Middle-class patronage expanded significantly during this period, and has been credited with the evolution of concert life and the market for music. The relationship with such patrons was complex, as musicians found themselves dealing with patrons much closer to their own social status, sometimes perceived as the class to which they themselves aspired, and at other times perhaps as being at a level below that which they wished to serve.

Private, middle-class patronage consisted of personal support of musicians' careers and the employment of music instructors. Public middle-class patronage could be collective support of a concert institution or membership in an anonymous audience. The identity of the middle-class musical consumers is difficult to pin down.[50] They ranged from the most precariously placed members of the "middling classes," or *petite bourgeoisie*, to those on the fringes of upper-class social circles; social distinctions were numerous and complex, and expressed by cultural activities and social exclusivity.[51]

Private patronage of musicians by members of the middle class occurred only rarely. In the early 1770s, a Mr. Gibson, partner in a Dublin musical instrument firm, took the young John Stevenson "under his protection," and, "after considerable difficulty procured admission for his protégé" as a chorister in the Christ Church choir.[52] Wealthy families occasionally hosted private concerts in their homes, but such attempts rarely attained the grand scale of the most distinguished private concerts. The most common form of private middle-class patronage remained the employment of music instructors.

Like the aristocracy, middle-class patrons sometimes sponsored concert institutions. Eighteenth-century concert series based on bourgeois support included the Castle Society, the Anacreontic Society, and the Academy of Ancient Music.[53] Most such concerts took place in the City, and their founding illustrates a self-conscious cultural distinction between aristocratic and middle-class culture. In the later decades of the eighteenth century, some of these musical institutions evolved from partially amateur men's singing-clubs to more professional subscription concerts which women could attend – part of the transition to sobriety and respectability in public entertainments.

As concert life started to revive after the revolutionary wars, another middle-class concert series appeared. Called the City Concert, in reference to its location and social base, it was founded in 1818. The incentive for the series seems to have come from wealthy merchants, and this "new" source of patronage was welcomed enthusiastically by a musical press unaware of the distinguished precedents for such a concert series:

We could never be brought to understand why the solid opulence of trade should not admit the same opportunities for intellectual cultivation . . . as the condition of the man of landed property or of the follower of the court . . . Every step therefore in the rapid progression which has for the last few years been going on towards the erection of the mercantile classes into an order distinguished by mental attainments as well as by the acquisition of wealth, has seemed in our estimate of things to add to the respectability as well as the strength of the country . . . we rejoice to see Music spring into the very midst of the city, and "at one brave bound" establish all its perfections, under the auspices of an almost entirely new class of protectors.[54]

The series began its first season with five hundred subscribers "including most of the principal merchants and their families," but very few aristocrats. Although the musicians, the programs, and, apparently, the performance standards were all excellent, the subscriptions declined drastically after the first season. Aristocratic patrons were not eager to mix with such a crowd, and the wealthy middle-class members of the audience were equally unwilling to appear in an audience shunned by aristocratic patrons. As one observer explained, "Every one knows how easily the bulk of mankind are led by artificial distinctions, in whatever class of society they are found – many satisfied an imaginary importance by joining a society which demanded for itself exclusive superiority, and many withdrew their names from the original association, lest they should be considered of an inferior order."[55] While wealthy members of the middle class were recognized increasingly as a potential support for concerts, the effectiveness of their efforts was undermined by their own social rather than musical aspirations, and by the loss of aristocratic patrons from public concerts.

The most common form of middle-class patronage was membership in a public audience. Determining the exact identity of this public is difficult. Ticket prices for concerts (as opposed to theatres) ranged from five shillings to one guinea, depending on the concert's pretensions and the price variations among the seats.[56] A season subscription to the eight concerts of the Philharmonic Society in 1830 cost six guineas.[57] Even the most successful members of the working class could not have afforded these prices. The extent to which skilled artisans could and did attend is less clear. According to William Weber, London artisans attended some relatively inexpensive musical performances, usually of choral groups, but these members of the middling class, like many professional musicians, could afford to attend concerts only rarely.[58]

Theatre tickets were priced lower than concerts. Relatively inexpensive tickets opened the galleries for the servants of wealthy opera-goers and to members of the lower classes. This was not a negligible expense, as is illustrated by the riots that followed an attempt by the Covent Garden management to raise the cheapest ticket prices from three and sixpence to four shillings in 1807. The notorious "Old Price" riots made the nightly performance virtually inaudible for more than two months, until the old price was restored.[59] Although the audiences at the Covent Garden and Drury Lane Theatres were undoubtedly of a lower overall social status than concert audiences, they cannot be considered working-class. The working classes may have been represented in these theatres, but they were more likely to be found at the smaller, more cheaply priced theatres and at more popular entertainments.

Contemporary musicians, theatre managers, and music publishers were deeply concerned with audience preferences. In this way, the audience exerted indirect patronage, which was used as a guide for artistic decisions and professional employment. Although the hiring of musicians for private aristocratic concerts was frequently in professional hands, public concerts and theatres commonly relied on managers and impresarios who were not musicians. Such managers often depended on audience reactions to guide their choices, rendering professional musicians vulnerable to prevailing musical tastes. McVeigh observes that throughout the late eighteenth century the quality of musical life was thought to be in decline, largely as a result of public taste. While contemporary despair on this issue was undoubtedly overdrawn, it reflects an ongoing struggle among the financial exigencies of theatres, concerts, pleasure gardens, and all the people employed by them; the musical sophistication of audiences from different social and educational backgrounds; and the varying artistic values and skills of performers and composers.

W. T. Parke, the first-chair oboist in theatre and pleasure garden orchestras in the late eighteenth and early nineteenth centuries, describes in his memoirs the sometimes bumbling techniques that were used to interpret audience preferences. He reports that at Vauxhall Gardens audience reactions replaced musical judgments:

In order to enable the manager (who was not a musical luminary) to form a correct judgment of the merits of his different singers, a person was appointed to commit to paper the number of encores elicited by each of them during the season; at the expiration of which, those who had obtained the greatest number were engaged for the following one.[60]

Predictably, "the inferior vocalists, not having the fear of lost reputation before their eyes, took care by circulating their orders amongst their friends, to carry away the palm; by which means it frequently happened that they, to the depreciation of the concern, obtained the preference." On another occasion a singer at Covent Garden asked Parke to omit the oboe cadenza immediately following the singer's solo, because it was depriving the singer of an encore. Though Parke found the request "mean and silly," he complied. He understood that "with some managers the encores of a singer go far towards securing a re-engagement, which may in some means account for anxiety to obtain them."[61]

Reliance upon audience response in lieu of musical judgment continued. An 1823 article in the *Harmonicon* described prearranged encores in the competition between a foreign composer, Bochsa, and two English ones, Bishop and Cooke, at the Drury Lane Theatre. The author attacked the low quality and lack of originality of Bochsa's compositions, adding

But it was encored! – yes, because Mr. Bishop's had been encored a few nights before: and, reader, if thou hadst seen [the] persons from whom the encoring and applause came – planted in different parts of the house – well instructed in the art of seeming to be in ecstacies, – accurately informed as to what was composed by M. Bochsa, what by Mr. Cooke, and scrupulously delicate and cautious in not giving any opinion of the compositions of the Englishman, – thou wouldst not have wondered … that the better and more sensible part of the town are not indefatigable playgoers.[62]

Note the assumption that the audience, left free to express its true reactions, would have perceived the true relative merits of the compositions and applauded them accordingly. This assumption was not universally shared, however, and the relationship between anonymous public patronage and professional musicians was frequently stormy. The public was often thought to fall short in its responsibilities, either because it was swayed by bad influences or was insufficiently educated. Increasingly, composers and performers saw conflict between their own musical values and audience tastes: "to second the reigning taste is the only miserable basis on which a composer can build or acquire credit in his art, and as upon this credit depends his subsistence, he is obliged frequently against his will, to suppress his natural genius, and his own particular instinct to seek the means of satisfying them."[63] Still, musicians rarely questioned the right of their anonymous patrons to influence the success of musical careers, suggesting instead the need for widespread musical education so that audience members could make tasteful choices.

The author cited below deplores the acclaim given to inferior singers for performances of mediocre songs. He attributes part of the responsibility to the public's faulty tastes, but refuses to blame the public entirely, insisting that the performers and composers could have struggled successfully against formidable odds:

New songs must be had, no matter what kind or sort they are... This, it may be said, is owing to the false taste of the public, and you ought not in justice to blame the singer for what he can neither avert nor oppose; true; but as it appears in the case of a popular singer before mentioned [probably Braham], that the public taste may be led astray, indeed it may even be formed by any one singer who possesses enthusiasm and ability enough to attempt the task, and as that performer's day is nearly gone by and his attractions on the decline, now is the time for the English singers to rouse themselves from the inglorious lethargy into which they have been plunged, and amid the numerous competitors from abroad, and the extraordinary passion for instrumental music which is daily gaining ground in England, let them prove my assertions untrue by their industry and their zeal.[64]

How the lethargic native singers were to combat such taste as well as the preference for foreign performers and the popularity of virtuoso instru-mentalists is left unexplained. Some observers also criticized musicians who succeeded by catering to low tastes:

Our artists have neither the high feeling, the emulation, nor the energy, to enter the lists against foreign talent. They voluntarily, to use a university phrase, degrade. They content themselves with the easier cultivation of less effective if not of lower styles. They sing to the pit and the gallery of the theatres, because the pit and the gallery roar out their honest and hearty acclamations – because they contend steadily and successfully for three encores – and because the manager will engage the man or woman who disdains not to sing in such a manner as to ensure being thrice encored. It is the money and not the music that is worshipped.[65]

A more moderate perspective was expressed in an 1823 article on the failure of a new concert series. The author noted that the programs lacked the "grandeur and passion" needed to draw the public, adding that "we must accompany to a certain length in order to lead the prevailing taste."[66] Whatever such a gentle courtship of public taste may have entailed, members of the musical profession seem not to have mastered the technique. Their failures continued to elicit self-criticism, either for pandering to public taste or for not pandering sufficiently. One musician blamed his English colleagues for performing foreign music. He questioned their "discretion in volunteering the extravagant patronage they do to foreign music... Professors enjoy the power of modelling the public taste, and I say English ability should be incited to produce."[67] In 1843, the dwindling fortunes of the Society of British Musicians concert series led the *Musical Examiner* to explain that the Society "has taken no lead in musical affairs – has in no way influenced public feeling – has in no way induced public patronage."[68] Note throughout the belief that professional musicians themselves were responsible for the reigning tastes and preferences, and that if they only chose to do so they could alter these tastes to their advantage.

Middle-class patronage was extremely important especially for those musicians with little access to aristocratic patronage. However, few if any professional musicians or concert series succeeded with middle-class patronage alone. The problem of discerning the public taste made dependence upon public patronage precarious. While public patronage was sometimes mediated by professional musicians, non-musical theatre managers and concert impresarios were more eager to cater to the public than to educate it. Since professional musicians were generally unwilling to concede their helplessness against public taste, they tended to blame other factors such as the sinister influence of upper-class prejudices (preference for foreigners), the distortion of musical values by superficial and opportunistic performers and composers (usually foreigners), or British musicians' own lack of initiative. As will be discussed in chapter 10, most of the solutions musicians proposed during this period looked not to the new and tyrannical public, but rather to more traditional patrons and patronage relationships.

Professional patronage

Although rarely mentioned, professional patronage is an important form of indirect patronage. It occurred when musicians offered employment to other musicians.[69] For example, the Master of the Music in the royal household was entirely responsible for selecting and managing the musicians of the King's Band.[70] Aristocratic patrons hired professional musicians (examples include George Smart and Domenico Dragonetti) to engage musicians for large-scale private concerts. Such musicians offered their colleagues not only employment, but also introductions to patrons, with the potential for other teaching and performing opportunities. Panels of professionals were recruited to audition and rank candidates for organist jobs, although church officials usually had the final decision. For example, Thomas Roseingrave gained the organist's position at St. George's, Hanover Square, in 1725 after a competition judged by Dr. Greene, Dr. Pepusch and Mr. Galliard, all leading professional musicians.[71] From the 1830s increasing numbers of professional women joined this tradition, exerting what has been termed "matronage" by forming close networks and providing teaching and performance opportunities for each other.[72]

The music directors in theatres, usually professional musicians, hired the orchestral players.[73] The successful theatre composer William Shield began his career as a violinist. When still young "he was employed as a leader of the concerts at Scarborough, where he became acquainted with several eminent performers from London, by means of whom he obtained a situation in the orchestra of the Italian Opera House."[74] Ultimately, the theatre's music director was responsible for hiring him, but the influence of the orchestra members also seems to have been important. William Gutteridge, a violinist and the leader of the Birmingham theatre orchestra in the early nineteenth century, was hired by T. Dibdin to instruct the chorus at the Surrey Theatre in London. This led to further connections, Dibdin eventually settling in Brighton to work for wealthy patrons in residence there. In 1823 it was reported that "Mr. Platts, a performer on the French horn ... has been engaged for the Oratorios, upon a very flattering report made by Mr. Braham of his abilities."[75] In the 1840s, speaking of the orchestral positions at the Opera and two other major concert institutions, H. J. Banister reported that "it requires considerable interest to obtain a situation in any one of the three."[76] Given that the music directors at these institutions were musicians, the "interest" he refers to was undoubtedly the influence and patronage of other professional musicians.

The absence of professional connections could severely hamper the development of a career. One despairing composer expressed his position as a professional outsider in 1829: "I am an isolated musician; unpatronized, uncountenanced, and unconnected with professional juntos of any kind. Unhackneyed in the business of choirs and orchestras, I have no ground to stand upon; no vote in any musical assembly, and no influence in musical politics."[77]

The main innovation in professional patronage was the collaboration of musicians to organize their own concert institutions, and thereby to establish a more independent relationship – professionally and musically – with amateur patrons. Many such concert series were launched in the eighteenth century. Most still depended on aristocratic patrons, but they were under professional control: the series organized by J. C. Bach and C. F. Abel; the Pantheon concerts, organized by Matthias Vento and Samuel Arnold; the Professional Concert; Salomon's concerts; the Vocal Concert organized by Samuel Harrison and Charles Knyvett; and several others.[78] These concert ventures represent an interesting mix of foreign and native enterprise. The Bach/Abel and Salomon concert series of course included German music and musicians, but the Pantheon programmed Italian and English music only, and the Vocal Concert performed English songs and glees.

The most important professional concert established in the early nineteenth century was the Philharmonic Society.[79] Founded in 1813 with an explicit professional as well as musical mission, its policies recognized the need for aristocratic patronage, but were also imbued – at least at the start – with radical democratic ideals reflecting artisanal/middling-class values as much as middle-class professional ones (see chapter 10). Since the founders included many eminent musicians, and since for performance of large-scale orchestral compositions it was "the only show in town," it attracted royal and aristocratic patronage as well as middle-class and professional audiences. For the same reasons, it drew an audience less concerned with social exclusivity. In 1821 it was reported that performance at a Philharmonic concert was "perhaps the severest test to which power can be brought, because the major part of the audience consists of professors or persons most immediately connected with music."[80] And in 1822, "the audiences at the Philharmonic are neither the 'great vulgar nor the small' – they are the cognoscenti – if there be any such in the whole realm – they go to hear and to enjoy."[81]

There were several other concert series initiated at least in part by professional musicians, but all struggled with the sparsity of aristocratic support and the small public audience. Such concerts included the abovementioned City Concert (1818–23), the British Concerts (1823), and concerts of the Society of British Musicians (1834–65). One observer wrote in 1818, "In the metropolis, it has been found difficult, not to say impracticable, to maintain even two or three [professional concerts]... In the country, where professors are few, it is next to impossible to support a professional concert."[82] The British Concerts, founded in 1823, are a case in point. There were two hundred subscribers at the outset, but they included very few members of the nobility; and the series by definition resisted the preference for foreign performers. Both were significant disadvantages:

We do not therefore say it is disgraceful to the rank of the country, that while an Italian Opera can boast the name of almost every family of distinction resident in London, an attempt made solely with a view to the encouragement of *native* talent, should find only the Earl of Essex and seven other persons of title amongst its supporters.[83]

The families of merchants were well represented among the patrons of this concert series, but, as illustrated by the difficulties of the City Concert, too great a proportion of merchants in the audience could undermine the fate of a concert series. In the 1830s and 1840s professionals began to organize chamber music concerts (the most notable being the Musical Union founded in 1845), which negotiated a new relationship between professional and aristocratic patrons. This mid-nineteenth-century synthesis will be discussed in chapter 10.

Church patronage

The conditions and characteristics of careers in church music will be discussed in chapter 5. The patronage of church music was by nature unlike the other types of patronage discussed so far, and deserves separate consideration. The most extensive provisions for hiring and maintaining musicians occurred in the original endowments of the cathedrals, and were interpreted and administered by the Dean and Chapter – clergymen, not musicians. S. S. Wesley, a leading church musician and organist, was greatly distressed by the problems of musicians' status and the quality of musical performance. He identified the problem explicitly as one of professional control: "The Clergy are the irresponsible directors of Cathedral music. The views of the highest order of musical professors are never brought to bear on the subject."[84] Professional patronage sometimes played a role: cathedral organists could be chosen on the basis of their musical reputation or by means of competitions judged by musicians, and in some instances organists participated in the selection of choir members and choristers; ultimately, however, the choice was made by the Dean and Chapter. Frequently the clergy sought little or no professional advice in such hirings, so musical standards remained low and the cathedral organist, especially one as professionally competent and serious as S. S. Wesley, felt demoralized:

Painful and dangerous is the position of a young musician who, after acquiring great knowledge of his art in the Metropolis, joins a country Cathedral. At first he can scarcely believe that the mass of error and inferiority in which he has to participate is habitual and irremediable... The painter and the sculptor can choose their tools and the material on which they work, and great is the care they may devote to the selection: but the musician of the Church has no power of this kind;

nay, more, he is compelled to work with tools which he knows to be inefficient and unworthy – incompetent singers and a wretched organ! He must learn to tolerate error, to sacrifice principle, and yet to indicate, by his outward demeanour, the most perfect satisfaction in his office.[85]

He argued for professional control over musical decisions in the church and exposed the clergy's inadequacy for the task:

[T]he very natural reflection must arise, that to confide funds to the clergy, for the joint support of religion and *something else*, must be wrong, because religion being of paramount importance, the clergy may, on an emergency, be tempted to deprive the *something else* of its due portion for the benefit of the object in which they are professionally concerned.[86]

Wesley had little power to influence decisions about church music, and he was virtually alone in his explicit assertion of such authority as an essential right and responsibility of professionals. The exercise of church patronage remained for the most part the province of non-musicians throughout this period.

Perceptions

Musicians' perceptions of patronage relationships centered on practical considerations such as wages and professional connections, and also on less intangible expressions of status. Their professional values dictated that they be paid for their services, even when this removed them from possibly profitable connections with wealthy patrons. But at the same time, connections with patrons as well as professionals were essential to a musical career, particularly if that career was to rise above irregular employment and financial insecurity. Church organists frequently depended on teaching work from members of the congregation. Musicians who played (sometimes gratis) at private concerts hoped to gain wealthy pupils, as well as patrons who would attend their benefit concerts. One observer wrote in 1818 that in London, "connection is considered by them [musicians] as the barrier against competition, and indeed as the very *pabulum vitae*."[87]

In addition, patronage relationships had varied implications for musicians' social and professional status. Employment by aristocratic patrons conferred only a dependent status-by-association, not necessarily the status and respectability of an independent professional. The deferential stance of many musicians toward wealthy and cultured patrons illustrates more traditional attitudes, as in this passage, warning musicians about the social distance separating them from their wealthy patrons:

Although generally persons of inferior birth and fortune, they suddenly become objects of public applause, and are called at once into the presence of rank and affluence, into an intercourse so close and immediate as to implicate a familiarity most dangerous to their habits, unless they are scrupulously guarded by that general self-knowledge, which includes also the knowledge of the relations in which we stand to those who surround us.[88]

Musicians sometimes preferred the treatment they received from aristocratic patrons to that of patrons with lower social standing. At first this may seem surprising, but few musicians were on an equal social footing even with many middle-class patrons, and it was noticed that aristocratic patrons were apt to be more sensitive to musicians' feelings:

Aristocrats regard the admission of professional people into their circle, merely as it contributes to their amusement. Still there is commonly a delicacy of behaviour which strives to cover this the true principle that brings the parties together, and to preclude its ever appearing to disconcert the individual. Talent is safe in the company of well-bred people, for the essence of good breeding is neither to say nor do an offensive thing.

The newly affluent members of the middle class, on the other hand, were sometimes eager to emphasize status differences:

The worser part of these sentiments, with regard to professors, have somehow or other crept downwards through all conditions, and hence it happens that the moment we pass from really elevated (or good) society, the character of the musician seems to suffer the degradation which so ill comports with the natural dignity of liberal art, and which the professor ought not to undergo.[89]

This view is filtered, of course, through professional musicians' own snobbishness, which may have led them to view the same behavior from aristocrats and bourgeois as refined condescension in the one case and boorish pretension in the other. Such attitudes were nevertheless consistent with the tendency of professional musicians to look back fondly to traditional patrons and to the old, elite status of the profession rather than to welcome a more modern definition of the profession and its accompanying new patronage relationships.

A simple dichotomy between private aristocratic patronage and public middle-class audience will not suffice for understanding musical employment. Shifting social and economic conditions combined with foreign competition made the patronage system extremely complex. Musicians' careers included a wide variety of patronage relationships, distinguished in the context of complex social values and perceptions. Although many musicians struggled to adapt creatively to new social, economic, and cultural contexts for music, many evinced a continued dependence on, and even preference for, traditional patronage relationships. Such inconsistencies lay at the core of musicians' equivocal social and professional status during these years.

4   Musical education

Throughout the eighteenth century musicians and observers of the musical scene called for reform and greater systematization of musical education, largely to help native musicians compete with foreigners. But because the institutions for educating and licensing professionals were of paramount importance in the achievement of professional status, such discussions were also part of the debate about the status and autonomy of music as a profession.

The main educational criterion for a member of the traditional professions was a liberal education, that is, the study of classical languages and mathematics, usually followed by a university education. The lower-status branches of these professions had less systematic educational requirements, and the necessary training was usually provided by apprenticeship. As the professions evolved during the eighteenth and nineteenth centuries, these routes were transformed. Gradually, the liberal education became a prestigious accomplishment which was not necessarily a prerequisite for a profession. At the same time, apprenticeship was gradually replaced by professionally controlled educational institutions which provided the necessary skills and credentials.

Unlike the liberal education of a clergyman, barrister, or physician, classical studies alone had never been sufficient preparation for the musical profession. Then, as now, aspiring musicians needed to begin their musical studies at an early age and required professional instruction in the craft of music for many years. However, like the traditional professions in the eighteenth century, music had high- and low-status branches that were attained by two different educational paths. Training for a career in church music began in early life with membership in a cathedral choir, which provided both classical and musical education. These years were followed by university study, culminating in ordainment and sometimes a musical degree. At the other end of the scale, secular singers and instrumentalists were generally trained by means of apprenticeships or private lessons; they received no classical education and sometimes little or no education of any sort other than music. There were no procedures for licensing qualified musicians and thereby controlling the size and character of the profession.

Each of the educational routes for musicians developed or declined in various ways during the eighteenth and early nineteenth centuries: the chorister and university route, apprenticeship, private lessons, study in Europe, and military training. The shortcomings of the existing institutions inspired numerous proposals for educational reforms, which will be discussed below, culminating with the founding in 1822 of the Royal Academy of Music.

Chorister training

Despite long-standing controversies about music's role in religion and the relationship between choirs and congregrations, separate choirs of paid singers were an essential part of the Anglican cathedral service, also known as the choral service. These choirs consisted of adult male singers and choristers (choirboys), usually in equal numbers, although the proportion varied. Paid choirs were maintained in cathedrals, collegiate chapels, and the chapels of the royal household. (Some parish churches paid singers, but in general parish choirs were staffed by local amateurs or charity children.[1]) A few choristers were employed to assist in performance of the Mass in the chapels of the London embassies of Catholic countries; in some secular concert series; and in theatres. In the 1760s two young musicians were employed at the aristocratic Concert of Ancient Music, and three sang in the chorus of the Drury Lane Theatre. But nothing indicates that the boys in these institutions received formal training.

A choir included six to eight boys who belonged to the choir from about the age of six until the time their voices broke. The choristers assisted at each performance of the service, usually twice a day throughout the week.[2] The criteria for selecting the boys varied. Where the organist successfully asserted his right to make the choice, musical aptitude and a good voice were the primary considerations. Where the Dean and Chapter used the selection process as an opportunity to exert local patronage, musical considerations were secondary, often to the choir's discredit.[3] In some instances, particularly the collegiate chapels at Oxford and Cambridge, preference was given to the sons of clergymen, but musical ability was also a criterion.

Wages and other benefits varied widely among the choral establishments. At Durham Cathedral the choristers received £8 to £9 and two suits of clothes annually.[4] The choristers of Lincoln Cathedral received only £2 to £3 a year and a gown every other year, but they were lodged and boarded with their music master.[5] The Westminster Abbey boys were paid from money given by the Chapter to the music master; he was required to pay the four senior boys a guinea a month, and the four junior boys fourteen shillings a month.[6] Wages were supplemented by what had probably once been the choristers' most important benefit, a free classical education. In general, the education consisted of elementary musical training and enrollment at the grammar schools endowed with the cathedrals.[7] Where there was no endowed school, private instructors were provided. For example, at Christ Church, Oxford, "since the foundation of the College there has always been a Master ... who instructs them [the choristers] in Latin and Greek. They are also taught Writing and Arithmetic... They are usually instructed in singing by the Organist four times a week."[8]

By the early nineteenth century, and probably earlier, the quality of the education offered to choristers as well as the number that took advantage of the opportunity had declined. For example, "Although the choristers [at Westminster Abbey] were by statute members of Westminster School, the attendance of some of them was a polite fiction, and they were little regarded."[9] At Canterbury Cathedral, the choristers had been officially excluded from attendance at the Royal Grammar School by 1824; instead they were taught music, reading, writing, and arithmetic at the Cathedral.[10]

Why had the quality of the choristers' education declined? The answer lies in the eighteenth-century development that had so powerful an effect on the musical profession – the decline in the importance and the performance standards of the Anglican service and the associated decline in the financial and professional status of church musicians. Although the once liberal choir endowments attached to the cathedrals had in many cases increased in value, the nominal wages of church personnel had remained the same. With decreased payments and a relative decline in the earnings and status of church musicians, the social origins and aspirations of the choristers seem to have declined as well. At Chichester in the 1820s a member of the Chapter wrote: "within living memory they [the choristers] were the sons of highly respectable persons, who esteemed themselves fortunate in placing them under the superintending care of the Dean and Chapter," but by the 1820s, "being in generally humble circumstances," they no longer chose to receive the free classical education that was available to them.[11] At Westminster Abbey, the boys no longer bothered with a classical education because "their parents (in many instances) are in such comparatively humble circumstances, that whatever advantage the boys may have derived from their attendance at the college is ... rendered nugatory by the circumstances of placing them out as apprentices in various professions or trades."[12] This impression is confirmed by one cathedral organist who complained in 1854 that choristers were "procured from a class of the community amongst which the delicacy of voice and utterance requisite is not easily found."[13]

Did the musical part of the choristers' education also decline? Or did it gain in relative importance, since the other parts of their education were being neglected? In addressing these questions, it will be helpful to consider what happened to choristers when they left the choirs. Traditionally, choristers who received a liberal education as well as musical instruction were equipped to study at a university. In most other cases, however, choristers appear to have become apprentices to non-musical trades after leaving the choir. Many received a bonus for "good behavior," ranging from £15 at Lincoln Cathedral to £30 at Salisbury Cathedral, and this gift was generally intended as an apprenticeship premium.[14] (The status of the trades that choristers joined varied with the size of the premium awarded.) The exception to this pattern could be found at establishments such as the collegiate chapels of Oxford and Cambridge, where choristers were frequently sons of clergymen, continued to receive classical educations, and had opportunities for scholarships at the university.[15] Some of them followed a primarily non-musical course of study and planned to be ordained; others returned to choral singing as ordained members of cathedral choirs (vicars-choral) or became church organists. Hackett reported of New College, Oxford, that "there is no place which has been more remarkable for supplying the various Cathedrals with valuable and efficient members; instances exist at this moment in Canterbury, York, London, Durham, Chichester, Hereford, Norwich, Salisbury, and Worcester."[16]

The choristers from the provincial cathedrals and collegiate chapels who chose musical careers almost always remained in the field of church music as organists, choirmasters, choir singers, and composers. There were four choral establishments, however, where chorister training was closely related to the secular musical world: the two London cathedrals, St. Paul's and Westminster Abbey, and the two royal chapels, the Chapel Royal at St. James's and St. George's Chapel, Windsor. A greater proportion of the choristers from these choirs came from professional music families and had the option of entering the world of secular music in London. The organists and adult singers in these institutions were professional musicians, and in fact were often leading singers in London's musical life, not only as members of the leading choirs, but also as performers in secular concerts. The standards both of musical training and of performance in these choirs were undoubtedly higher than elsewhere.

Furthermore, the experience of church music that was acquired by the choristers in these choirs seems to have been supplemented by secular performances for which they were subcontracted by their music master. In 1785 the Chapel Royal boys, dressed in full livery, performed at the aristocratic Concert of Ancient Music.[17] In 1798, special provisions for the boys' transportation and supper were made for those occasions "when the boys return home from singing at the Oratorios, the Antient music, or any other concert, public or private."[18] The employment of choristers, which drew some criticism in the early nineteenth century, was undoubtedly valuable experience for a musical career. William Hawes, the choirmaster of St. Paul's, defended the practice in 1814 by emphasizing that he was "a Teacher of Music, and that he conceives the Choristers' attendance at such Concerts and Oratorios is an important part of a Musical Education, and a great source of improvement to them."[19]

In sum, by the late eighteenth and early nineteenth centuries, chorister training had diverged from its original purpose as a method of training respectable, if not always affluent, boys for a high-status profession that required both liberal and musical training from an early age. At some of the provincial cathedrals, chorister work became merely a benign form of child labor that could also provide a rudimentary education. At the most musically prestigious institutions such as the Chapels Royal and the two London cathedrals, choristers gravitated to the varied employment opportunities that were offered by London's secular musical world, rather than to the church and university route. Only at the collegiate chapels of Oxford and Cambridge did choristers continue to follow a more traditional educational path, which converged at many points with the preparation for a career as a clergyman.

University education

University degrees of Bachelor and Doctor of Music were granted in England as early as 1463, before comparable credentials in music were offered by any of the Continental universities.[20] It appears that in previous centuries the universities may have occupied a more important place in musical activities, especially relating to the church. Traditionally, university music degrees were addressed to the needs of clergymen: "the original office of the university music professor was to instruct those intending to enter holy orders in the principles of church music."[21]

From 1750 to 1850, university degrees remained prestigious credentials for musicians, at least for composers of church music and organists. They were not a source of practical musical education, however, as they required no residence or formal course of study. Even the four musical professorships, one each at Oxford, Cambridge, Edinburgh, and London (the Gresham chair), seem to have played little role in training musicians. In 1843, one musician observed the extent to which such positions were usually irrelevant to the mainstream of musical life: "Neither of these give the professor the command of an orchestre [*sic*]. The first three I conceive to be little other than sinecures, beneficial to the holders, but useless to the art."[22] The professors generally only gave a few lectures a year, and the position was largely an honorary one, with no salary until 1868.[23]

Candidates for degrees were required to have practiced music as a profession for a specified number of years (seven for the bachelor's degree, five more for the doctorate) and to submit a musical composition. Like chorister training, university degrees were unavailable to women. In 1856, Elizabeth Stirling, a successful organist and composer, submitted a composition for the bachelor's degree in music at Oxford. The work passed the examination, but "there was no power to confer the degree."[24] The examinations were officially opened to women in 1878, although they still could not receive the degree.

The vast majority of musicians earning such degrees during this period were church musicians, but there were a few exceptions. Composers for the English theatre such as Thomas Arne and Samuel Arnold received D.Mus. degrees from Oxford in 1759 and 1773, respectively. The nineteenth-century English theatre composer, Henry Rowley Bishop, received an Oxford B.Mus. in 1839 (at the age of fifty-three), and then a doctorate in 1853, the latter when he was no longer at the peak of his career and was apparently having financial difficulties. Occasionally, Oxford awarded honorary musical doctorates, sometimes to foreign musicians; examples include the virtuoso flutist Frederick Hartmann Graff in 1789 and Haydn in 1791. Otherwise foreign musicians were unlikely to seek out such degrees, partly because of the strong connection with the English tradition of church music. A notable exception was the violinist George Augustus Bridgetower. Born in Poland, the son of an African father and a European mother (although Sainsbury reports rumors that he was the son of an Indian prince), he emigrated to London around 1790 at about the age of twelve, soon established himself as a performer, and proceeded to amass the credentials most coveted by English musicians: royal patronage, membership of the Royal Society of Musicians (1807), and a B.Mus. from Cambridge (1811). (He later met Beethoven, giving the first performance of the Violin Sonata in A which Beethoven originally intended to dedicate to him, but after some misunderstanding dedicated instead to Kreutzer.)

The certification as well as the status associated with university degrees led to a brief attempt, in the early 1790s, to use the degrees for professional self-definition and exclusiveness. Originally suggested by Thomas Sanders Dupuis, organist and composer to the Chapel Royal, the new group was called the Society of Musical Graduates and met several times a year to discuss musical and other matters.[25] The cohesiveness of the group was shaky from the start, however; one of the members, Samuel Arnold, had recently been appointed conductor of the aristocratic concert series, the Academy of Ancient Music, in place of another degree holder, Benjamin

Cooke. Consequently, it took some efforts to persuade Cooke to join the group. J. W. Callcott's accounts of the meetings reveal a high sensitivity to issues of status, some confusion about the professional mission of the group, and a good deal of drinking and merriment. Callcott conceded that "It is true in some moments when the power of wine conquered that of reason, all improvement of the mind ... was stigmatized with the title of parish business."[26] For the most part, the Society grasped at exclusiveness but with very little sense of professional mission; in fact, at one point, because it was suspected that "some improper persons designed to take their degrees for the purpose of intruding themselves into the Society it was resolved that no new members should be added to the lists." At the other extreme, the renowned bass choral singer Richard Bellamy suggested that the group go beyond conviviality and cliquishness to a truly professional role in guaranteeing standards: "that no person should be elected to any musical place in the Cathedrals of this Kingdom without a previous testimony of their abilities from the Society of Musical Graduates." Perhaps too far ahead of its time, the suggestion was described by Callcott as "not only ridiculous but impossible to put in execution."

In short, university degrees became increasingly irrelevant to musical careers during the eighteenth and early nineteenth centuries. Relatively few musicians held degrees (sixty-four B.Mus. and forty-eight D.Mus. degrees were awarded between 1750 and 1850), and they were linked with church music at a time when that branch of the profession was declining in social and economic status. Although degrees were impressive professional credentials for musicians with established careers, the connection with a declining branch of the profession meant that degrees could guarantee neither status nor success; nor could they function as a potential mechanism for professional licensing or certification. Not until the mid-nineteenth century were there reforms in the standards and examinations for the musical degrees. The numbers of musicians who earned such degrees increased significantly from around 1870.

Apprenticeship

Although it was possible for some choristers to gain employment as church organists when they left the choir, most required further training. The most common route for ex-choristers and other students was apprenticeship.[27] Seventy-eight musicians in the catalogue trained as apprentices; sixteen of them began as choristers. By the late eighteenth century, these two routes, chorister and apprenticeship – the one traditionally characteristic of the more exclusive ranks of the profession, the other of the lower artisan-type musical career – were frequently combined. For those who identified music primarily with the composition and performance of church music, however, the idea of apprenticeship could seem incongruous and demeaning. Sir John Hawkins, the eighteenth-century historian of music, expressed disapproval of any link between the musical profession and occupations having a guild/apprenticeship system. In reference to the founding of a musicians' guild by James I he wrote, "By this act of regal authority the only one of the liberal sciences that conferred the degree of Doctor, was itself degraded, and put upon a footing with the lowest of the mechanic arts."[28]

Nevertheless, by the time this passage was written in the 1770s apprenticeships were common in all branches of the profession. In many cases church music apprenticeships were little more than formal agreements for private lessons. Secular music apprenticeships were more like those in the skilled crafts and the lower ranks of the other professions. The following passage describes the type of apprenticeship that was characteristic of singers and instrumentalists preparing for secular careers in London:

The common method of ensuring the tuition and introduction of public singers is by binding them under articles for a given number of years to a person competent to the object by knowledge and connection... The pupil gives a sum (or not, as it happens); the master instructs, makes engagements, and receives a moiety of the money earned during the term of the articles... The pupil is pushed into musical society, and advantaged by hearing every concert or performance to which the master can obtain gratuitous admission.[29]

Apprenticeships traditionally began at the age of fourteen and continued for five to seven years.[30] The fee varied widely; £25 was sufficient for most crafts and trades, including music, until the 1840s (all the indentures paid for by the Royal Society of Musicians were £25), but some students were apprenticed without a fee, perhaps because they already seemed likely to earn the teacher substantial profits from their performances.[31] On the other hand, an apprenticeship with a famous musician, or with one known to have valuable professional or patronage connections, was undoubtedly much more expensive. In addition to the premium, there was a penalty, which could be several hundred pounds, if apprentices failed to serve the full time for which they had been bound. One method of overcoming the expense of a good apprenticeship was for students to be bound to their musical fathers or other relatives. The decision to article a student to a relative, when private lessons were just as feasible, suggests the degree to which a formal apprenticeship was valued as a professional credential.

Unlike chorister training, musical apprenticeships were open to girls. Most female music apprentices were preparing for careers as stage singers. However, while all of the six female apprentices in the catalogue aspired to careers as stage singers, not all of them were apprenticed to singers or singing teachers. One aspiring singer, Miss Travis, was an articled apprentice to the aristocratic directors of the Concert of Ancient Music; they "provide her with an Italian and a Singing master, pay all her expenses, make her a handsome present at the close of the season, and permit her to form engagements entirely for her own emolument."[32] Apprenticeships were rarely acceptable to the families of middle-class female students, however, at least partly because of the connection with theatre work.

As was true of apprenticeships in other trades, there were numerous instances of mistreatment, or of the failure of the master to instruct as had been agreed. Masters were not always sufficiently expert in the area the apprentice intended to study. Around 1811, one singing student, Miss Fearon, served her apprenticeship to Charles Cobham, a London orchestral violinist, who "drew his ideas of vocal art chiefly from the branch of music he exercised, and cultivated execution principally, and that execution by no means in the best manner."[33] (She later continued her studies in Italy, returned to London in 1827 as Mme. Feron, and reputedly received £40 a night for her performances on the English stage.) Even worse, the renowned organist and bass singer William Horsley was bound for five years to a master who was "passionate and indolent to an extreme degree, and entirely neglected the instruction of his pupil, who was, at all times, most happy to escape from his violence."[34] And some apprentices received no instruction at all, but were hired out at the beginning of their terms:

A master advertizes, or otherwise lays out for apprentices, male or female, having good voices and wishing to become "candidates for theatrical fame." He meets with some indigent person, who engages upon the conditions... The moment the article is signed, he writes to a number of country managers, who he informs that he has a very promising pupil to bring out, and solicits their aid. He instructs (or *parrots*, as it is technically termed) the poor boy or girl in the music and dialogue of one or more popular characters ... and whips them off to the first company that assents to their introduction. If they succeed, and are engaged, he takes half the salary; if they fail, the coach-hire is all the loss... I believe there is an individual now making some hundred pounds per annum by such means.[35]

The apprenticeship system was nevertheless an important training route for musicians, particularly those who aspired to secular London careers as stage singers or orchestral instrumentalists. Its success as instruction and as an introduction to the profession varied with the apprentice's abilities and the master's musical attainments and professional connections. Even under the best conditions, however, apprenticeship had serious shortcomings as training for musical careers. Apprentices had few opportunities for informal performance with other musicians, and it was limiting to study with only one musician for five to seven years, especially since few musicians could teach all the areas of music a professional needed to master:

> Shut out from all communion with fellow-students, those who shewed an aptitude for music were obliged to bind themselves to some Professor for a term of years, paying a large premium, and sacrificing afterwards, for years, a portion of their hard earnings; and all this but for one branch of their art, harmony, the essential foundation to make a musician, being often entirely neglected.[36]

It was at least partly this sense of the limitations of apprenticeship that led to proposals for educational reforms.

Private lessons

The most flexible and widespread method of musical education was the private lesson – undoubtedly the most important source of early training for children of professional musicians, and especially for women. But to have private lessons it was necessary to find a teacher and to have money for lessons. The first problem should not be underestimated, as there were relatively few musicians working in provincial England until well into the nineteenth century. Furthermore, the cost made extensive private study inaccessible to large numbers of aspiring musicians. One solution was to find a wealthy patron to pay for a number of years of study, but although there are a few examples of this kind of patronage it was extremely uncommon. More often a student worked (frequently gratis) with a relative, usually a parent or sibling. Of the 548 musicians in the catalogue known to have studied privately, 118 (21.5 percent) studied with a relative. This was one of the many advantages enjoyed by the children of professional musicians in their preparation for musical careers.

As many contemporaries observed, private study alone was insufficient to train a professional musician. Hence the invaluable role of the experience of public performance that was enjoyed by the choristers in the major London choirs and by apprentices who attended and assisted at concerts and theatres. But even with such musical experiences, private lessons and apprenticeships could not address all the necessary branches of study. The need for systematic training that would continue where these institutions left off was an important motivation behind the educational reforms proposed throughout this period.

Foreign study

An alternative form of musical training for English students was to study in Europe, where there were many renowned teachers and conservatories.

As one contemporary reported, the cost of instruction was lower than in England,[37] and at least in Italy it was observed that there were many more opportunities to hear great performances at reasonable prices. However, such students had fewer opportunities to make valuable connections with London musicians,[38] and since it was expensive to travel and live abroad they needed wealthy patrons or some other source of income. There are a few examples, particularly in the eighteenth century, of royal and noble patronage for foreign musical study. Those who went abroad in the nineteenth century tended to be from middle-class families who could afford a year or two of foreign study.

The eighteenth-century examples are most often singers, especially women, who went to Italy for the training they needed for theatrical performance. Singers continued to account for the majority of such students in the nineteenth century, although a number of nineteenth-century composition students studied in Germany. Students continued to choose foreign study even after the founding of the Royal Academy of Music in 1822. Many were children of professional musicians, such as Clara Novello, daughter of the organist, composer, and publisher Vincent Novello, and Clara Kathleen Barnett, daughter of the composer of English operas John Barnett. They became successful singers who later emigrated to Italy and America, respectively. As Clara Barnett wrote many years later, she was sent to Germany because her parents believed that was where "the most thorough musical education was to be obtained and under better conditions than in our own country."[39] The advantages of foreign study seemed particularly important for female singers. As one editorial explained,

For a long period the female in this country, if she relied on a purely *home* education, was placed under great disadvantages. There was no existing native Opera, and the education commonly bestowed on an English girl would but ill qualify her for the brilliant arena of the Haymarket. Therefore the dramatic style, that in which fame and emolument awaited the successful competitor, as it rarely formed a branch of tuition, so it continued to languish in undeserved neglect.[40]

In contrast, some observers objected to "that opinion every where prevalent in England, that it is essential to artists to visit foreign countries, receive foreign instruction, and earn a character in foreign lands, and in Italy especially, before their countrymen can be expected to see and apprettiate [*sic*] and applaud their merit."[41] The prevalence of this opinion nevertheless led increasing numbers of students to go to Italy, Germany, or France for at least a short time to gain not only European training but also the status conferred by European credentials.

Military training

A small number of musicians (nine from the catalogue) learned their art as members of military bands.[42] Military bands had no explicit educational plan, but their members could learn from the daily experience of work with other musicians. The unprofessional, haphazard nature of this method of studying music is illustrated by Edward Frost, who joined a recruiting party as a fifer in 1794, "having previously learnt to play a few tunes." He then also learned the clarinet, and after four years was selected for a regimental band.

He now began to feel the effects of harmony (not having heard a military band before) and directly set about composing marches and other military pieces, in which he succeeded tolerably well as to the melodies, but the arrangements in parts were certainly curious; for, having heard musicians talk of *discords* without explaining their relations to harmony, he imagined that no two intervals, disagreeing in themselves, could be tolerated together; his chief care, therefore, was to avoid all discords, consequently his productions were monotonous enough.

His understanding of harmony gradually improved with experience, but

he found that, to be able to arrange music effectively for a band, it required a knowledge of the various instruments to be introduced, and this he was not able to obtain till he was appointed master, which situation he enjoyed about twelve years; when, by experience, he found that even the worst performer in a band may be set off to the best advantage.[43]

Frost was the bandmaster from 1803 to 1815, after which the regiment disbanded, and he became a music teacher. It is revealing that he first had to be appointed bandmaster in order to have an opportunity to study band instruments and arranging.

Some of the musicians of this period who began in military bands did have opportunities to study with experienced musicians. Most became bandmasters, some were private teachers, and one went on to be a stage singer. But the system of military music was too unstructured to offer any kind of systematic training for musical careers until the foundation of Kneller Hall, a school for military musicians and bandmasters, in 1857.

Educational reforms

Throughout the eighteenth and early nineteenth centuries there appeared numerous proposals for an English conservatory of music. They expressed a number of interrelated but not necessarily compatible ideals, and were motivated by the pragmatic goals of providing musical education, challenging foreign competition, and improving the social and professional status of musicians. Such attempts were characteristic of many aspiring professions seeking control over training and licensing. As Larson explains, the goal of professions that proposed educational reforms was "to unseat the traditional professional elites and to separate themselves from the trades. Their progress involved nothing less than the creation of a graded system of comprehensive education and the reorientation of its higher-level institutions."[44] But musicians were in a peculiarly disadvantageous position to accomplish these goals, because entrance to the profession was completely open and educational routes were so varied. The reform proposals, which combine the strategies of the newer professions with nostalgia for the education and status of the traditional elite professions, reflect such complexities. The ongoing conflict between ideals and the numerous obstacles to achieving professional status culminated in the usurpation by aristocratic patrons of the plans for a music school.

Eighteenth-century plans for an English music school tended to focus on the specifics of musical training and especially the need to produce English musicians who could compete with foreign musicians in the secular market. Even early in the century, the reliance on foreign musicians was obvious, particularly at the Italian Opera. Daniel Defoe, writing in 1728, was troubled by this situation, primarily because Italian singers were so expensive. He proposed that an orphanage – Christ's Hospital – select promising students and give them a systematic musical education. The governors of the institution were to choose thirty boys, "of good Ears and Propensity to Musick."[45] Six would be trained in wind instruments, sixteen in strings, and eight in voice, organ, or harpsichord. All would eventually study composition. After seven or eight years of study, the students' educations would be extended by formal apprenticeships, though still connected to the hospital. At one point he adds that "For the greater Variety they may, if they think fit, take in two or more of their Girls where they find a promising Genius, but this may be further consider'd of."[46] For Defoe, not a professional musician himself and therefore not particularly concerned with status, foundlings seemed perfectly appropriate candidates for joining the musical profession. Because Defoe is addressing the dominance of foreign musicians chiefly in the secular/theatrical world, there is no mention of the classical education that had traditionally been part of chorister training. Fifty years later Charles Burney made a similar proposal, inspired by his visits to the Venetian conservatories (orphanages that trained female musicians to a high level of professional skill). The institutions proposed by Defoe and Burney might have produced English musicians to compete with foreigners, but would have done nothing to raise the social status of the profession. For that, one must turn to proposals made by musicians, who tended to address not only the pragmatic concerns of Defoe and Burney but also issues of professional status.

In the 1750s the cathedral organist and conductor William Hayes identified the main problems as foreign competition and the general lack of regard for musicians in English society. His solutions were to obtain market control and to establish a professional music school, both under the auspices of the Royal Society of Musicians. Market control would be established by rather extreme measures:

I could heartily wish there were an Act of Parliament made, that no Music whatever should be published, (upon Pain of incurring a considerable Penalty) before it had undergone a severe Scrutiny of the Governors and Assistants belonging to the Musical Charity. And if that could not easily be obtained that the Society would make a Law among themselves, forbidding any Member of the said Society to publish his Compositions, until they had been approved of by the Major Part of the aforesaid Governors and Assistants, upon Pain of Expulsion, and being forever deprived of any Benefit they might otherwise be entitled to as Subscribers ... it unquestionably would not only *preserve* but also *promote* the Reputation of the Science they profess.[47]

In addition, the RSM would fund a school for "such Boys and Girls, who shew an early Genius in the several Branches of Music, indiscriminately, whether Musicians Children or otherwise."[48] He hoped to challenge foreign competition: "might not this enable us in a few Years to pay back with *Interest* what we have *borrowed* from foreign countries at too large a *Premium*?"[49] The Academy would be limited in size, and educate its students from the ages of seven or eight until their early twenties. He also stipulated that the children should receive complete educations, including reading, writing, arithmetic, grammar, and religion, "it being the Misfortune of many Musicians to be extremely ignorant in most of these Qualifications."[50] It is noteworthy that by "complete education" Hayes does not mean a classical education. This is all the more extraordinary since Hayes was an esteemed representative of the traditional, high-status career in church music. (He had been raised as a chorister at Gloucester Cathedral, and later became master of the choristers at Magdalen College, Oxford, where he received a B.Mus., became Professor of Music, and, in 1749, received the D.Mus. degree. In addition, one of his sons was a chorister at Magdalen.) In suggesting reforms characteristic of later professions – market control and a professionally focused training – and recognizing the very limited scope for the ideals and status of the traditional professions, Hayes was remarkably astute about the underlying disadvantages faced by musicians, and far ahead of his time.

After Hayes's surprisingly modern ideas for reform and Burney's more traditional foundling strategy, comments by musicians continued to illustrate the conflicts between the ideals of the traditional and emerging professions. Musicians were always in competition with foreigners, who appeared more cosmopolitan and better educated than their English colleagues. As a result, musicians in the early 1800s argued increasingly that broader education was an essential component and would make musicians more suitable for the company of great and cultured patrons. One anonymous journalist explained in 1818,

first, that it [music] is a liberal art which requires the aid and support of a liberal education; and secondly, that as the profession is sure to be associated more or less intimately with persons of high birth, affluent circumstances, and enlarged acquirements, it is essential to its prosperity that the mind should be trained to elegant pursuits and attainments, as well as to a just sense of what is due to character, independently of a particular science.[51]

This author recognized, however, that "few indeed are those who combine general knowledge with excellence in art," adding that "upon such knowledge, nevertheless, depends all the estimation they can hope to enjoy in society, beyond the short-lived admiration which the exercise of particular talent immediately excites."[52]

Contemporary writings emphasized that musicians were, and needed to be, highly educated. During its first years, the *Quarterly Musical Magazine and Review* announced,

The Profession at large, we are happy to say, admit that the circulation of our work has done more towards diffusing a philosophical view of the advantages which music, both as a science and as an art, both as to its own character and as to the character of its professors, may derive from a connection with letters, than any other attempt that has hitherto been made to advance all these important objects.[53]

In 1826 the same author reaffirmed the importance of a broader educational background, as he happily observed "the growing connection between literature and music":

Nothing we will venture to assert can so effectually confirm the principles of a sound musical education, and contribute to establish the professional character upon so sure a foundation as this union ... by this union we entertain the most sanguine expectations that musicians will ere long take rank with other artists on the score of intellectual acquirement and moral and social respectability – a place which has but too long been denied them.[54]

The preoccupation with liberal educations for musicians was connected with the often-mentioned image of the "mere fiddler," musicians whose non-musical education was so limited that they embarrassed colleagues and patrons alike as soon as they spoke. This criticism frequently applied even to rudimentary education, as in William Hayes's provision for basic instruction. However, when the criticism of the "mere fiddler" became a recommendation that musicians have liberal educations and "literary attainments," it represented less a modern professionalizing strategy than a nostalgic retreat to the values and criteria of the old elite professions.

Calls for a national music school appeared with increasing frequency in the early nineteenth century. One such proposal was made in 1811 by Joseph Kemp. Educated as a church musician (chorister at Exeter Cathedral in the late eighteenth century, organist of Bristol Cathedral from 1802 to 1809, and holder of degrees in music from Cambridge), Kemp had moved to London and shifted his energies to composing theatre music and publishing a system of music pedagogy. He was concerned above all with the problem of foreign competition:

I have, with other masters, proposed a College similar to the Conservatories of Italy and Germany, and all we require is a *free Seminary* to meet our endeavours, being resolved not to make profit an object to the exclusion of genius. If the erection of a building, or the purchase of a house adapted to the purpose, be provided by public contributions, or some other means, a Musical College may raise the profession to a summit it has not yet attained, and afford amusements such as have not yet resulted from the English school – such as will vie with those of other nations, whose excellent performances are in a great measure the result of a systematical education in a national seminary.[55]

In 1822 F. W. Horncastle, trained as a chorister in one of the London choirs and employed as organist at Armagh Cathedral, drew up a "Plan for the Formation of an English Conservatorio."[56] This plan makes explicit the need for both systematic musical education and broader education. His school would have fifty pupils, starting around the age of eight (as in chorister training). Half the students would live at the school and pay no fees except for an initial expense of £20; in other words, they were "apprenticed to the governors of the institution." The other half would not board and would pay for their own tuition, with the expectation that they would eventually receive financial support. There were to be twenty-four teachers in a variety of subjects (see table 7). The emphasis is clearly on musical training, and the large number of composition teachers reflects the sense of many contemporary English musicians that this was an area in particular need of improvement in the educational system. Horncastle goes on to explain that in existing institutions, specifically the London choirs, "in the necessary miscellaneous learning in which a true musician, perhaps above all other artists, ought to be a proficient, there is a great deficiency."

Despite the absence of classical studies in his curriculum, he argues that

A liberal education, in the truest sense of the word, is absolutely necessary to form composers of any eminence; it is this that exalts their taste, enlightens their understanding, and assists their judgment. There is a certain refinement, not only in the manners, but in the thoughts of those who have been well educated, that never can be found in persons not so fortunate; it makes a man anxious for the society of his superiors, solicitous for his own improvement and respectability in life.[57]

Table 7. *Curriculum of music school proposed by F. W. Horncastle, 1822*

vocal instruction: church and chamber
vocal instruction: dramatic
piano
organ
violin
cello
flute
oboe
bassoon
composition: vocal music (glees, madrigals, etc.)
composition: oratorio
composition: operas and chamber music
composition: instrumental overtures, symphonies, etc.
composition: organ music
composition: piano
composition: stringed instruments
theory (starting with thorough bass)
lecturer: once a quarter, on various topics
schoolmaster: reading, writing, accounts, English grammar
French
Italian
Latin
lecturer: poetry and "belles lettres"

Such notions tell us much more about musicians' social values than about musical education. After all, Horncastle laments that "low company appears to have been the ruin of many men of genius who had received inferior education," and then includes Mozart among his examples. The confusion of social and musical values is one of the persistent themes of the musical profession during this period.

Finally, Horncastle describes his ideas for funding and structuring the school. He proposes a solution that would both provide financial support and preserve professional control. Musicians would appeal for patronage to the King, and with that backing "the next step would be to appoint a committee of professors, who should choose from among themselves a treasurer, secretary, &c. to receive subscriptions, distribute notices and plans of the establishment." When funds were sufficient, the school could open. A plausible enough plan, but this route to professional self-sufficiency and training was not to be the model for the first English music school, the Royal Academy of Music.

Since Horncastle was in Ireland, he may not have been aware that members of the Philharmonic Society were simultaneously drafting a different plan. A committee (including Henry Bishop, J. F. Burrowes, Henry Hill, C. Kramer, Charles Neate, Vincent Novello, Cipriani Potter, and T. F. Walmisley) had been appointed to review a number of different proposals for a Royal Academy of Music, and in a memo dated March 13, 1822, that committee expressed its preference for the plan drawn up by T. F. Walmisley, since it was "calculated to produce the most beneficial Effects to the Musical Profession, and the Musical World in general."[58] Most of the brief plan concerns finances and management of the school, with every detail designed to preserve professional control. Contributions would be raised from members and associates of the Philharmonic Society and from wealthy patrons who would receive in exchange admission to concerts and lectures. Operating funds would be similarly acquired, with further support from the Philharmonic Society. Additional money-making ventures included benefit concerts, lectures, and student exhibitions, and half the profits from student engagements outside school. The administration of the school was to be conducted entirely by professional musicians.[59] The Philharmonic Society plans were not realized, however, as a rival plan – sponsored and designed by aristocratic patrons – appeared on the scene.

The Royal Academy of Music

The only school established to train musicians during this period was the Royal Academy of Music, founded in 1822. Like earlier initiatives, the RAM was designed to remedy the deficiencies of English musical training and to produce graduates who could compete effectively with foreign musicians. But from the start the RAM was planned, funded, and managed by aristocratic patrons. While patrons shared professional concerns about musical education, and were increasingly put off by the high fees charged by foreign musicians, especially at the Italian Opera, they did not share musicians' values or concerns about social and professional status.

In non-musical circles the aristocratic control of the RAM was greeted favorably. A leading London newspaper remarked: "We look upon the entire exclusion of professional feelings from this body, as a sure token of the sagacity with which its appointment has taken place, and of the success by which its distributions will be attended … who can answer for the jealousy and suspicion that would be entertained of the same extensive influence in mere professional hands."[60] But some professional musicians were outraged and apprehensive about the aristocratic initiative for the RAM. One article in a music periodical, after reviewing the rules and curriculum of the RAM, argued that

The plan is radically faulty in planting an expensive permanent establishment far beyond the real purpose and the real necessity ... in discarding the experience and the judgment of the profession, whose character and interest are deeply involved in the effects of such an institution, and in the virtual assumption of the whole power and patronage by the sub-committee.[61]

The author of this comment also expressed serious doubts about how long the RAM would last.

Students entering the RAM would be between ten and fifteen years old, literate, and have some aptitude for music.[62] They were required to supply their own instruments, except for horns, cellos, double basses, pianos, organs, and harps.[63] There was a regulation that "each student must, at the time of admission, come decently clothed, and continue to do so, as the establishment will not charge itself with any expense on that head."[64] Boys and girls were admitted in equal numbers, though they had separate faculties and curricula (as we shall see below). After a year of study, the students were examined to determine if they should continue. The length of the program varied for each student but the average was from four to seven years (not unlike an apprenticeship). In the original regulations of the school the attendance fee was to be ten guineas upon entrance, and five guineas for each additional year. Children of professional musicians were to pay five guineas upon entrance, and two guineas for each additional year.[65] But these prices turned out to be unrealistic, since by 1824 the fee had risen to £40 a year, which made the school even less accessible for families of poor to moderate income.[66] There were a few royal scholarships available through the school and several students received some form of aristocratic patronage for tuition and in gaining admission.

It was generally necessary to audition before being admitted, although one account of the auditions reported that "In the examination of these youthful candidates no great deal of talent was manifested, except by the son of Mr. T. Cooke, who distinguished himself much, by performing upon several instruments."[67] Social and professional connections were also helpful, however. William Henry Holmes, the son of a professional musician in Derbyshire, had performed as a child for the local nobility and gentry, and

having been heard by the late Archbishop of York and Mr. Charles Knyvett [a professional musician], who both took an interest in his welfare, through their kind interference he was made know[n] to his late Majesty George IV, through Sir William Knighton, and on the opening of the Academy in 1823 was at once nominated a student on the Foundation [i.e. he received a scholarship], on the recommendation of his Majesty.[68]

He later became a prominent London pianist and composer. Other examples include Henry Brinley Richards, who entered the RAM in 1834 "with the assistance of the Duke of Newcastle,"[69] and John Thomas, who was placed in the school in 1840 "through the influence of the Countess of Lovelace."[70]

Every effort was made to ensure the respectability of the school. The original rules and regulations stated that the first priority would be religious and moral instruction. The stated reasons for this stem from English cultural perceptions about musicians: "It is well known that there exists not a profession whose members are more exposed to every species of temptation than that to which the pupils of the Academy have devoted themselves. In proportion to the peril should be the precaution of guarding the tender mind, by a sound, moral, and religious education."[71] Second in importance was the study of the English and Italian languages, writing, and arithmetic.[72] Furthermore, careful arrangements were made for the segregation of male and female students: "the upper stories are already so arranged, that the apartments in which male and female students will be accommodated, admit of no communication: the same observation applies to the entrances, as two doors will be provided, one for the girls and one for the boys; the garden also, which is very spacious, will be divided by a wall."[73] As a result, the school could be attended by girls (and boys) whose middle-class families would not have considered apprenticeship or stage careers for their children.

The daily schedule for the students was long and inflexible, even by contemporary standards. One journalist noted that the intensive schedule "employs almost every hour of the pupils' time, leaving no more relaxation (and perhaps by some it will be thought hardly enough) than health of mind and body imperatively requires."[74] The curriculum was broad by the standards of musical education at the time, although there was some criticism of the program for not including more non-musical studies.[75] When the school first opened in 1823, the curriculum was very limited (see table 8).[76] The mingling of native and foreign teachers is also noteworthy, although apparently the initial plans included more foreigners and more eminent English players; the school could not afford to pay the fees for the most famous musicians, however, and "In practice . . . most teaching was done by 'obscure natives' rather than 'eminent foreigners.'"[77] Boys were required to learn two instruments: "as the desire to acquire a knowledge of those instruments which are the most likely to lead to rank and emolument in the profession would produce an uniformity fatal to some of the best purposes of the school, every boy is taught to perform on some other."[78] (It is difficult to know how this rule was enforced in the early years of the school.) Girls usually studied singing, although several studied piano and a few chose the harp. Both girls and boys had harmony teachers, but there

Table 8. *Curriculum and teaching staff of the Royal Academy of Music, 1823*

(as recorded in the *Quarterly Musical Magazine and Review*, 1823)

Boys	
Harmony and composition	Wm. Crotch
	Lord
Piano	Potter
	Haydon
Singing	Crivelli
Violin	F. Cramer
	Spagnoletti
Cello	Lindley
Harp	Bochsa
Hautboy	M. Cooke, sr.
Italian	Caravita
	Cicchetti
Writing music	Goodwin
Girls	
Harmony and composition	Wm. Crotch
	Lord
Piano	J. B. Cramer
	Beale
	Mme. Biagioli
	Miss Adams
Singing	Mme. Regnaudin
Harp	Bochsa
Italian	Caravita
	Cicchetti
Dancing	Monsieur Finart
Writing music	Goodwin

seem to have been serious shortcomings in the theoretical studies, probably even worse in the girls' programs of study. H. C. Banister, who attended the RAM from 1846 to 1851, described the complete absence of counterpoint from the curriculum in the school's early years:

At that period [*circa* 1830], the importance of that branch of study [counterpoint] was hardly recognized by the authorities of the Institution; although, subsequently, when I was a student, it was part of the regular curriculum for those who aspired to become composers. Even then, however, it was understood that it needed not to be included in the course of study of female pupils.[79]

Even with the thin curriculum, students had the advantage of being in contact with professional musicians and other students. There were regular public concerts given by the school, at which the more advanced students performed. Such opportunities were clearly an improvement over the isolated condition of the private student or the apprentice.

Some native musicians were dismayed by the initial choice of instructors; this was heightened by the appointment of the great French harpist, Nicolas Bochsa, as secretary of the school. Bochsa, whose checkered past included a conviction for forgery, had created a rage for harp playing in London after he fled from France to avoid imprisonment in 1817. Native musicians objected that

The professed intention of this school was to give encouragement to British Musical talent, and to render the annual importation of foreign performers, of all descriptions, for the use of our theatres, concerts, schools, &c. unnecessary. This argued a very patriotic and praiseworthy design, and revived the drooping hopes of many a half successful labourer in the English field of sounds, who had been struggling against Italian, German, and French competitors the greater part of his life... At first ... it was not to be credited, that the very first step towards encouraging native artists could be to tell them, that amongst the whole of them, no one could be found to read and write *English* so well as a French harper who had resided some half dozen of years in London.[80]

The debate about Bochsa's appointment raged in a number of periodicals. One author took a more sympathetic view, arguing that while many of the native musicians had kept aloof from the proceedings (perhaps because of resentment of the aristocratic control of the project), Bochsa had been extremely active in raising subscriptions, participating in discussions about the principles upon which the school should be run, and bringing in a large number of applicants.[81] In fact, among the original students who auditioned, the majority applied to study harp with Bochsa.[82] The debate seems to have died down, and Bochsa continued in the position for four years, at which time he was involved in a scandal and was "dismissed on account of public attacks upon his character which he was unable to deny."[83]

For many years, the school struggled on many fronts. As Cyril Ehrlich explains, "the RAM suffered a meagre and precarious existence. Most of its troubles stemmed from poverty, but grandiloquent and muddled aspirations, incompetence, and petty rivalries all played their part."[84] The power struggles that continued until almost 1860 between the aristocratic and professional priorities for the school, as well as the ongoing financial weakness of the institution, severely compromised the standards of instructors, students, and musical education. The RAM did not begin to match the quality of musical training available in the best European conservatories. Ehrlich also suggests that in the early decades the school was largely ineffectual in supplying top musicians to the London music scene, noting particularly that only a very small proportion of mid-

Table 9. *Curriculum and teaching staff of the Royal Academy of Music, 1838*

(as recorded in the Royal Academy of Music, *A List of Pupils Received into the Academy*, 1838)

Principal:	Cipriani Potter
Leader and director:	F. Cramer
Conductor:	C. Lucas
Harmony and composition:	H. R. Bishop, C. Potter, J. Goss, C. Lucas, A. Devaux, T. M. Mudie, G. A. Macfarren
Italian singing:	Signor Crivelli, Signor Carrara, M. Benedict, Signor Negri
English singing:	Sir G. Smart, W. Knyvett, J. Elliott, J. Bennett, Mrs. Burnett
Sight singing and concerted music:	J. Elliott
Pianoforte:	Mrs. Anderson, J. B. Cramer, I. Moscheles, C. Potter, W. H. Holmes, Miss Dorrell, Miss Foster, Mrs. W. Seguin, W. S. Bennett, A. Devaux, W. Dorrell, T. M. Mudie
Harp:	J. B. Chatterton, W. Lord, E. J. Neilson
Violin:	F. Cramer, N. Mori, C. A. Seymour, H. G. Blagrove, C. A. Patey
Violoncello:	R. Lindley, C. Lucas
Double bass:	J. Howell
Clarionet:	T. L. Willman
Flute:	W. Card, J. Richardson
Oboe:	G. Cooke, J. Keating
Horn:	Signor Puzzi, H. Platt
Bassoon:	J. Tully
Trombone:	J. Smithies
Trumpet:	T. Harper
Italian language:	Signor Barracco

nineteenth-century London orchestral instrumentalists were RAM graduates.[85] Little significant challenge to the dominance of foreign musicians was launched.

This dark picture of the school's accomplishments should not be overemphasized, however. By 1838 the curriculum had expanded considerably, with English musicians now forming the mainstay of the teaching staff (see table 9).[86] Some graduates of the RAM rapidly joined the upper ranks of the profession, others became leading musicians in London, and still others found lucrative teaching practices in provincial towns. Once the school expanded its curriculum beyond the limited fare of the initial years, RAM graduates had a distinct advantage over other English music students. A RAM education in itself conferred some degree of respectability and status, due as much to the connections students made there as to the musical education offered by the school.

The RAM improved the status of the profession in a number of other ways, despite the setback to professional autonomy in the school's original organization. The school provided a small step toward the kind of systematic training and certification some musicians had been calling for; it provided a new high-status form of employment for musicians as instructors at the school; and its graduates were relatively free from the prejudices attendant upon musicians who had been trained as apprentices. The RAM may even have helped to institutionalize a secular, especially concert-based, career track to replace the reduced prestige of careers in church music.

However, its most dramatic contribution was for women musicians, whose options for musical education were much more limited. The opportunities for musical training, the concern for propriety and respectability, and the associations with aristocratic patrons opened doors for a new generation of female singers and pianists who started pouring into the London musical scene in the late 1830s. They formed close networks, performed in concerts together, and extended a helping hand to the next generation of female musicians. A number of them were involved in founding the Royal Society of Female Musicians in 1839.[87] In the ensuing decades, some of the leading women musicians of the time were associated with the RAM, both as students and instructors.

Still, the RAM alone could not completely overcome the challenges faced by musicians during this time of sweeping social change, and it certainly did not further the agenda of those musicians who looked longingly back to the traditional professions. The aristocratic patrons who founded the RAM believed, perhaps more so than middle-class patrons, that musicians and respectability were compatible, and that musical skill did not have to be achieved at the expense of basic education. However, there was no provision for classical studies or anything approximating a liberal education. The aristocratic vision for professional musicians admitted that carefully selected musicians might become respectable members of the middle class, but not that they were candidates for either traditional forms of gentility or the independence of nineteenth-century professionals. Such competing visions did not begin to resolve until the second half of the nineteenth century, with the proliferation of new music schools and professional organizations.[88]

The evolution of careers in church music was closely intertwined with the history of the Anglican Church, which experienced its own upheavals and transitions during this period. There has been much debate in recent years about the role of religion and the church in eighteenth-century British thought and society; many scholars now question the traditional view of eighteenth-century Britain as an increasingly secular society, noting instead the degree to which religious ideals and concerns continued to pervade most aspects of the culture.[1] Recent studies have also tempered the notion of a radical contrast between the neglect and decay of the eighteenth-century church and the debates and reforms of the nineteenth-century Oxford movement.[2] Despite these important revisions, however, the condition of church music and musicians in the eighteenth century lends support to the view that in at least some respects the church experienced a period of decline.

Church musicians enjoyed a number of advantages not shared by their secular colleagues: membership in the traditional, high-status branch of the profession linked to the cathedrals and universities; relative freedom from association with cultural anxieties about gender, foreigners, and immorality (women were largely excluded and foreigners unlikely); and connection with the long and esteemed history of a distinctly English tradition of church music. George Hogarth, writing in 1838, expressed the beliefs of many native musicians when he wrote that "England is ... entitled to boast that her cathedral music is superior to that of any other country, and that, while the music of the church in Italy, and even Germany, has degenerated, ours retains the solemn grandeur of the olden time."[3]

The economic and artistic conditions for church music seem to have declined considerably, however, reaching a low point in the early decades of the nineteenth century, and the status of church musicians often compared unfavorably with that in other branches of the profession. The university music degrees sought by many church musicians seemed increasingly irrelevant as credentials for status and employment in the profession at large. By the early 1800s complaints about the conduct of the choral service, lawsuits about the diversion of choir funds by clergymen, and tirades against the decline of the religious branch of the profession had become common. One observer wrote in 1824:

[W]hat wonder that our cathedrals are desolate? what wonder that our canons and our prebendaries and our singing-men and singing-boys, outnumber their congregation? what wonder that the service is slovenly performed? . . . what wonder that sacred composition has almost sunk into desuetude? what wonder that our secular musicians consider it a disgrace to be attached to the service of the church? what wonder that our enemies assert that music is now to be heard only in the theatre? Better far to shut the doors, sell the organs for old metal and fire wood, and turn the surplices into some more useful apparel, than thus to disgrace the science and bring its professors into utter contempt.[4]

Even the valued distance from the world of secular (and foreign) music seems on occasion to have been called into question. After all, given the perceived social dangers of music, its appropriateness to religious worship had perennially to be defended. Acknowledging these dangers, an anonymous author wrote in 1753 that it was especially important to avoid "the Mistakes of those Gentlemen, who, to gratify the Vanity of some and the idle Curiosity of others, blend the Music of the Temple with that of the Opera, as if the Airs of the one were essential to the Devotion of the other, and that nothing could or ought to be performed in the Service of the Choir without the Sanction of the Opera."[5] His objections pertained not only to musical style:

[S]uch is our Attachment to the Opera, such our Disregard or Neglect, (not to say Contempt) of God's Service, that we can compliment the one at the Expense of the other! . . . interrupt the Devotion of the Church, to compliment Foreigners! – A fine Compliment, indeed! but to whom? – not to Men of our own Country, of our own Church and Religion, but to Foreigners, Men of a different Communion, and for the most part of a Church made up of nothing but Pomp and Pageantry![6]

In general, though, it was precisely the separation of church music from such concerns and its place in a long, prestigious, university-linked, distinctly English, and exclusively male tradition that provided church musicians with their special status in the profession. Even the style of singing employed in the church separated this musical tradition from the contemporary secular realm. The methods of vocal production used gave rise to a distinctly "white," "pure," sound with very little vibrato which has been described as the English choral, or cathedral, tone.[7] (Twentieth-century representatives of this style include, for example, the King's Singers and performers of early music such as the soprano Emma Kirkby.) As will be discussed in chapter 6, such differences in tone quality were associated at the time with a whole range of national, gender, and social values. The exclusive use of such vocal techniques and sounds in the music of the church was linked with the special status that church music and musicians enjoyed, even as the material conditions of their careers declined during these years.

Organists

Of the 971 organists for whom documents survive, 71 percent were employed primarily as organists, although they usually had other employment, particularly as teachers. Others (29 percent) combined posts as organists with several other types of musical work.

Most of the organists in the records were male, although there were a few exceptions. At least thirty-nine women worked as organists during these years. The 1954 edition of Grove's *Dictionary* states that Emily Dowding, organist of Temple Church, London, from 1796 to 1814, was probably the first woman organist in England.[8] There were, however, at least six earlier ones: Miss Greatorex, from a large musical family, who became the organist of St. Martin's Church, Leicester, in 1774;[9] Mary Hudson, organist at two London churches from 1790 to 1801;[10] Ann Valentine, organist of St. Margaret's Church, Leicester, from about 1785;[11] and two others working in London churches in 1794 (Miss Theophania Cecil at St. John's Chapel, Bedford Row, and Miss Burton at Piercey Church, Rathbone Place. In 1818, M. Horth was hired at Cripplegate Church, London, after a contest among thirteen candidates.[12] There are thirty others from the 1820s to the 1850s. Many of them came from professional musical families, had studied with relatives, and became the primary organists of churches after years of deputizing for fathers and brothers. Three had studied at the Royal Academy of Music.[13] Like male organists, they often had varied careers as singers, pianists, teachers, and composers.

Although the majority of organists worked for churches, cathedrals, or royal chapels, there were several other sources of employment, most of them religious. Schools and colleges employed organists in their chapels, as did hospitals, asylums, other public institutions, and the foreign embassies of Catholic countries. When Vincent Novello was the organist at the Portuguese Embassy from 1791 to 1822, "it became a fashion to hear the service ... and South Street, on a Sunday, was thronged with carriages waiting outside, while their owners crowded to suffocation the small, taper-lighted space within."[14] And by 1820 the Bavarian chapel had begun to charge sixpence and one shilling, respectively, for two galleries inside.[15] Aristocrats occasionally employed organists in private chapels; although

Table 10. *Sources of employment for organists*

Royal chapels	16
Cathedrals[16]	244
Churches	751
Other	65

rare, many of these appointments occurred in the second half of the nineteenth century (for example, Joseph Hart and George Elvey[17]), when such forms of patronage are often assumed to have decreased. Table 10 indicates the relative numbers employed by each type of institution.

Organists also performed in a few secular settings such as the eighteenth-century London pleasure gardens, Vauxhall and Ranelagh. Even London concerts sometimes employed organists. Samuel Wesley (the nephew of John Wesley and son of Charles Wesley, the hymnwriter) "received six guineas a night . . . for playing the organ at the oratorio concerts at Covent Garden Theatre with an additional four guineas for playing a concerto 'between the Acts.'"[18] There are several other examples of recital and theatre work by organists from the 1790s to about 1820. Benjamin Jacob, Samuel Wesley, and William Crotch performed at organ recitals to large audiences from 1808 to 1814;[19] John Watts played organ at concerts;[20] and John Wall Callcott was the organist at the Covent Garden Theatre in 1794.[21] However, secular employment for organists began in earnest only with the nineteenth-century growth of cities and the construction of substantial town halls, which were often equipped with cathedral-sized organs. From about 1840 towns such as Birmingham, Liverpool, Brighton, Glasgow, Leeds, and Newcastle upon Tyne employed municipal organists at competitive salaries. W. T. Best, a pioneer in this area, was employed at St. George's Hall, Liverpool, in 1855 and later at the Royal Albert Hall, London: "He alone among English organists of his day recognized and developed the secular uses of the instrument. He never held a cathedral appointment . . . he was pre-eminently a recitalist."[22]

For most of the period from 1750 to 1850, however, such opportunities were rare, and the training, employment, and musical orientation of most organists were directed toward church music. The professional duties of church organists varied with the size and importance of the institutions where they were employed. Their main duty was of course to perform the choral service – at cathedrals twice daily, at many churches only once a week. In the establishments where there was a full choir, the organist was usually the choirmaster as well. Only in the London cathedrals and the Chapels Royal were two positions – Organist, and Master of the Children

– sometimes divided between two musicians. The highest-status church and cathedral organists also composed church music and many had attained university music degrees.

Organists were selected by a variety of methods and criteria. Sometimes the Dean and Chapter of the cathedral made the choice; at other times professional musicians were called in as experts; and occasionally the parishioners themselves chose the candidate. It seems to have been assumed from an early date that appointments should be based on musical ability, which was determined by formal credentials and reputation, by employing the organist for a probationary period, or by contest.

For the necessary credentials, it was generally an advantage to have been employed in a choir as a child, and to have had experience as an organist; one or more university degrees were helpful in obtaining positions at the most prestigious institutions. Again, the London cathedrals and the royal chapels were exceptional in that they tended to hire organists and composers who had achieved prominence in the more cosmopolitan and secular London musical world.

Especially at the more prestigious institutions, organists might be employed on probation for a time before the appointment became official. Thomas Capell was on probation as organist of Chichester Cathedral for three years before his appointment was made official.[23] Sometimes an organist acted as a deputy for the official organist for years, so was already well known to the congregation and simply took over the position when the former organist retired or died. For example, when Henry Westrop became too ill to continue working after forty years as an organist at the church of St. Edmund King and Martyr in London, he continued to receive the stipend because he was "allowed to send a deputy and his daughter is at present doing the duty."[24] After his death a year later in 1876, Kate Westrop continued as the organist there for eleven years.[25]

A great number of appointments, even in the early eighteenth century, were decided by means of competitions. The use of these competitions in choosing organists is significant in that it reveals early assumptions that advancement in the musical profession was, or should be, based on ability, and that the best judges of this ability were professional musicians. Depending upon the number of candidates and the care that was taken in judging them, these contests could go on for several weeks. In some cases, outside experts (i.e. professional musicians) were brought in to listen to the performances and rank the candidates. Vincent Novello "was frequently appointed umpire at competitions for organists' situations, from his know[n] discrimination in judgment, as well as his great care and justice in decision."[26] Sometimes the experts' opinion was final, while on other occasions their conclusion was only used as a recommendation; local

favorites could be chosen even if they were not preferred by the professionals. In 1837, for example, an organist named Thomas Adams acted as
judge in a contest for a position. But when he picked an organist who was
not from the parish, "his opinion was consequently rejected, expense
uselessly incurred, and a member of the profession wantonly insulted, by
the return of a lady, whose only recommendation was that of residing in
the parish."[27] The final decision belonged to the officers of the cathedral,
but in some churches it was left to the parishioners. John Purkis, after a
three-day competition at St. Olave, Southwark, in 1793, was elected by a
majority of 111, which suggests a rather large participation in the decision.[28]

The wages earned by organists varied widely. One source reported in
1857 that organists at parish churches received an average annual salary of
£50, while cathedral organists were paid about £150 and were sometimes
provided with a house as well.[29] The organists of Magdalen College,
Oxford, received £60 in the late eighteenth century; the salary was raised to
£80 in 1820, £105 in 1838, and £150 in 1848.[30] Bangor Cathedral organists
received £40 in the eighteenth century, £60 by 1812, and, as a result of a
lawsuit, an increase to approximately £120 by 1819.[31] S. S. Wesley wrote in
1849 that cathedral organists received about £200, but he may have been
offered higher salaries on account of his reputation.[32] The highest salary
was that of W. T. Best, who received £300 in 1855 (soon raised to £400) as
organist of St. George's Hall, Liverpool.[33] The salaries of organists in
London churches increased even less than those of cathedral organists,
however. John Purkis at St. Olave, Southwark, and Jacob Cubitt Pring at
St. Botolph, Aldersgate, both earned £30 in 1793, as did Thomas Smart at
St. Clement Danes in 1798. John Ambrose earned only £20 in 1794 at St.
Ann's, Limehouse.[34] Fifty years later, however, the same John Purkis, now
at St. Peter's Church, Walworth, received only £40.[35] In addition to their
regular salary, organists sometimes earned extra fees of £4 to £6 for tuning
the organ and any other keyboard instruments in the church (Edmund
Olive at Bangor Cathedral and Edmund Larkin at Peterborough Cathedral).[36]

Most organists needed to supplement their salaries in various ways.[37] As
one observer pointed out in 1824, if a church organist had only one
position, "he may look for a subsistence, but he will find none. Hence the
pluralities complained of, which none can more bitterly lament than many
of the individuals retaining them."[38] Many parish church organists held
positions at two or more churches, and even cathedral organists might be
employed at other churches in the neighborhood. Thomas Bedsmore,
a mid-nineteenth-century organist at Lichfield Cathedral, worked at
several churches in the vicinity.[39] Thomas Attwood Walmisley combined

employment in the chapels of four Cambridge colleges by working the following Sunday schedule: "St. John's at 7.15 a.m.; Trinity, 8; King's, 9.30; St. Mary's, 10.30 and 2; King's, 3.15; St. John's, 5; Trinity, 6.15."[40] However, holding more than one job usually depended on the deputy system, in which an aspiring musician received a small payment for substituting for the official organist.

Although the deputy system could work well, especially among family members, it could also be exploitative. In 1824 one author viewed the deputy system as part of a spiral of declining wages and status: the low level of organists' salaries made multiple jobs essential, and "the existence of these pluralities tends to the still farther depression of the character of church musicians... Much must inevitably be left to be done by deputies with inferior talents, and yet more 'beggarly' stipends."[41]

Organists also supplemented their salaries with private teaching. The prestige and connections of a cathedral organist could provide very lucrative employment opportunities. S. S. Wesley reported in 1849 that "in populous and wealthy districts [the organist's salary] forms but a small item in his actual income. If he be a clever pianist and teacher of singing, an industrious use of these acquirements will produce him from one to two thousand pounds a-year."[42] Robert Janes, organist of Ely Cathedral from 1831 to 1866, had a large number of students throughout Norfolk and Suffolk, and "in later years was wont to relate how he rode long distances on horseback to fulfil his engagements ... it is said that his income at this time could not have been expressed in less than four numerals."[43]

Particularly in London, positions as an organist were frequently combined with a wide variety of other kinds of musical employment. In 1794, when Joseph Major was twenty-two, he was organist of Knightsbridge Chapel, taught music at two schools, and had other engagements (performing and/or teaching).[44] In 1779 William Smethergell was organist of two churches, had engagements as a private teacher, and was a principal tenor singer at Vauxhall Gardens.[45]

Like most musicians, organists often became impoverished, especially in old age. A few did have some kind of pension arrangement when they retired. When the departing organist was respected and liked, for instance, the new organist might be expected to split the salary with the outgoing one. After John Keeble succeeded Thomas Roseingrave as organist of St. George's, Hanover Square, in 1737, Roseingrave continued to receive one half of the organist's salary until at least 1750.[46] In 1818, when Reginald Spofforth retired as organist of Southwell Cathedral, he was allowed £25 a year in recognition of his many years there. (His successor was paid £30 a year, which was exceptionally low for a cathedral organist at that time.[47]) Thomas Forbes Walmisley at St. Martin in the Fields and Robert Turle at

Westminster Abbey both received pensions when they retired in 1854 and 1882, respectively (the latter after fifty years of service).[48]

Yet even cathedral organists sometimes found themselves in extreme poverty. Financial struggles were particularly common for London musicians who had enjoyed several sources of income and were later reduced to living solely on their organist's pay. In 1798 Thomas Smart appealed for assistance because he was ill and had "but Thirty Pounds a year coming in as Organist of St. Clement Danes to Support Himself, a Wife, and son aged Twelve Years."[49] William Duncomb sent a similar plea in 1814, "as I am destitute of every professional emolument my Organists situation excepted."[50]

Despite the decline in some aspects of the careers of church organists, they still offered some professional advantages over secular employment. Appointment to a position as an organist had an implied tenure of office; the few examples of dismissals occurred very early in this period, and were due to gross negligence of duties, never to musical inadequacy. At Exeter Cathedral an organist was dismissed after fifty years "for his long absence and disorderly life."[51] An organist at Peterborough Cathedral was dismissed in 1777 "for negligence in the duties of his office,"[52] and at Lincoln Cathedral in 1771 the organist was "arraigned and reproved for playing one Anthem while Mr. Binns was singing another" and for "insolence."[53] Also, in contrast to theatre musicians, whose association with the stage made them morally suspect, organists' association with religion enhanced their status and respectability, making them more eligible for private patronage as teachers. Organists at some provincial cathedrals achieved prominent social roles. Edward Orme, organist of Chester Cathedral in the mid-eighteenth century, was a Freemason, a Deputy Herald of the city, and served a term as Sheriff.[54] By the nineteenth century, local organists tended to focus more specifically on musical activities, and they frequently became the leaders of local musical life, conducting choral and orchestral societies and directing preparations for regional music festivals. As one source pointed out, "the value of such appointments [organist posts in parish churches] is greater than would at first appear, especially to the youthful aspirant to musical fame, as they give a certain position, and are calculated to afford an advantageous introduction."[55] In sum, the education and musical attainments of organists, as well as the material circumstances of their careers, varied as widely as those of most branches of the musical profession. Many benefits accrued specifically from their position in the church, but this alone was rarely sufficient.

Choir singers

Institutions that performed a full cathedral service employed choirs: the royal chapels (London and Windsor), the cathedrals of London, Dublin, and the provinces, and the chapels of Oxford and Cambridge. Cathedral choirs were restricted to male singers, with the upper lines sung by boys, although some of the parish choirs made up of charity-school children may have included girls as well as boys.[56] The three professional female choir singers in the catalogue were not part of the daily performances of the Anglican choral service. One was a member of the Royal Academy of Music's student choir, which performed at a London chapel in the 1840s.[57] The other two were clearly soloists rather than members of the choir, but they did sing in a religious setting: Miss Povey, a theatre singer who was also the principal singer in a Catholic chapel in London, and an Italian singer, Signora Marinotti, who combined concert work with singing at the Catholic chapel of the Spanish ambassador.[58] From time to time, free-thinking professional musicians pointed out the musical shortcomings of exclusively male choirs. S. S. Wesley wrote that boys' voices "at the best, are a poor substitute for the vastly superior quality and power of those of women."[59] And John Hullah, the mid-nineteenth-century pioneer in musical education, argued that "A choir implies not only Tenors and Basses, but *Sopranos* and *Contraltos*. Of whom are the latter to be composed? In cathedrals, as everybody knows, the sopranos are all boys... The cathedral system ignores the existence of half the creation, and that the most musical half."[60] Such arguments were, and in many cases remain, well ahead of the times.

Most of the choir singers in the catalogue represent the more prestigious metropolitan institutions. Although they were not particularly well paid compared to secular singers, they were much better off than singers in provincial cathedrals. In addition they had more opportunities to supplement their wages from the choir with other forms of musical employment.

The highest-paid singers were at the Dublin cathedrals, where the nominal salaries had kept pace with the value of the choir endowment. In the early 1800s, "each of the vicarages [includes vicars-choral] at Christ Church was altogether worth £222 per annum, while the Stipendiary Choirmen or Supernumeraries each received £150 per annum."[61] These were extraordinarily high salaries for choir singers at that time. Because of this fact, an attempt was made to divide the money between two choirs instead of one. However, "it was soon discovered that the once famous choirs were going to seed: the diminished incomes failed to tempt over and keep good singers from England, and an inferior set of men were attracted to the Cathedrals."[62] The experiment was ended and the high salaries restored.

The salaries of singers at the Chapel Royal, London, were probably among the highest in England, but they were much lower than the Dublin salaries. In 1818 the singers received £73, although "after paying deputies and other charges, the net income does not exceed £56."[63] At Westminster Abbey the singers received £10 a year throughout most of the eighteenth century. There were requests for higher salaries in the 1790s, resulting in raises of £10 to £20 during that decade.[64] It is clear that other fees and benefits were paid to the choir members, so that these figures probably underestimate the overall income. For example, John Sale Jr. received £5 a year for some time before 1819 from the rent of a house that was apparently owned by the Abbey.[65] In 1838 the salaries for two new singers were £90 each,[66] and this salary probably reflects not only a rise in income over the earlier period, but also a consolidation of numerous fees and wages collected by each singer.

But choir singers, like other musicians, depended on more than one source of income. It was not unusual for the most successful singers to hold multiple choir appointments, although the scheduling must have been very difficult. Nicholas Steele in 1780 and Israel Gore in 1789 held posts in both Windsor and London.[67] In the 1790s several musicians sang in more than one of the leading London choirs and sometimes at Windsor as well (Edmund Ayrton, William Clark, John Friend, John Gibbons, John Moore, and John Sale Jr.). In the early 1800s John Jeremiah Goss obtained appointments to the Chapel Royal, St. Paul's, and Westminster Abbey; other examples include the Reverend James Lupton in the 1830s and Henry Whitehouse in the 1850s.[68] These multiple appointments drew some criticism on the grounds that they decreased the quality of each performance:

It is not to be imagined that the same person can repeat the same service several times in the same day, with equal ardour and attention. Besides, if he be singing in the abbey [Westminster] he may feel apprehensive lest he should be too late for the Chapel Royal; or if performing in the latter place, he may have . . . some misgivings, whether it will be in his power to snatch a hasty morsel, and arrive, breathless, in time for service at St. Paul's.[69]

While some singers did dash around to fulfill their engagements, others relied on the deputy system, especially when they had posts in both London and Windsor. Richard Clark had an active singing career in 1814 based entirely on deputizing for other choir singers: "he is engaged as a deputy for Mr. Bartleman at the Chapel Royal, Mr. Sale at St. Paul's and Mr. J. B. Sale at Westminster Abbey."[70]

The men who were employed by these institutions often sang professionally in other settings and had a variety of musical occupations. They rarely sang at theatres or pleasure gardens, although there were a few exceptions. Perhaps partly as a result of the cultivation of the distinctly English choral type of voice, they tended to remain in the realm of religious music, singing in oratorio concerts and others such as the Concert of Ancient Music; examples include James Bartleman, William Knyvett, Horatio Michaelmore, and Jonathan Nield. Many of them also had extensive teaching practices. John Sale Sr., for example, who was a lay clerk at St. George's, Windsor, taught many royal pupils.[71] Some singers also performed as church organists, or even, in a few cases, as orchestral instrumentalists. William Hawes, who was a Chapel Royal chorister in the 1790s, became a singer at Westminster Abbey and the Chapel Royal, and played the violin in the orchestra of the Covent Garden Theatre (he later became Master of the Choristers at St. Paul's, then at the Chapel Royal, was a music publisher for a while, became the music director at the Lyceum Theatre from 1824 to 1836, and wrote a great deal of music both for the church and the theatre).[72]

The majority of professional choir singers in the early nineteenth century were much less fortunate. In fact, there are few categories of musical career in which a decline in social and economic status is more apparent. Although choir singers had once been relatively well paid, early nineteenth-century inflation reduced their salaries to below a subsistence wage: "While the salaries of all other persons connected with the church have advanced, according to the different value of money wrought by time, those of her 'singing men' remain very much the same as they were a century and a half ago . . . it is totally inadequate to the decent maintenance of a musician and his family."[73] Even at Westminster Abbey one source reported that "as a rule [the choir singer] was a pluralist hack scratching for a living,"[74] and the picture was much gloomier at many of the provincial cathedrals. At Bangor Cathedral, choir singers received £10 a year in 1811, which was increased to £15 the next year.[75] A source of 1824 estimated that choir singers in general received £30–£40 per year for their twice daily services, and deplored the decline of church musicians' real wages relative to the value of money and the cost of living.[76] Apparently, the singers had been reduced to a "'beggarly salary' . . . [which] would in many instances scarcely pay a journeyman blacksmith for his time."[77] A similar judgment was made by the organist S. S. Wesley, when he complained that choir singers were paid "at the rate of inferior mechanics and day-labourers."[78]

Furthermore, while traditionally Anglican choir singers appear to have been ordained, and enjoyed a degree of status based on their role in the religious service, by the late eighteenth and nineteenth centuries this level of religious education had become relatively rare. The most important choirs of London and Windsor were exceptions, for in 1794 they contained at least seven choir singers who were ordained: Wildon Champness, William Clark, Henry Fly, John Gibbons, John Moore, Waring Willett, and a Reverend Clark. This was not the case for provincial cathedrals, however, with the exception, apparently, of Hereford Cathedral. William Gardiner, visiting the cathedral around 1802, wrote with apparent surprise: "I was informed that the vicars-choral were all clergymen, and that no one could hold that office, or become organist, but a graduate of the university. Having visited nearly all the cathedrals, this was the first instance in which I found educated persons appointed to those offices." Gardiner discovered some conflict, though, between the singers' musical and pastoral commitments, because at the Sunday service he "found an inferior performer at the instrument, and was told that the gentlemen choristers were all absent, being gone to do duty at their respective livings in the neighborhood; and that Sunday was the only day in the week the cathedral service was not performed," upon which he "left Hereford with gloom and disappointment."[79]

As professional and social status declined and choir singers resorted to non-musical and non-church-related employment, one observer asked in 1824, "what wonder that the singers are frequently taken from the lowest order of society? what wonder that they unite some handicraft business with their profession, in order to eke out a scanty subsistence?"[80] Two decades later, S. S. Wesley complained further that "the constant vibration of the lay clerk between his shop and his Cathedral, as at present, is productive of serious results; rendering him, but too often, a tradesman amongst singers, and a singer amongst tradesmen,"[81] concluding that "there exists not a class in England more degraded and bereft of the port and dignity of manhood than the men by whom the daily worship of God is now carried on in our Cathedrals."[82] Not until the 1840s would a "choral revival" begin to reverse this century-long downward trend in the standards and status of church music and musicians.[83] Meanwhile, the decline of musicians' earnings and social status depressed what had been the most prestigious branch of the musical profession, and symbolized for many musicians a decline in the status of the profession as a whole.

Church music composers[84]

Composers of church music were traditionally drawn from the high-status branch of the profession, and they usually derived their primary financial support from employment as organists, although the Chapel Royal also specifically designated some musicians as composers. The almost total absence of women from this category reflects the importance of chorister training and the general exclusion of women from careers in church music.

Of the sixteen women in the catalogue who wrote religious music, most wrote and published hymn tunes, although two, Mary Ann Virginia Gabriel and Charlotte Sainton-Dolby, composed mostly secular music but strayed into the sacred realm of cantata and oratorio.[85] Only one woman, Clara Angela Macirone, wrote a choral service, cited in one biographical source as the first service written by a woman that was actually used in the church.[86]

By the mid-eighteenth century there was already an esteemed tradition of cathedral music by English composers. In fact, there seems to have been an evolving sense of this tradition as a canon, preparing the groundwork for the introduction of that idea in the secular realm.[87] For example, the middle decades of the eighteenth century witnessed a project to compile and publish cathedral music, edited by William Boyce. This work was expanded and reissued by Samuel Arnold in 1790.[88] (It is intriguing to note that, according to William Weber, Arnold was also at the forefront of the canonizing impulse in concert life.[89]) Another revised edition, prepared by the organist, composer, and music historian Edmund Rimbault, appeared in 1843. The leading players in this movement worked at the Chapel Royal as well as numerous institutions in London's secular musical world.

By the late eighteenth century, however, composition of church music had become less central to musical life. This was due in part to the erosion of the education given to choristers and to the neglect of the choral service in general. Even musicians who trained in this tradition devoted little time to composing music for the church. One important reason was financial. Even cathedral organists had to combine various kinds of employment in order to earn a living, and this left little time for study and composition. There were few financial or professional incentives to compose church music. The career of Thomas Thompson, the organist of the cathedral of St. Nicholas in Newcastle upon Tyne in the 1820s, seems to have been typical: "The unceasing round of his professional avocations, to those who know the full extent of his engagements in teaching, will sufficiently account for his not having attempted the higher walks of composition, which, to a country professor, are too often neither productive of profit nor fame."[90]

The lack of incentives to compose church music was identified by contemporary observers as another symptom of the decline of the Anglican church and its musical institutions, and was also used to explain the decline in the quality of the repertoire. As E. H. Fellowes wrote, "in the eighteenth and nineteenth centuries the standard both of composition and performance was allowed to degenerate to a deplorable extent."[91] S. S. Wesley believed that many more composers would choose to devote themselves to church music if the status and earnings of church musicians were improved: "It is necessity, not choice, that has driven our finest musicians to compose for the theatre, or to occupy their time in tuition, as affording the most lucrative return."[92] Another observer wrote in 1824 that the few musicians who devoted themselves to the study and composition of church music did so

at the certain risk of continual poverty... What rewards are held out, what honours are conferred on those who labour in the untilled field? True, the degrees of bachelor and doctor of music are still known, at least in name; but how rarely are they sought and obtained!... Is it that our church musicians are too poor to raise the necessary funds to defray the expences, which perhaps amount to as much as most of them get in the service of the altar, perhaps for *years*? And do not our *seculars* find so much encouragement in another direction as to render them indifferent to this honourable testimonial of talent? and does not this circumstance account for the low estimation in which musical degrees are now by *worldly* musicians notoriously held?[93]

While a small number of musicians, including the leading cathedral organists, continued to study and compose in the tradition of the Anglican choral service, the decline of the religious branch of the musical profession combined with the deplorable conditions of the choir and low performance standards left few incentives to pursue the calling of a composer of church music. Only with the energetic reforms of the Victorian age – some of them aimed primarily at musical reclamation, others, such as the Oxford movement, directed at religious issues – was there a revival of the English cathedral music tradition. These reforms were accompanied by improvements in the professional status of church musicians, but evolved from the fragmentation rather than the collective success of the profession.[94]

6   Secular musicians: singers

Secular singers, both male and female, inhabited a wider and less protected world than that of the exclusively male performers of English church music. More than any other branch of the profession, theatre and concert singers stirred up the national and gender anxieties that pervaded British musical life. The 841 singers in the catalogue (199 of them women) worked in a variety of settings (see table 11).[1] While many combined two or more employment categories, the educational and social differences between the singers in choirs and those in theatres made the combination of religious and theatrical employment less common.

Singing careers lay along a broad continuum of musical context and content, nationality, gender, respectability, earnings, social and professional status, and vocal style. The affective power of the voice, the combination of female and male performers, the long-standing association of theatres with immorality, and the striking contrasts between English and Italian styles of singing intensified the importance of such distinctions. At one extreme, the choir singers inhabited a respectable, religious, male musical landscape characterized by the vocal techniques specifically associated with English church music. Next along the continuum were mainly English male and female singers who performed religious music such as oratorios as well as secular works in concerts. These singers were more likely than stage singers to come from slightly more prosperous and/or professional backgrounds, to have been trained in private lessons or at the Royal Academy of Music, and to enjoy a higher social status. In contrast, singers in the English theatres generally came from lower social origins, had been trained as apprentices, and occupied a lower social stratum, reinforced by their association with the theatre. Nonetheless, the existence of the English theatres and the cultivation of a distinctly English vocal style, even in a theatrical setting, offered an alternative to the Italian Opera, which occupied the far end of the continuum. Italian singers represented foreignness, a vocal style which to some listeners seemed to clash with British ideas of gender and musical propriety, and yet these singers received the highest possible earnings.

Table 11. *Numbers of singers in various employment settings*
n = 841

	Male	Female	Total	%[a]
Choir	291	3	294	35
Stage	149	128	277	33
Concert	309	116	425	51
Music hall	1	0	1	0.1
Employment unknown	55	11	66	8

[a]Many singers are counted in more than one category.

Concerts

Concert, or orchestral, singing was an increasingly important form of musical employment in the nineteenth century. Concerts featured a wide range of repertoire, from Italian opera arias to oratorios to English ballads. With the exception of the oratorios performed in the theatres during Lent, however, concerts generally did not take place in either a theatrical or religious setting. In the eighteenth century the flourishing of public and private concerts provided many opportunities for singers, and while concert life dwindled during the wars with France, afterward more concert series appeared. In addition, the provincial choral festivals, which began in the eighteenth century, gained momentum in the nineteenth. Professional London singers often traveled to these music meetings as the soloists in oratorio performances.[2]

Most of the singers (238) in the catalogue who performed in concerts also pursued musical employment as organists, instrumentalists, teachers, and composers. Stage and choir singers alike performed in concerts, which offered a middle ground between music for the church and music for the stage. And in contrast to the Opera and the church, concerts employed both foreign and native musicians. Few singers built careers entirely on concert singing, and most of those who did were women who preserved a certain social and professional status by distancing themselves from the theatres.

Compared to the salaries commanded by the leading stage singers, concerts in general brought modest earnings. Still, some of the late eighteenth-century London concert series offered competitive fees for the top singers. A few such stars such as Lucrezia Agujari and Gertrude Mara received eighty to ninety guineas per night and the proceeds from a benefit concert, while the more typical fee for soloists seems to have been between ten and twenty guineas.[3] Occasionally the fees offered by a concert series could lure a singer away from the Opera entirely, as in 1781 when the

Table 12. *Fees for singers at Philharmonic Society concerts, 1822*

Name	No. of performances	Paid (£.s)	Per concert (£.s)
Mrs. Salmon	3	93	31
Miss Goodall	4	29.8	7.7
Mme. Camporese	3	47.5	15.15
Mme. Caradori	2	31.10	15.15
Mme. Ronzi de Begnis	1	15.15	15.15
Mr. Vaughan	2	14.14	7.7
Begrez	4	29.8	7.7
Antonio Sapio	2	14.14	7.7
Thomas Bellamy	1	7.7	7.7
Angrisiani	1	7.7	7.7
Zucchelli	1	7.7	7.7
J. B. Sale	2	10.10	5.5
Kellner	1	5.5	5.5
Terrail	2	6.6	3.3
Nelson	2	6.6	3.3
Master Coles	1	3.3	3.3

Pantheon concert paid the tenor Giovanni Ansani £300 for the season.[4] The highest concert salary in the eighteenth century appears to have been paid to Auguste Vestris: 700 guineas for one benefit performance and fifty guineas for travel expenses.[5] But these cases were exceptional, and the standard fees had not increased much by the early nineteenth century; in 1822, the Concert of Ancient Music paid £100 for the combined services of three leading female singers, Mrs. Salmon, Miss Stephens, and Mme. Camporese.[6]

Concerts alone were rarely lucrative enough to be the primary focus of singers' careers. Charles Horn, after first choosing a concert career, "soon found it neither met his wishes, nor answered his expectations in a pecuniary point of view, upon which he at length resolved to appear before the public as a theatrical vocalist."[7] The fees paid to solo singers at provincial music festivals appear to have been higher, but partly because the singers participated in several performances over two or three days. In 1814 at the Chester Festival Angelica Catalani received £420, Mrs. Salmon £160, and Messrs. Bartleman and Braham £220 and ten shillings each.[8] In 1824 fees to the leading singers at the Newcastle Festival were as follows: Braham £189, Miss Stephens £189, and Mrs. Salmon £168.[9] These and the Concert of Ancient Music seem to have offered the highest concert fees available at the time. Table 12 presents the fees paid to all the vocal soloists at the Philharmonic Society during the 1822 season.[10] Note that Mrs. Salmon and Mme. Camporese received somewhat less than their fees from the

Concert of Ancient Music. Note also that the list includes both Italian and English singers, that the highest salary went to an English woman singer, and that almost all were paid in guineas (one pound and one shilling) rather than pounds – perhaps a symbol of professional status.

Concert singing offered neither the job security of choir employment nor the wealth brought by success on the stage, but it did have compensations. As a supplement to other forms of singing career, concerts gave singers opportunities to increase not only their income but also their connections, leading to more engagements and students. Some concerts had snob appeal, since the Ancient Concerts and private concerts were the only sources of direct aristocratic patronage for most English singers. And further, even in the predominantly non-aristocratic oratorios, Philharmonic concerts, and provincial festivals, the freedom from association with the theatre made these performances an attractive form of employment for musicians, particularly women, who were not inclined to take the social risks of association with the stage.

Concert singing evolved as a primary career focus in the nineteenth century, particularly for women musicians. Frequently graduates of the Royal Academy of Music, they sang at the Ancient Concerts, Philharmonic Concerts, and provincial music festivals, occasionally performed in Europe (for example at the Gewandhaus Concerts in Leipzig), and specialized in the oratorio repertoire. Two leading exponents of such a career are Elizabeth Rainforth and Charlotte Sainton-Dolby. Their status and reputations enabled them to build large and respectable teaching practices which probably made up the greater part of their incomes.

Successful male singers were less likely to specialize exclusively in concert singing, because the stage entailed fewer risks for them and because they also had access to choir employment. But they, too, supplemented their vocal work with other musical employment. In the 1790s, Charles Knyvett Jr. sang at the Ancient Concerts and the Vocal Concerts, and he was a deputy choir singer at the Chapel Royal. He also gave singing and piano lessons, and in 1802 became the organist of St. George's, Hanover Square.[11] During the same period, John James Ashley sang in private concerts and in the Lenten oratorios presented at Covent Garden; was organist of Tavistock Chapel; played violin, viola, and drums; taught singing and piano; and composed songs and other music.[12] In 1835, John Orlando Parry reported that he was "engaged, as a principal singer at most of the Concerts in London, and at several provincial meetings. He performs on the Harp and Pianoforte, and has much private teaching."[13] He also appeared as a ballad-singer, presented a one-man show in the 1850s, composed operettas, and took a job as an organist in 1853.[14]

Concert singers were a relatively high-status branch of the musical profession, ranking between the religious and secular music worlds. They were better placed to supplement performance with lucrative teaching practices, so they had more opportunity than stage singers of providing for times of unemployment. (There were exceptions, of course. The extremely successful concert singer, Mrs. Salmon, was destitute for at least the last ten years of her life.[15]) In most cases concert singers' careers were as varied as those of other musicians. The one important exception is the careers of some nineteenth-century women concert singers who, by specializing in concert work, navigated a delicate course through the various social risks for women in the profession.

Theatres

Stage singers performed at theatres and pleasure gardens. Forty-six percent (128) of stage singers were women, the highest proportion of women in any type of musical employment except teaching. Many of the men and women in this category also pursued other forms of musical employment, such as teaching, but these were usually secondary, with singing the focus of the careers.

The most important and prestigious institution for singers and other secular musicians was the aristocratically supported Italian Opera.[16] Because the music and the spectacle at the Italian Opera was essentially an imported cultural product, the vast majority of the singers employed there were also imported, usually from Italy. The large salaries attracted some of the Continent's most renowned singers, recruited by the manager of the Italian Opera through a Europe-wide network of professional singers, Italian schools and teachers, and aristocratic patrons.[17] Sometimes these singers emigrated permanently, but more often they came to London only for the season. Although only a few settled in England, their positions and high salaries made them visible and influential members of the London musical scene. They became musicians with whom English singers had to compete for all kinds of patronage.

Salaries of opera singers varied widely.[18] Sometimes, especially for the top singers, the salaries were augmented by the proceeds from benefit concerts. The success of these concerts varied as well.[19] A few women commanded the highest salaries. In 1794 the top two salaries were paid to Brigida Banti and Anna Morichelli, who each received £1,400 and one or two benefits. Banti later earned salaries up to £1,700 and a benefit in the 1800–1801 season.[20] Comparable payments went to Josephine Grassini, record-breaking salaries to English singer Elizabeth Billington in 1803–4 and 1805–6 (£2,625), and the highest of all to Angelica Catalani, who earned £2,500 in 1806–7 and £5,250 in 1807–8.[21] Such salaries, benefit concerts, and sometimes also public and private concert engagements in London raised such singers far above the economic level of most professional musicians.

The next level, still extremely lucrative, includes male and female singers earning £800 or more for the season. In 1794, Giuseppe Viganoni received £1,400 and a benefit,[22] although he appears to have been paid less (£800 and a benefit) in subsequent years.[23] Other singers received salaries ranging from £100 to £800. After the first decade of the nineteenth century, the secondary singers were paid from £150 to £900, depending on how many performances they gave, and how popular or indispensable the management thought them to be.[24]

Very few English singers achieved success at the Italian Opera. Examples include Elizabeth Billington, John Braham, Maria Dickons, Michael Kelly, Catherine Stephens, and Ann Selina Storace. But in general it was very difficult for English singers to obtain even one opportunity to sing there, and rarer still for them to succeed. This was attributed by contemporary observers to a combination of factors: aristocratic preference for all things Italian and prejudice against English singers; the influence of the leading Italian singers on engagements; and the failure of English musicians to attain the standards of vocal, musical, and dramatic performance which were expected at the Italian Opera. All of these explanations were true to some extent. English musicians were powerless to change the first two, but the third did cause some aspiring English singers to study in Italy and gain experience in the smaller local and municipal theatres there. For example, a Miss Fearon studied singing unsuccessfully with a London violinist around 1820. She then went to Italy where she studied and sang for many years; upon her return to London as Mme. Feron, although she never broke into the Italian Opera, she received £40 a night at the English theatres.[25]

The musicians who chose this route rarely found a place at the Italian Opera. But they offered competition to native-trained musicians for employment in English institutions. Examples include Fanny Ayton, John Braham, Michael Kelly, and Catherine Stephens. The most successful of them worked at the two patent theatres in London: Covent Garden and Drury Lane.[26] In the eighteenth century, they might also perform at smaller, rival theatres such as the Little Theatre, the Haymarket, and the Lyceum, and at the outdoor pleasure gardens such as Vauxhall and Ranelagh. In the early nineteenth century, newer rival theatres provided increasing employment for stage singers. Finally, itinerant singer/actors could find employment with provincial theatres and touring companies.

The wages of singers at the English theatres varied widely. The most successful of them had generally studied for some time in Italy, may have performed briefly at the Italian Opera, and had access to a wide variety of professional engagements. Catherine "Kitty" Stephens earned thousands of pounds in the 1820s and 1830s. Her earnings from summer theatre and concert work in the provinces alone were estimated to be £2,500.[27] And these figures were thought to be conservative, "for it was publicly said that Miss Stephens netted £5,000 by her visit to Ireland alone, and Miss Wilson is lately reported in the journals to have made £4,000 by a similar jaunt."[28] The Miss Wilson referred to was another young stage and concert singer of the time, and reputedly made £10,000 from all sources in 1821, the year of her debut.[29]

Such examples were hardly typical, of course, and may well be exaggerated. Most singers pursued much more modest, patchwork careers. William Pearman, a tenor who was born in Manchester in 1792, offers a view of a singer who "came up through the ranks" with gradual but steady success. When still a child, he went to sea as a cabin-boy, and received no formal music training. Eventually he tried to find work as an actor, and, as was typical of work at non-patent theatres, he also had to sing. He sang for a while at Sadler's Wells theatre in London, and then worked in the provinces, singing at theatres in Newcastle, Bath, Bristol, and others. He made his operatic debut in London in 1817, and subsequently received regular employment at Drury Lane and Covent Garden.[30] While Pearman never even approached the earnings, status, or fame of the leading English singers, he did obtain regular employment as a stage singer.

The brothers James and Charles Bland illustrate the improvised career paths of stage singers. Sons of a popular London stage singer, Maria Romanzini Bland, they began as singers in London theatres in 1826. Charles's debut at Covent Garden may have been too ambitious; he was not very successful and was not employed for the next season. He obtained work in provincial theatres until the 1831–32 season when he again tried the London stage, and was employed for several years at the Olympic and at Astley's Theatre.[31] James, on the other hand, made his debut in an English opera at the Lyceum and later performed at Drury Lane. Unlike his brother, he was able to find sufficient work in London. In 1831, however, "he appeared at the Olympic as an actor and singer in burlesque with such success that he gradually abandoned serious singing and became the acknowledged representative of the kings and fathers in the extravaganzas of Planché and others."[32]

Many stage singers' careers were even more varied, encompassing other branches of the profession. John Braham, who sang one season (1796) at the Italian Opera before continuing his studies in Italy, returned to England in 1801 to become not only a leading singer in the English theatres, but a successful opera composer as well. He commanded high salaries, at one point receiving £1,000 to sing at Vauxhall Gardens in 1826.[33] He lost the very large fortune he had amassed from his musical career, however, when he invested heavily in two theatres.[34]

Less commonly, singers combined work in all performance settings: choirs, concerts, and theatres. Thomas Bellamy, the son of a prominent London choir singer, received his early training as a chorister at Westminster Abbey in the 1770s. He worked as a concert and choral singer until 1794 when he became a stage-manager in Dublin and part-proprietor in several theatres in Ireland and the English provinces. From 1807 to 1817 he sang in English operas at Covent Garden and Drury Lane. In 1819 he became the choirmaster at the Spanish Embassy chapel, and in 1820 he obtained a prestigious engagement as principal bass at the aristocratic Concert of Ancient Music.[35] Unusual for its combination of theatrical and choir employment, Bellamy's career illustrates the close connections between the leading London choral establishments and the London secular musical world.

Although the principal singers of the English stage combined a wide variety of engagements, English singers enjoyed fewer opportunities than Italian singers for employment outside the theatres. The English theatres gave more performances in the course of a week and the managements were less willing to accept absences by singers who preferred to fulfill other engagements. But at the King's Theatre the Italian singers enjoyed more flexible arrangements, eliciting some criticism:

The engagements . . . are much too loose, and permit by far too much allowance to private engagements. The best singers are found nightly at one, two, and even more public and private concerts, and the consequence is, that the opera is paralyzed by the indisposition of these very singers. The English Theatres experience much less of this evil, and for the simplest of all reasons – every failure subjects the defaulter to heavy forfeitures. And why should not foreigners, upon whom so much less labour is imposed, be submitted to similar conditions?[36]

Italian singers were in great demand at concerts, particularly private ones and musicians' benefit concerts, since their presence or absence often determined the success or failure of those concerts. It seems that without some Italian names on the program, English singers and instrumentalists could not hope to profit from their benefits:

The great passport to public favour, and it is as sudden in its exaltation of the fame of singers as it is great in power, is the King's Theatre – this has been frequently the subject of remark, but this season has confirmed it more than ever with regard to the effect upon the Benefit Concerts. We are warranted in saying that even where the most extensive personal connection has seemed to favour the artist's right to public patronage, the concerts have failed from the absence or the opposition of the leading stars of the opera.[37]

Below the level of even the modest careers described above, the singers employed in small roles and in choruses received very low wages. In 1821, the chorus of thirty-six singers at the King's Theatre received approximately £500, about £13 to £14 a year each.[38] In 1828, the sixteen men and twelve women in the chorus earned between £600 and £700, or about £23 each.[39] These singers may have had non-musical sources of income like the provincial choir singers, or they may have been singing in a chorus to supplement other types of musical employment. Ralph Shaw, who sang in the Drury Lane chorus, also performed on the oboe and the bassoon in the 1780s and 1790s.[40] A more prominent musician, John Danby, seems to have made a career of chorus singing in addition to being an organist and a successful composer of glees. He sang in the chorus of Drury Lane Theatre, but also in non-theatrical choruses at the Concert of Ancient Music, the Lenten oratorios, and the Academy of Ancient Music concerts.[41] It was rare, however, for theatrical chorus singers to have musical employment in the high-prestige concert series, and they undoubtedly occupied a low rank, both economically and socially, in the musical profession.

In conclusion, the social and economic status of stage singers is a study in wide contrasts. As has been shown, the leading singers of the Italian Opera and the English theatres could earn fortunes, especially when they combined stage singing with other kinds of lucrative employment such as private concerts and teaching. Further down the scale of professional success on the stage, careers become more varied, and, although the records are more scarce, earnings seem to have been quite low. Even the highest earnings were not always sufficient to compensate for the insecurity and irregularity of singers' employment. The most successful sometimes mingled in aristocratic social circles, although this was less true for English singers. There were even a few (usually female) singers, such as Anastasia Robinson and Clara Novello, who achieved dramatic upward social mobility by marrying aristocrats.

There were social risks for singers as well, particularly for women. Even the greatest English singer of this period, Elizabeth Billington, was libeled by rumors and pamphlets in the 1790s, and her supporters had to go to great lengths to defend her reputation.[42] The appearance of female stage singers who were both respectable and financially successful was paradoxical given the persistence of such ideas. It was generally assumed that only financial exigency would lead anyone, particularly a woman, to choose the musical profession, especially as a stage performer. John Ebers, the manager of the Italian Opera in the 1820s, expressed this opinion in justification of one Italian singer's exorbitant salary demands:

Like every other singer, however amiable and estimable, she [Camporese] was griping in her demands on the treasury, in forming her engagements. Nor is there any real inconsistency in this. For the only object which can induce a woman of character and education to come on the stage being the hope of emolument, the organ of acquisitiveness may naturally be expected universally to develop its power with proportionate strength.[43]

Because the middle-class prejudices against the stage extended to men as well, male stage singers also risked some loss of social status.

Cultural values and the voice

In addition to the challenges of finding training and employment, secular singers had to navigate a range of associations linking national identity, social status, gender roles, and styles of vocal production. Simon McVeigh points to the difficulties inherent in any discussion of national tastes and styles, and this is particularly relevant during a century when musical idioms and preferences evolved considerably.[44] However, he finds evidence of distinctive national values expressed in the eighteenth century. By the early nineteenth century, observers and critics of the musical scene became preoccupied with such issues, in particular the complex associations among national temperaments, vocal styles, and gender.

As discussed in chapter 1, gender, class, and national identities were closely related, and music occupied an uneasy place among these concerns.[45] Singing in particular inspired anxieties about gender and national identity. The reasons for this are many and complex, including the preeminent position of Italian singers in the London musical scene, the necessity for mixing women and men in performances of theatrical and choral works, and the sheer physicality – the undeniable role of the body – in the act of singing. English critics described Italian singing as affected, voluptuous, overly sensual, emotionally unrestrained, and effeminate. English singing on the other hand was pure, chaste, sober, and manly. For example,

To the Italians belong passion, force, transition, variety, and general splendour. To the English, sensibility tempered by an invariable sense of propriety, purity, delicacy, and polish. The emotions raised by the first are strong, but liable to sudden disgusts ... the last are more equable, and please most on reflection; in few words, the one is theatrical, the other orchestral – the one lies as it were beyond, the other within the range of our natural domestic pleasures. Italian music is now also much more voluptuous than English.[46]

The reference to "natural domestic pleasures" clearly indicates the underlying concern that music remain consistent with the values of middle-class respectability. Not surprisingly, the unrestrained character of the Italian theatrical style was even more unsettling when the singer was a woman: "We speak of the exercise of the art, as 'sound and chaste.' These are amongst our highest epithets of commendation: we are shocked at dramatic vehemence; it appears somewhat allied to what is coarse and unbecoming, particularly in our female singers."[47]

The same author acknowledged that the English were indebted to the Italians for the technical foundations of singing, but also described specific vocal techniques that continued to distinguish the two national styles. He claimed that the Italians explored a wide range of vocal sounds for dramatic purposes, while the English cultivated a tone that was more pure, arising from neither the head nor the chest, "but from a region somewhere between both, where it receives its last polish."[48] He continued with a discussion of vowel pronunciation, intonation, dramatic use of portamento, the trill (or shake) and other ornamentation. Ornamentation in particular had long been a focus for such national comparisons and criticisms. McVeigh notes that already in the last decades of the eighteenth century, English taste tended at best to be suspicious of virtuosity and ornamentation, a suspicion linked to some extent with xenophobia.[49] While ornamentation was accepted as a means of intensifying the affect of certain passages, early nineteenth-century critics remarked that beyond a certain point the resulting "wailing, complaining effect is to our ears effeminate,"[50] and that it was employed less often by English singers for that reason. The same author recommends that the English should "appropriate what is best in Italian art, and still preserve the pure and manly energy which, after all, is the capital characteristic of our legitimate composition and execution."[51]

The gender values expressed in such statements dazzle with their inner contradictions. Italian singers – both male and female – were considered disturbingly effeminate. The purity and chaste sound idealized for English singers – both male and female – was described as manly. Even today the ideal for English choral sopranos tends to suggest the tone of the boy soprano voice "with its straight, vibrato-less quality."[52] It is difficult to escape the conclusion that the gender-role concerns and ideals expressed by early nineteenth-century critics illustrate a certain aversion to unrestrained femaleness – whether in reaction to the voluptuous and sensual singing of women or the notion – articulated since the early eighteenth century – that musicians, foreigners, and male homosexuality were somehow linked. It is arguable that the vocal aesthetic articulated by early nineteenth-century critics mirrors the cultural, gender, class, and national identities forged during the tumultuous social reshuffling of the time. We can observe in the prescriptive aesthetic of vocal production the struggle to define not just a British, but specifically a middle-class, identity distinguished from the aristocracy and legitimized in its claims to power by social propriety, restraint, and manliness.[53]

The French also struggled to understand and identify differences in national vocal aesthetics. Their characterization of Italian singers is remarkably similar to that of English critics, although their comments about French singers focus primarily on vocal style, and do not appear to include the same moral concerns and gender anxieties that pervade English vocal/musical criticism during these years.[54]

The application of such values to singers is pervasive in the musical press of the 1820s, and posed particular challenges for women musicians. Since the audible and powerful assertion of the body by women singers unavoidably subverted contemporary beliefs about appropriate gender roles, they had to construct a careful balance among competing social, cultural, and musical values.[55] The successful career of Catherine "Kitty" Stephens illustrates the close links between the ideals of domesticity, propriety, and an English vocal style. The daughter of a London carver and gilder, she studied first with a well-known Italian singing teacher, Gesualdo Lanza, and later with the English singer and composer Thomas Welsh. She seems to have combined some of the technical attributes of the Italian school with a distinctly English tone, and performed on stage, at concerts, and in oratorios. Sainsbury's 1825 biographical entry reports that

The peculiar bent of her talent seems to be towards ballads and songs of simple declamation; in a word, towards that particular style which is generally esteemed to be purely English ... It is impossible for any thing to be more pure, more chaste, than the simplicity with which Miss Stephens gives such songs as "Auld Robin Gray," "Angels ever bright and fair," and "Pious orgies," of Handel.[56]

The purity of her tone extended to ornaments, which were "correct and pleasing ... there is little of the coarseness of the stage to be discovered." In other words, Stephens manages to be a professional musician, on the stage, and yet still not undermine English middle-class values:

There results from the whole of Miss Stephens's performance a certain grateful sense of pleasure, somewhat analogous to the sensation experienced and the sentiments inspired by the conversation of a polished, sensible, and well-bred person ... her title to the regard she earns so industriously and so honourably, is supported by a purity of mind and character correspondent to her professional manner. Such characters as Miss Stephens prove sufficiently, that the public exercise of talent is not incompatible with the grace, the ornament, and all the virtues of domestic life.[57]

The artistic limitations created by these social and national anxieties must have been considerable for native musicians. Partly as a result, foreign singers continued to play a significant role in London's musical life. By the 1840s one writer admitted candidly:

There is a something wanting in our English singers which I cannot precisely define

– but which must, until it be remedied by some better method of general education, invariably leave them far in the rear of the continental artists – especially the Italians and the French ... I like to hear the Misses Rainforth, Birch, and Dolby, very well – *occasionally*, and in a certain school of music, but my ears are too cultivated to remain satisfied with them, and only them, at the first English Concerts – to the exclusion of others so much their superiors, whose only fault seems to be their foreign birth.[58]

While the shortcomings of the system for musical education undoubtedly played a role, the necessity for singers to plan their careers and modify their vocal and dramatic style to appease the underlying anxieties of their audiences must have had a stifling influence on their musical development.

Conclusion

The careers of singers illustrate central themes in the history of the profession: the crumbling institutional framework for choir singers; the potential for high earnings in the secular musical world combined with the insecurity and low social status of theatre work; and the emergence of a new performance venue, the concert. Concerts provided a high-status, respectable setting consistent with musicians' social and professional aspirations, bridging the social and moral chasm between church and theatre. Accompanied by distinctive styles of vocal production, each of these career paths navigated the social, aesthetic, national, and gender anxieties of the culture, arguably to the detriment of musical values and aspirations.

Instrumentalists commanded neither the high salaries of singers, the potential earnings of teachers, nor the respectability of organists. Their careers were associated with apprenticeship training, relatively poor earnings, and an artisanal social status. The plight, particularly of orchestral instrumentalists, inspired much comment in contemporary writings. One musician in 1822 blamed the aristocratic prejudices which had "given currency to the belief that an instrumentalist is a weak or unworthy member of society."[1] And twenty years later, an irate editorial in the *Musical Examiner* asked,

What would a concert be without the presence of these ill-requited labourers?... What would all the Rubinis, Grisis, and other such notables, in the universe be worth without the unacknowledged, but *indispensable* aid of that ill used, and almost despised body of *musicians* (necessarily, much more so than singers), at which vocalists and anythingists, so they be soloists, toss their heads, and turn up their noses? – Nothing ... And yet this eminently useful body, in the absence of which, any musically inclined person would leave a concert room in less than five minutes after entering it, is looked down upon with almost contempt by vocalists, etc. who are only superior, inasmuch as they are *better paid*.[2]

Table 13 presents the numbers of musicians employed in various categories of instrumental work. Note that only thirty-six (3.2 percent) of the instrumentalists in the catalogue were women. This was because orchestral instruments were not considered proper for women to play. Occasionally, foreign women who played the violin came to England, but they did not succeed in establishing careers. In fact the renowned opera and concert singer, Mme. Mara, had arrived in England as a violinist, but "became a singer by the advice of the English ladies who disliked a female fiddler."[3] Most of the women instrumentalists in this period were pianists or harpists.

Many male instrumentalists in the eighteenth and early nineteenth centuries performed professionally on more than one instrument, and sometimes on several. It was not unusual, for instance, for a string player to accept employment on any of the orchestral string instruments. There

Table 13. *Instrumentalists in various types of employment*[4]
n = 1,115

	Male	Female	Total	%[a]
Theatre orchestras	508	2	510	46
Concert orchestras	536	0	536	48
Military bands	84	0	84	8
Royal "bands"	83	0	83	8
Soloists	83	24	107	10
Chamber musicians	30	3	33	3
Dance bands	21	0	21	2
Accompanists to theatres or concerts	16	2	18	2
Civilian bands	3	0	3	0.3
Other	2	0	2	0.2
Specific employment unknown	197	7	204	18.2

[a]Many instrumentalists worked in more than one category, so the total of the percentage column is greater than 100%.

were many musicians who performed on both string and wind instruments. Walter Clagge (Clagget), a member of the Covent Garden orchestra in 1784, listed his instruments as "violin, cello, viola, double bass, oboe, flute, clarinet, etc."[5] And John Christian Rost, a member of the same orchestra forty years later in 1821, claimed proficiency on the trumpet, trombone, horn, violin, tenor [viola], etc.[6] Although orchestral appointments were usually for a specific instrument, Rost's contract with Covent Garden in 1818 listed violin, trumpet, bugle-horn, and trombone.[7] When the brothers George and Daniel Schutze applied for membership of the Royal Society of Musicians in 1783, each claimed to be able to play "all instruments."[8] This kind of versatility was more characteristic of orchestral and military musicians than of soloists or chamber musicians, and it became less common in the nineteenth century as higher standards led to greater specialization.

Soloists

Ten percent of the instrumentalists in the catalogue performed as soloists, undoubtedly the highest-status group among instrumental performers. Concerts featuring solo instrumentalists tended to be relatively sophisticated in terms of the music, the patrons, and the audiences. Furthermore, as was true of the most respectable types of musical employment, there were proportionately higher numbers of foreigners, of women, and of graduates of the Royal Academy of Music in this group. The number of women in this category reflects both the relatively more respectable setting of the concerts, and the tendency for women musicians to perform on solo instruments (mainly piano and harp). Their numbers were negligible before the 1820s, but increased significantly after that date. The numbers of RAM graduates and foreigners among this group reflect the relatively high standards and keen competition among musicians who established themselves as soloists.

Most were pianists such as J. B. Cramer and Lucy Anderson, although harpists and violinists also performed as soloists. Instruments other than piano, harp, or violin were usually played as solo instruments by foreign virtuosi, who performed fantasias or other show pieces; such performances were popular well into the first half of the nineteenth century. And no mention of solo instrumentalists in early nineteenth-century London would be complete without reference to Domenico Dragonetti, whose performance on the double bass and duo concert appearances with his friend the cellist Robert Lindley were widely admired.[9]

There was a wide variety of payments, from the most generous (used to woo eminent foreign musicians to London) to the willingness of many great musicians to perform gratuitously or for nominal fees at the most prestigious concerts, including the first decade of the Philharmonic Society concerts.[10] In the 1790s, solo violinists at the most prestigious concerts earned impressive salaries. Viotti received 550 guineas for a season of twelve or thirteen performances at Salomon's concert series. More typical was a fee between five and ten guineas per night, received by Wilhelm Cramer and Giovanni Giornovichi at the oratorio concerts and private concerts.[11]

Solo performances during this period were rarely one-person recitals, but were usually part of a large, varied concert including singers and other instrumentalists. The first successful solo piano recitals in England did not occur until Charles Hallé's performances in his London home around 1850.[12] It was not that the idea of a piano recital had not occurred to anyone, but that the few attempts had been financially unsuccessful. In 1822, one musical observer pointed out some of the difficulties which solo performers faced:

[T]he two greatest . . . pianists of late years have been Mssrs. Cramer and Kalkbrenner; the first of whom has frequently complained when pressed to play in public, that he was tired of doing so, for that whenever he did play, it did not induce fifty persons to purchase tickets beyond his own immediate scholars and connections! And as to the second, so long as he played in public without pay, he was in demand; but no sooner did he fix a moderate price for his labour, than he was deserted by those who give concerts.[13]

In general then, before 1850, solo recitals were not offered with any hope of financial gain, but were rather means of advertising in the hope of establishing reputations and expanding teaching practices.[14]

Chamber musicians

Because chamber music, like solo performing, required a few highly skilled performers and a relatively small audience, chamber music lent itself to exclusive, private concert settings. That opportunities for the performance of instrumental chamber works were nevertheless very limited in this period may be partly explained by the growing familiarity with, and preference for, large orchestral concerts, the relative difficulty (for performers and listeners) of the chamber works of this period, and the greater popularity of vocal as opposed to instrumental music. There was some perception by the 1840s that the vitality of chamber music had been greater in the late eighteenth century:

Despite the advance of art, chamber instrumental music, in the days of George III, was more in vogue than at present. The patriarch Dragonetti had his two-guinea subscription concerts at the houses of the nobility. Salomon, and the leading men of his time, were nightly engaged in similar entertainments; and where there is now no territory sacred to the promulgation of this species of music in the mansions of our modern wealthy amateurs, there were at least a dozen in the period alluded to ... For a long lapse of years the quartet and other chamber music found no other existence than in the public concerts of the Philharmonic Society, until the effects of the gorgeous symphonies of Beethoven totally unfitted the hearers for the delicate and exquisitely fine cabinet productions intended only for a chamber.[15]

Only a few attempts to present chamber works in public performances occurred during this period: Ella gave six *soirées musicales* in each of the 1829 and 1830 seasons. From the 1830s, there were two string quartets offering concerts: the Dando, Lucas, Blagrove and Gattie, and the Mori, Watts, Moralt, and Lindley quartets.[16] Various pianists introduced individual chamber music *soirées* (Ignaz Moscheles, Charles Neate, William Henry Holmes, and others). John Ella established the Musical Union in 1845, a concert series which combined high professional standards with aristocratic patronage.[17]

Given the limited number of musicians required for such concerts, few instrumentalists could build careers solely as chamber musicians. Only thirty-three musicians in the catalogue are known to have performed in chamber music concerts, and there are only seven whose sole known form of professional employment was in chamber music. The majority were string players, with a few pianists and wind players. Only three of this number were women, all pianists. Even more than in the solo arena, foreign musicians dominated the chamber music scene. All seven of the instrumentalists who worked exclusively as chamber musicians were foreigners, who make up nineteen (58 percent) of the thirty-three who played chamber music at all. Fifty-seven percent of the British chamber players (eight) were graduates of the RAM. Chamber musicians, like soloists, represented an elite of musical skill and training.

Private aristocratic and royal concerts

Instrumentalists were sometimes hired to perform in the homes of wealthy patrons at private concerts. Some of the concerts were of a high professional caliber, usually organized and conducted by a leading member of the profession who therefore provided substantial professional patronage. For example,

A conductor (Sir George Smart, Mr. Greatorex, and Sig. Scappa, are much employed in this way,) is consulted as to the engagements of performers, which are of course according to the extent of the arrangements and the number of amateurs [i.e. the audience]. It is left to him to form the bill, or the donor of the concert makes such suggestions as he thinks proper.[18]

These concerts employed full orchestras, featured the favorite singers and/or instrumentalists of the season, and, except for their exclusive settings and audiences, were indistinguishable from many public concerts. Such concerts were frequently offered as subscription series. For example, in 1807,

subscription concerts, conducted by the elder Sapio,[19] were given at the houses of some of the nobility, in which Madame Catalani was the principal singer. The first took place at the Marchioness of Stafford's, on the 4th of March. Salomon led the band, and Mr. J. B. Cramer presided at the piano-forte. The company, including the Prince of Wales and several of the royal dukes, were of the first distinction.[20]

In other instances, however, musicians were hired merely to supply background music, or to perform intermittently during a party. The treatment and the pay they received varied with the pretensions and pocketbooks of the hosts. Some musicians, particularly foreign ones, seem to have been willing to perform at such parties without a fee, simply for the potential connections with other patrons. Such a practice sometimes became exploitative, as in the case of Mlle. Pallix, a French harpist, who was hired to play at a private party and "was placed among the performers, played twice, but obtained neither further notice nor refreshment, and in fine, was put into a coach with three other musicians, who were set down at their houses, and at last Mlle. Pallix was deposited at her lodgings."[21] She had to bring a lawsuit in order to obtain her six guineas in payment.

Eighty-three musicians in the catalogue performed in royal concerts.

Thirty-six (44 percent) of them are known only from the record of their royal employment, while forty-two (50 percent) are also known to have worked in theatre and/or concert orchestras. Although the numbers are relatively small, the keen competition for these jobs meant that the musicians were frequently well known and otherwise well employed.

Royal appointments were valued for their security, competitive wages, and high professional and social status. The social benefits of contact with the royal family were great. Professional status was enhanced as well, even though the role of the musicians in this setting seems to have resembled a pre-professional, servile model of employment rather than the more independent role of public concert performers. In the late eighteenth century, the members of the King's Band were required to perform frequently, and to dress in livery.

For all the prestige of royal association, the salaries of royal musicians do not seem to have been higher than those of theatre musicians. The highest went to the conductors and composers who were responsible for the music and arrangements. In the 1760s, C. F. Abel received the generous sum of £200 a year as chamber musician to Queen Charlotte.[22] However, the conductor of the band in 1778, a German flutist named Charles Weidemann, earned £100 a year, which was no greater than the salary of the leader or harpsichordist in any of the top theatres.[23] The rank and file instrumentalists also seem to have received rates comparable to, but not exceeding, those of theatre orchestras. For example, Samuel Henry Okell, who played horn, violin, and viola, was a member of the King's Band in 1800, for about £40 a year.[24]

In general, these instrumentalists were established members of the mainstream London profession. Like other musicians, they depended on diverse forms of employment such as orchestral jobs, teaching, and sometimes positions as organists. For example, John Parke, an eminent oboist, was a member of the Opera orchestra in the 1760s and of the Drury Lane and Vauxhall Gardens orchestras in the 1770s, and performed at all the main concerts in the 1780s and 1790s in addition to being a member of the King's Band. Several decades later, in 1848, the same situation still obtained. Edmund Thomas Chipp was a violinist in Her Majesty's Private Band, was the organist at St. Olave, Southwark, and gave private lessons in violin and piano.[25]

Six of the royal musicians in the catalogue were also military instrumentalists, three of them in the band of the Coldstream Guards in the 1830s and 1840s. For example, in 1834, Charles Godfrey, a member of His Majesty's Band, was also first bassoonist at the Drury Lane Theatre and Vauxhall Gardens, and bandmaster of the band of the Coldstream Guards.[26]

As in other categories it is instructive to note the proportion of foreigners. Not surprisingly, twenty-three (27.7 percent) were foreign, and the number would be even larger if it included the musicians' children. Two families in particular enjoyed more than one generation of royal patronage. Of the fourteen members of the Griesbach family in the catalogue, those known to have been employed at court were J. F. A. Griesbach (1769–1825), J. W. Griesbach (1772–?), and J. H. C. Griesbach (1762–?), all German-born; and their English-born sons, Charles James (1797–1853), George Ludolph Jacob (1757–1824?), and John Henry (1798–1875). Another such family, the Kellners, were similar, with three English-born sons obtaining royal employment. Again, there was a disproportionate number of foreign musicians who enjoyed such patronage.

Orchestral musicians

By far the largest group of instrumentalists consisted of orchestral musicians employed by the Italian Opera, other theatres, and the pleasure gardens. Throughout this period, other concert institutions performed orchestral works as well. The Salomon concert series, which presented Haydn's London symphonies in the 1790s, is a well-known example, and there were several others in the late eighteenth century, including the Professional Concerts and the Vocal Concert.[27] The Concert of Ancient Music, which mainly featured vocal soloists, employed an orchestra of forty-three musicians when it was founded in 1776;[28] private concerts also provided orchestral accompaniment for singers. The most important one from the perspective of professional development was the Philharmonic Society, established in 1813.[29]

All these sources of employment were seasonal: the presence of patrons in town and the theatrical season extended from approximately late autumn to late spring. Some orchestral musicians therefore found alternative summer employment in London or in provincial theatres. The Haymarket Theatre in London had a patent for the summer performances only,[30] which enabled musicians such as William James Castell to supplement his position as a double bass player at the Adelphi Theatre (London) in the winter by working at the Haymarket in the summer.[31] Many provincial theatres employed London musicians: in 1790 George Gillingham stated that he "Plays the Principle [sic] Second Violin at the Theatre Royal Covent Garden and Leads the Band in summer at the Theatre Birmingham."[32] Examples in other provincial towns were Thomas Entwisle, a string player who was employed at the "Theatres Royal Drury Lane and Liverpool" in 1798,[33] and a horn player named Perry who listed his employment in 1794 as Sadler's Wells Theatre and the Edinburgh and Bath theatres.[34]

As with singers, there seems to have been some status distinction be-

Table 14. *Sources of employment for orchestral instrumentalists*

	Male	Female	Total
Theatres (and pleasure gardens)	157	1	158
Concerts (and festivals)	175	0	175
Both of the above	245	0	245

tween musicians employed by theatres and pleasure gardens on the one hand, and those employed in concerts and festival orchestras on the other. Table 14 presents the numbers of orchestral musicians in the catalogue who worked in these settings. The largest category worked in both types of orchestra, and is undoubtedly even larger than the table suggests, because there are few musicians for whom all sources of employment are known. This might suggest that there is no significant difference between the two types of employment. However, there are musicians in the concert category whose freedom from association with the entertainment and the clientele at theatres and pleasure gardens made them more acceptable as performers at high-status concerts, including private concerts, and as teachers. Musicians who exemplify such careers include William Tebbett, who stated in 1782 that he "performes on the Violin Tenor [viola] at several private Concerts [and] lives with His Grace the Duke of [Marlborough] as private Musician";[35] John Hobbs, who wrote in 1784 that he "Plays at the An' [Ancient] Concert and is employed yearly by Sir Watkin Wm. Wynn";[36] Richard Huddleston Potter, who in 1785 was organist of St. Bride's Church and played the flute at "Mr. Crosdale's and other private Concerts" and had a large number of students;[37] and John Jolly, who in 1816 played organ, piano, and violin, and wrote that he "is Organist of Stockwell, deputy Organist of Westminster Abbey[,] is engaged at the Antient and Vocal Concerts, has Two Schools and other private Scholars."[38] Members of theatre and pleasure garden orchestras, on the other hand, were not as likely to enjoy private patronage or even to have church appointments, particularly at high-status institutions. In other words, although there is not a clear line dividing the two types of employment, some careers focused on one or the other type of performance setting, with important implications for earnings and status.

The careers of orchestral instrumentalists were patchwork affairs that combined numerous forms of employment in an attempt to provide a subsistence. Yet instrumentalists' jobs were so time-consuming as to limit the opportunities for other work. The Italian Opera performed several nights a week, not counting rehearsals, while Covent Garden and Drury Lane seem to have given performances five or six nights a week during the season (thirty-five weeks, or 200 nights) with rehearsals during the day.[39]

The time taken up by these relatively ill-paid jobs was a significant draw-back, as one musician pointed out in 1843: "a situation in any theatrical orchestre [*sic*] is, on account of the rehearsals, incompatible with any considerable amount of private business. In years that are past, many have resigned even the Opera on this account."[40] The Philharmonic concerts, on the other hand, had eight performances a season, and the other concert series seem to have been on a smaller scale as well. Musicians who worked primarily with concert institutions therefore had more time for other engagements and for teaching.

The wages of orchestral instrumentalists varied with the institutions that employed them. Still, it was clear to contemporaries that the big earnings went to singers, not to orchestral players. In 1822, a writer for the *Quarterly Musical Magazine and Reveiw* concluded that singers were so overpaid that managers and concert impresarios had little left to pay the members of the orchestra. It reported that "at the Ancient concert Mrs. Salmon, Miss Stephens, and Mme. Camporese, are engaged nightly at a sum amounting to very near £100. I think ... that the whole instrumental band do not receive more than an equal sum."[41] Such differences were also striking in the theatre orchestras. In the 1790–91 season of the Italian Opera, the entire orchestra of forty-two players averaged £31, twelve shillings and sixpence per performance, far less than was earned by the leading singers.[42] In 1843 the financial prospects for orchestral musicians still seemed restricted, according to the cellist H. J. Banister:

The engagements most generally sought after, on account of their regularity and supposed permanence, are the Opera, and the Ancient and Philharmonic Concerts. These together will produce a man in the ranks from seventy to eighty pounds a year; the salaries varying a little, according to circumstances and standing. Truly a pitiable result. – It will be understood I am not speaking of the principal instruments... A situation of the ordinary kind, in the orchestre [*sic*] of either of the royal theatres, will produce the happy occupant from fifty to sixty pounds a year, as the price of nine months' severe servitude.[43]

Other available evidence confirms Banister's figures, although it suggests somewhat more variation in wages depending on the importance and location of the theatre or concert series. For example, while Walter Clagge [Clagget] received £2 a week from Covent Garden during the 1784 season,[44] which would have produced £70 for the season, Thomas Kaye, a horn player at Colman's Theatre in 1798, earned only £30 a year.[45] The incomes of theatre instrumentalists outside London, even in cities such as Edinburgh and Dublin, were much lower, partly because there were probably fewer performances each season.

Rank in the orchestra also made a significant difference in wages. First-chair players received higher salaries for most instruments, while the leader (first violinist), who through the first decades of the nineteenth century occupied a position of great responsibility in the orchestra, was paid extremely well.[46] For example, François Hippolyte Barthelemon was offered £500 a year to be the leader of the Ancient Concert orchestra in the 1770s.[47] Wilhelm Cramer earned much less, £150, to lead the orchestra of the King's Theatre (Italian Opera) in 1779,[48] but by 1794 he and G. B. Viotti were each earning £300 for the leader's position there.[49] Johann Peter Salomon also earned £300 for leading the orchestra there in 1799–1800.[50] The leader's salary was about the same in 1808 when Weichsell received £315,[51] although the salary seems to have declined afterwards; in 1821 Spagnoletti, who was the leader there for many seasons, earned £250.[52] Harpsichordists, who sometimes led the orchestra, were also well paid. Vincenzo Federici, who played the harpsichord at the Italian Opera in 1796–97, earned £200 for the season,[53] and in 1808 Giacomo Ferrari earned the same fee.[54] Top-rank performers on other instruments sometimes commanded salaries that were significantly above those paid to rank and file orchestral players. One notable example was the virtuoso bass player Domenico Dragonetti, who received £150 as first double bass at the Italian Opera in 1821,[55] and also received exceptional wages from the Philharmonic Society for over twenty years.

The range of orchestral wages and the influence of rank on salaries is illustrated by the following tables. Table 15 presents the contents of twenty-three one-year contracts between orchestral musicians and the music director of the Covent Garden Theatre in 1818.[56] Tables 16 and 17 present the wages paid to all the members of the Philharmonic Society Orchestra in 1819 and 1840, respectively.[57] Rank clearly determined wages at both institutions. The bassoonist John Mackintosh, who was the first-chair player at Covent Garden and the Philharmonic Society, earned fourteen shillings a night (or a yearly salary of £140) at the theatre compared to the second bassoonist Edmund Denman's five shillings (5s) and tenpence (10d) a night (or £58 a year). At the Philharmonic, Mackintosh earned £28 7s for the season compared to the second bassoonist Mr. Tully's £14 3s 6d. Clearly a first-chair position in the theatre provided a substantial income, especially in combination with a Philharmonic Society job, while the lower-paid players barely earned a subsistence income. Note the exceptional wages, even for first-chair players, which were paid to Lindley, the first cellist, and Dragonetti, the first double bass, at the Philharmonic Society. In 1819 they each earned £52 10s for eight concerts, while in 1840 Lindley still received £52 10s and Dragonetti £63. They were both so well known (and in fact frequently played duets together in concerts) that they commanded well above the normal first-rank salary, which ranged from £21 to £28. Another exception was the first oboist,

Table 15. *Wages for orchestral musicians at the Covent Garden Theatre, 1818*

Name and instrument	Nightly salary (s.d)	Estimated annual salary for a 200-night season (£.s)
W. Henry Kearns, violin (leader in absence of Mr. Ware)	14.	140
John Mackintosh, bassoon	14.	140
William Parke, oboe	10. 6	105
Charles Wodarch, cello	10.	100
Joseph Birch, flute	9. 2	91.10
Thomas Wallis, trumpet and bugle-horn ("It is understood that Mr. Wallis shall receive an additional sum of Five (5) shillings per night, for those nights on which he is required to perform on the *Keyed Bugle*.")	9. 2	91.10
Thomas Brown, violin (principal 2nd)	8. 4	83
Joseph Young, violin	6. 8	66
John Woodcock, violin	6. 8	66
Joel Bowden, violin	6. 8	66
Thomas Watkins, violin	6. 8	66
James Bowden, violin	6. 8	66
Robert Spencer, violin or viola	5.10	58
J. G. H. Hoffman, violoncello or violin	5.10	58
George Wells, violin	5.10	58
Samuel Underhill, oboe	5.10	58
Edmund Denman, bassoon	5.10	58
Cornelius Bryant, French horn	5.10	58
George Hopkins, clarinet or violin	5.10	58
John Rod Polglaze, trumpet or bugle-horn	5.10	58
John Rost, violin, trumpet, bugle-horn, trombone	5.10	58
Thomas Chipp, kettle drums or harp ("It is understood that Mr. Chipp shall tune the Piano-Forte's of the Theatre whenever required")	5.10	58
Samuel Pritchard, trombone or bugle	5.	50

Griesbach, who earned £42 10s 6d. Note also the extraordinary salary paid to the leader, Mr. Weichsell – £157 10s – for fewer than eight concerts. Such fees were paid to other leaders in subsequent years, usually visiting foreign violinists such as Louis Spohr in 1820 (£262 10s) and Kiesewetter in 1821 (£262 10s) and 1822 (£157 10s).[58]

In the early decades of the Philharmonic Society, players accepted lower

Table 16. *Wages of musicians in the Philharmonic Society Orchestra, 1819*

(8 concerts, 8–10 rehearsals)

Instrument	Name	Salary (£.s.d)
Leader	Weichsell	157.10
	Mori	42
	Loder	31.10
Violin (firsts)	Dance	28. 7
	Watts	28. 7
	Mountain	28. 7
	Femy	16.10. 9
	Gattie	20. 9. 6
	Ireland	21. 5. 3
	W. Griesbach	21. 5. 3
	Betts	21. 5. 3
	Wagstaff	21. 5. 3
	Sanderson	20. 9. 6
	Robberacht	20. 9. 6
Violin (seconds)	Cobham	14. 3. 6
	Nicks	14. 3. 6
	Simonet	14. 3. 6
	Litolf	14. 3. 6
	Collard	14. 3. 6
	T. Leffler	7.17. 6
	Fliesher	14.14
	Anderson	2. 7. 3
	Rawlins	14. 3. 5
	T. Leffler Jr.	1.11. 6
Tenor (viola)	Ashley	28. 7
	Challoner	21. 5. 3
	F. Ware	18. 8
	Lyon	21. 5. 3
	Calkin	20. 9. 6
	Daniels	19.13. 5
	J.(?) Leffler	2.12. 6
Cello	Lindley	52.10
	C. Lindley	28. 7
	C. Ashley	27. 6
	Eley	21. 5. 3
	Calkin, James	21. 5. 3
	Binfield	21. 5. 3
Contrabass	Dragonetti	52.10
	Iouve	21. 5. 3
	Anfossi	28. 7
	Taylor	21. 5. 3
Flute	Ireland	28. 7
	Cutting	14. 3. 6

Table 16. (*cont.*)

Instrument	Name	Salary
Oboe	Griesbach	42.10. 6
	M. Sharp	14. 3. 6
Clarinet	Willman	28. 7
	Mahon	14. 3. 6
	Baerman	12.12
Bassoon	Mackintosh	28. 7
	Tully	14. 3. 6
Horn	C. Tully	21. 5. 3
	Leander	21. 5. 3
	Charlton	5.15. 6
	Kelner	14. 3. 6
	Nolbrath	7.17. 6
	Puzzi	10.10
	Harper and Schmidt [trumpets]	21. 5. 3
	Hyde [trumpet?]	13.13
Trombone	Mariotti	21. 5. 3
	Dressler and Smithies	9. 9
Drums	Jenkinson	21. 5. 3

wages than they were likely to receive in other orchestras.[59] By 1840, the wages paid by the Philharmonic Society appear to have become more standardized. The base fee was higher – £19 13s 9d compared to £14 3s 6d in 1819 – while the top salaries were overall a little lower or the same. However, some of the wages were lower than they had been in 1819: Mr. Challoner, a viola player, had earned £21 5s 3d but had been reduced to £19 13s 9d, and Mr. Calkin, another viola player, also earned less in 1840. The drummer in the earlier year was paid £21 5s 3d, while Mr. Chipp earned £19 13s 9d in 1840. Overall, the nominal salaries of these musicians changed very little during this twenty-year period. In the next few years, budget problems at the Philharmonic led to severe reductions in the fees for the leaders as well as those for the principal players.[60] While a few players, such as Dragonetti, refused to accept the cut in pay, most seem to have continued, undoubtedly with some loss of morale.

In the long view, musicians' incomes must be interpreted in relation to issues such as job security. Although there are several musicians in the preceding tables who retained their positions for a considerable period, orchestral musicians in fact had no guarantee of regular employment. The main sources of job insecurity for orchestral musicians were competition from other players, the financial problems of theatre and concert institutions, and illness.

Table 17. *Wages of musicians in the Philharmonic Society Orchestra, 1840*

(8 concerts, 9 rehearsals)

Instrument	Name	Salary (£.s.d)
Leader	F. Cramer	52.10
	*Loder	52.10
	T. Cooke	52.10
Violin (firsts)	Tolbecque	19.13. 9
	Blagrove	30. 3. 9
	*Wagstaff	26. 5
	Eliason (7 concerts, 6 rehearsals)	14.19. 3
	A. Griesbach	19.13. 9
	Guynemer	19.13. 9
	E. Thomas	19.13. 9
	W. Cramer	19.13. 9
	*Gattie	19.13. 9
	N. (?) Mori	19.13. 9
	Richards	19.13. 9
	Patey	19.13. 9
	J. (?) Banister	19.13. 9
Violin (seconds)	Watts	26. 5
	*Mountain	26. 5
	C. Reeve	19.13. 9
	Dando	19.13. 9
	Kearns	19.13. 9
	Willy	19.13. 9
	Pigott	19.13. 9
	*Anderson	19.13. 9
	Westrop	19.13. 9
	*Litolf	19.13. 9
	A. Macintosh	19.13. 9
	W. Blagrove	19.13. 9
	*Nicks	19.13. 9
	Marshall	19.13. 9
	J. Calkin Jr.	19.13. 9
Viola	Moralt	26. 5
	Hill	20.14. 9
	Sherrington	19.13. 9
	Glanville	19.13. 9
	*Challoner	19.13. 9
	*Calkin	19.13. 9
	*Daniels	19.13. 9
	Abbott	19.13. 9
	Alsept	19.13. 9
	S. (?) Calkin	19.13. 9

Table 17. (*cont.*)

Instrument	Name	Salary
Cello	*Lindley	52.10
	Crouch	26. 5
	Rousselot	26. 5
	*C. Lindley	26. 5
	Lucas	19.13. 9
	Hatton	19.13. 9
	*Jas. Calkin	19.13. 9
	*Binfield	19.13. 9
Double bass	*Dragonetti	63
	*Anfossi	32.16. 3
	Howell	19.13. 9
	Wilson	19.13. 9
	C. (?) Smart	19.13. 9
	Flower	19.13. 9
Flute	Ribas	26. 5
	Card	19.13. 9
Oboe	H. Cooke	35
	Keating	19.13. 9
Clarinet	*Willman	35
	Williams	19.13. 9
Bassoon	Baumann	35
	*Tully	19.13. 9
Horn	Platt	35
	Rae	19.13. 9
	Kielbach	19.13. 9
	*Tully	19.13. 9
Trumpet	*Harper	35
	Irwin	19.13. 9
Trombone	*Smithies	13. 2. 6
	Smithies Jr.	13. 2. 6
	Albrecht	13. 2. 6
Piccolo	Price	13. 2. 6
Drums	Chipp	19.13. 9

* Present in the orchestra in both 1819 and 1840

Orchestral jobs remained coveted positions for many instrumentalists, and competition for them was keen. In the case of theatre orchestras, the responsibility for hiring players seems to have rested solely with the music director, almost always a musician himself and often a composer as well. It seems likely that one-season contracts were typical. All but one of the Covent Garden contracts in table 15 were for one year (Thomas Wallis's was for three years), and each contract had to be renegotiated for the next season.

As mentioned above, another problem for orchestral instrumentalists was the uncertainty of the employer's financial condition. By the 1820s, John Mahon, who had once been an active London professional,[61] was struggling to support himself and his family in Dublin. He was seriously affected by the financial difficulties of the theatre at which he was employed. In December 1826, Mahon recorded:

My Salary at the Theatre Formerly was two Guineas per week, but it has been twice curtaild, and now it remains at the small sum of £1.6s. per week, and that only when they perform six nights a week, when they perform only 2 or 3 nights, I am paid according to the number of nights.[62]

A year later, in December 1827, he was earning even less:

My salary at the Theatre has been cut down to one Guinea a week, which in some weeks, when the Theatre is open only 3 or 4 nights in the week, amounts only to 14s or less, according to the number of nights they perform, besides which, there has been three month's vacation, in addition to Passion week, and the principle [*sic*] fast days in Lent.[63]

Although the orchestral players at the leading London theatres were relatively safe from this kind of wage variation, such insecurity was typical of many other London theatres and certainly of those outside London. As one musician wrote in 1843,

Uncertainty ... hangs over the produce of orchestrel [*sic*] labours. Is the scene the orchestre of a theatre? Continual apprehension, now-a-days, is entertained of being put upon half salary, or of the abrupt closing of the house, through non-success. Again: the possession of a situation one season, is little or no guarantee for its retention for the second.[64]

The policy toward orchestral players who became ill seems to have depended primarily on the kindheartedness of the music director. In 1788, John Addison discovered this when he

was attacked with a severe fit of the Gowt which continued upwards of seven weeks [during] which time he Rec.d no salary tho' engaged as a Performer in the Royal theatre of Edinburgh for they neither pay there the Musicians nor actors in case of Sickness, or other accidents which may disable them from performing.

Addison only learned of this policy, which was not what he had experienced as a London theatre musician, when he requested his salary,

upon which he was refused payment and further told that it was not the custome now at least in London whatever it might have been heretofore: Mr. Addison answered he could not think it was a truth which they declared for that he was a performer in Drury-lane for a number of years in Mr. Garrick's management and during that time was several times sick himself and knew others in like case who were always paid.[65]

He then inquired about the policy in London and found that in fact sick players were still paid in some instances. But in London, if the player had to be replaced, he could lose the fees and sometimes the job as well. For instance, the London oboist J. F. A. Griesbach appealed for financial assistance to a benefit fund in 1823, on the grounds that "I have not received anything from the Opera House for the last ten nights nor do I expect anything more, as there has been another person engaged who would insist on receiving the whole."[66] The abovementioned John Mahon, who played the violin in the Dublin Theatre Royal in the 1820s, became a liability in the orchestra because of his poor eyesight and stiff fingers. He realized that he would be dismissed:

When last I wrote to you, I told you that I expected to be discharged from the Theatre, and soon after many broad hints, that it would be more respectable for me to withdraw myself, than to wait untill I was put out, therefore having caught a severe cold, I took the opportunity of retiring, and I have not been in the Theatre the last nine days.

He was soon completely destitute, but a letter from him in March of that year reported that

a friend of mine has had a conversation with the Proprietor of the Theatre on my account, and he has agreed that I may remain in my situation at the Theatre as long as I find it convenient, therefore, altho I am not adequate to the situation, I will for the present accept his kind offer, and next week I will resume my former situation.[67]

In general, it seems there was no consistent policy for dealing with orchestral players who were too sick or old to continue working, though they did occasionally receive special consideration.

Benefit concerts

Benefit concerts, a feature of London's musical life throughout the late eighteenth and early nineteenth centuries, were presented for a variety of reasons: some were to create profit and publicity for an individual musician; some were to help a musician who was ill (or to assist his family); and others were to raise money for charitable institutions.[68] The money-making potential of these concerts depended on the gratuitous assistance of all the musicians, which meant that many instrumentalists (and singers) performed without pay much of the time. John Ella, a violinist, wrote in 1845:

we [Ella] were constantly invited to lend our humble aid to some meritorious artist, and notwithstanding the arduous occupations of Opera, Ancient, and Philharmonic duties, private instruction, editing Musical Journals, and directing Musical Societies, we have, during the last twenty years, performed *gratis*, at no less than two hundred and eighty concerts![69]

Despite the free labor, however, benefit concerts were often financially unsuccessful. The Philharmonic Orchestra gave a benefit in 1829 for the family of a Mr. Gledhill, who had been a violinist in the Philharmonic and King's Theatre orchestras. They apparently netted £400 from the sale of 800 tickets.[70] However, this sum probably does not take into account all of the expenses of the evening. Another source reported that

> with all the gratuitous assistance professors are accustomed to extend each other, if the concerts are upon a good scale they seldom cost less than from £100 to £140 per night. The charges for the rooms, and those attending the making the particulars sufficiently known, always amount to half that sum. Hence it is only the professor whose reputation, connection, or musical promise can command numbers, that is really advantaged. Most, even of the second class, find their benefit a loss, and consequently these concerts would be fewer were it not that the desire of being known and the power of obliging and forming connections, are sufficient inducements to hazard the chance.[71]

Even when the aim of the concert was charity, the result could be far from successful. In 1819, Charles Cobham, a violinist at the King's Theatre, Drury Lane, Ranelagh Gardens, and the Philharmonic Society, died from a stroke.[72] His widow, who was left with five young children, decided to attempt a benefit concert, and proceeded to obtain musicians, rooms, public posters and so on for the concert. Although a number of well-known musicians participated, the results were disappointing, as she wrote afterward: "had I supposed my Concert would have produced so little I never would have undertaken the immence [sic] trouble I did for until the last day I despaired of gaining my expenses and gave away many Tickets in order that the room might not appear quite empty."[73]

The reason for such failures was partly that there were so many such concerts, increasing steadily from the 1820s on. As one observer wrote in 1828,

> Not many years ago the benefit concerts were considered as rewards for service, and even performers of long standing hesitated before they adventured to advance their claims. The contrary is now the fact. A benefit concert is now regarded in two lights: as a mode of introduction to teaching, and as affording a chance of making money – if the second does not hit, the first may. So frequent indeed are these advertisements of names, that not to take a benefit seems to place an artist below the rank which all are willing to occupy.[74]

Thus, although benefit concerts cannot be included among the more profitable forms of employment for instrumentalists, they did provide showcases at which young artists could make unofficial debuts and older musicians could advance their careers.

Military bands[75]

In the mid-eighteenth century military bands were very small, often consisting of no more than fifes and drums, with the drummers sometimes playing fife and drum simultaneously.[76] By the 1770s and 1780s, however, numerous wind instruments had been added, including oboes, clarinets, French horns, bugle-horns, and bassoons. By the early nineteenth century, the band of the Grenadier Guards consisted of "oboes, clarionets, French horns, bassoons, trumpets, and serpents, and the fifes and drums played occasionally with the band." There might also be "black 'time-beaters,' who played the bass drum, tenor drum, side drum, and cymbals."[77] The growth in the size and the make-up of the bands was not, however, accompanied by any standardization of instrumentation or repertoire until late in the nineteenth century.

Eighty-four musicians in the catalogue performed in military bands. There were of course no women, and only five of this group were foreigners. It is important to note that, during this period, military musicians were often civilians, many of whom had active professional careers in the mainstream of civilian musical life. (Thirty-four [40 percent] appear to have been primarily military musicians while forty-four [52 percent] were also employed in theatre and/or concert institutions.) When the Scots Guards were formed around 1815, its band members "were professional musicians; they resided at their private residences and not in barracks, and only appeared in uniform when engaged on military duty or fulfilling engagements as the band of the regiment."[78] The same was true for the bands of the Grenadier Guards, the Royal Horse Guards, and others.[79] This accounts for the large proportion of military instrumentalists who also performed in orchestras. In 1785, for example, Hezekiah Cantelo, whose main instruments were trumpet and bassoon, was employed at the Drury Lane Theatre and Vauxhall Gardens in addition to being in the band of the First Regiment of Foot Guards.[80] By 1794 he was also employed at the leading London concerts such as the Ancient Concerts and the Professional Concerts.[81] Thomas Wallis Jr. played the clarinet and horn in the Third Regiment of Foot Guards from 1794 until at least 1801, belonged to the Sadler's Wells orchestra, and from 1818 to 1820 played trumpet and bugle-horn in the Covent Garden band.[82] A later example is William Handley, who reported in 1839 that he played the trumpet and *cornet à pistons*, belonged to Her Majesty's Band of the Coldstream Guards and was engaged to play the first trumpet at the Drury Lane Theatre and at the English Opera House.[83]

Sometimes the civilian character of the band led to conflict, as with the band of the Coldstream Guards in 1783. At that time, the band consisted of "two oboes, two clarionets, two French horns, and two bassoons, selected from the King's and patent theatres. They were civilians hired by the month, their only military duty being to play the King's Guard from the parade in St. James's Park to the palace and back."[84] However, when officers were unable to obtain the band's services at other functions, they replaced it by importing a full band of German musicians from Hanover. This somewhat larger group, consisting of "4 clarionets, two bassoons, two hautboys, two French horns, one trumpet, and one serpent,"[85] became established in London, and began a tradition of importing German band musicians, especially bandmasters, to staff English military bands. The trend toward importing German bandmasters seems to have been one way to raise the standards of military band performance in lieu of standardizing and professionalizing military music and musicians in England, a process which did not begin until the second half of the nineteenth century. Nevertheless, the majority of the military bands throughout this period were British.

Dance bands

Only twenty-one instrumentalists in the catalogue performed in dance bands. In general this seems to have been viewed as the work of hack musicians or those who could find no other employment. Exceptions are the families of Scots fiddlers such as the Gows and the Macfarlanes, who were renowned for their composition and performance of dance music. The case of George Broad illustrates the degree to which dance music was a kind of "last resort." When Broad, who had been employed at Drury Lane and Vauxhall Gardens in 1806, found himself poor and unemployed, he inquired about the quadrille season in Dublin from his colleague, Thomas Kelly. Kelly wrote to him that "the Quadrille Business has been very good for the last Month and continues so … I have two Balls a week in the Castle, I have had 27 good Balls already … and Calvert wants a bass player, I think he would engage you."[86] So Broad borrowed £10 to travel to Dublin for the dance season. John Mahon also moved to Ireland, but he barely subsisted for several years, mainly by playing quadrilles.[87]

A hint of the relatively low professional status of musicians who subsisted primarily on the "quadrille business" is suggested by the following. A musician inquired regarding the seating arrangements at a benefit concert dinner: "Mr. Forbes wishes to be placed in Mr. Potter's or Sterndale Bennett's or Rovedino's parties and not with the Quadrille Gentlemen[,] not being in that line of the Profession himself."[88]

Conclusion

Instrumentalists were essential to most musical performances, but in general they were not accorded the status or remuneration attainable by many singers, teachers, and organists. Only those with the musical skills and professional connections to obtain employment as soloists or as chamber musicians enjoyed the status of successful musicians among other branches of the profession. While on the secular side solo work and chamber music concerts offered new, higher-status performance settings comparable to oratorio concerts for singers, the opportunities in these areas remained extremely limited. The financial insecurities and the low social and professional status of the predominantly apprentice-trained instrumentalists typify the persistently artisan social identity of this important group of musicians.

Most musicians depended on several types of employment. Teaching, with which many musicians supplemented performance income, was in some cases lucrative enough to become the musician's sole or primary occupation. Composing, on the other hand, was less reliable. Some musicians may have wished to build careers primarily as composers, but they most generally had to combine composition with other forms of musical employment. Other musicians expanded their activities beyond performing, teaching, or composing, to include entrepreneurial ventures as publishers and sellers of printed music, and even the musical instrument trade.

Teachers

Most professional musicians worked as teachers at some point in their careers. The 1841 census lists three thousand music teachers, reaching five thousand by 1851; the number would be even greater if it included the part-time teaching of most of the individuals classified in the census as "musicians."[1] One writer pointed out that "not only [do] all those engaged in our orchestras employ themselves in teaching ... but our leaders and solo performers find it expedient to betake themselves to the same occupation."[2] The musicians who worked exclusively as teachers, and not to supplement other work, were either relatively unqualified or unfortunate musicians who had to rely entirely on the uncertain income from a few students, or the most successful teachers who amassed such lucrative practices that they could devote their energies entirely to teaching. In short, music teachers could experience extreme insecurity and destitution, or they could accumulate wealth and even attain a relatively high social status.

Teaching was a particularly important form of employment for women musicians, more than is indicated by the catalogue which includes only 109 (12.5 percemt) women teachers. The census figures for 1841 and 1851 provide a more complete picture (see table 18).[3] Teaching was one of the few completely respectable forms of musical employment for women

Table 18. *Number of women music teachers*

	1841	1851	1861
United Kingdom	789 (24%)	2,606 (45%)	3,103 (56%)
London	438 (29%)	1,125 (52%)	1,296 (60%)

because it did not involve public performance. Furthermore, women teachers may have had an advantage over men in obtaining students, since there are indications that some middle-class families preferred their daughters to have female teachers. Eight of the women teachers in the catalogue, all former students of the Royal Academy of Music, worked in the traditional career of governess, five of them specifically musical governesses.[4]

By far the largest number of teachers gave private lessons, but they could also work at schools, from grammar schools, which employed one music master or mistress, to schools that specialized in music, and, at the highest level (after 1822), the Royal Academy of Music. School appointments were valued for the dependable income they provided; payment was made by the school and the teacher was less likely to be victimized by the unreliability of individual students or the possibility of parents reneging on the tuition.[5]

Teachers' wages, security, numbers of pupils, and qualifications in music or skills in teaching all varied widely. Particularly during the early nineteenth century, when an increasing number of middle-class families required music lessons for their daughters, the numbers of people advertising themselves as teachers rose, and there were few safeguards and standards to ensure competence. One observer complained that it was very difficult to screen out the numbers of aspiring but unqualified teachers. He noted that many women with very little musical training attempted to obtain employment, at least partly based on music teaching:

It cannot be denied, that while there are many ladies who possess considerable talents and judgment, the great majority, whether acting as private teachers or governesses, are incapable of giving musical instruction in a manner truly beneficial. It is not uncommon for a female, after she has gone through the usual routine of a boarding school for two or three years, to seek for a "situation," and to announce "music" among her other qualifications.[6]

Attempts to take undue advantage of the market for music lessons were not restricted to women, however. One of the common abuses was for musicians to teach instruments they did not play, but for which lessons were more in demand – usually the most popular ones for young ladies – piano, voice, and harp.

Almost every performer on the violin, violoncello, double bass, or flute, will now give you lessons on the piano forte or in singing; players on wind instruments will teach you the harp, and players on the harp will teach you wind instruments – to which, if desired, some of them are ready to add *"the science of harmony and the art of composition"*! Even our music-sellers' assistants join in the confusion, and many a young gentleman who has furnished you with a waltz in the morning will attend to teach it to your daughter in the evening.[7]

But the incentives to tap the market for lessons remained compelling. In the 1780s, Benjamin Blake, who had been a successful orchestral violinist for many years,

on losing his royal patron the duke of Cumberland ... began to study the application of the piano-forte, so far as was necessary to qualify him for teaching, for he never professed that instrument as a performer. To this undertaking, he was advised and zealously instructed by his friend William Dance; he also received much useful information from Messrs. Charles Frederick Baumgarten and Muzio Clementi. Thus assisted, in 1792, Blake commenced teaching; in 1793 was engaged at Camden-house boarding school, Kensington; and soon, by his success, found it necessary to resign all his orchestral engagements, and attend to teaching only, which he continued till 1820.[8]

The overall earnings of teachers depended, naturally, on the rates they charged and the number of pupils they had. Both of these in turn depended on teachers' professional reputations, geographical locations, and the social classes that made up their clientele. There seems to have been a continual perception that teachers' rates had declined during recent decades, and the printed sources offer conflicting evidence. G. F. A. Wendeborn wrote in 1785: "Those ... who earn part of their livelihood by teaching, have seen formerly, as it is said, better times than at present. I have heard of some receiving a guinea, or half a guinea for a lesson, who now, perhaps, must be content with five shillings."[9] The music teachers who commanded a guinea a lesson in the 1780s were undoubtedly the few at the top of the profession. However, a very similar observation of declining wages was made by Samuel Wesley in 1830:

The inferior masters were used to receive two guineas for eight lessons and two guineas entrance also. Three guineas for eight lessons was a very usual price with masters of the higher order, and four for those of the highest. At different periods I myself have received a guinea a lesson, and from some pupils as much as twenty-five shillings; whereas now [1830] the prices are so dwindled down that three shillings and half-a-crown per lesson are offered and accepted, through the influx of musical pretenders by whom England is now deluged.[10]

It is possible that the heightened competition for pupils in the 1820s and 1830s did force down the minimum fee that some musicians would accept. However, one musical journal reported that the rates of some teachers rose during the first decades of the nineteenth century:

[T]he teacher, who in the metropolis 25 years ago used to think himself well paid at 3s.6d. or 5s.3d. per lesson, ... now aspires to a guinea; and although there are still many good masters at half-a-guinea, yet nearly all those who consider themselves *in the first class* require a guinea per lesson.[11]

In 1848 John Ella noted that his *matinées*, at 5s 4d, were one-quarter the price of a singing lesson.[12] Overall, it seems that by the mid-nineteenth century, one guinea had become an acceptable and respectable base fee for lessons from the better teachers.

While the price of private lessons may have been lower outside London, provincial teachers faced an even greater disadvantage – the scarcity of pupils. In 1818, one writer considered the logistics of attracting various sorts of patronage, and noted that "the expense of tickets becomes a momentous consideration to all but the most affluent, who are now a days (particularly in the provinces) *the many* to whom the teacher of music is to look for his support."[13] Some teachers compensated by traveling long distances to find enough students. Robert Janes, for example, organist of Ely cathedral from 1831 to 1866, "had a very large teaching connection in Norfolk and Suffolk, and in later years was wont to relate how he rode long distances on horseback to fulfil his engagements."[14] In other instances, groups of provincial residents would recruit a reputable musician from London by promising a minimum number of pupils. Charles Hallé wrote that in 1848, when a resident of Manchester tried to convince him to move there, "I determined to give it a trial; on the condition, however, that a fixed number of pupils (not a small one) should be enrolled to begin work from the day of my arrival ... Not a week had elapsed when I received the news that the pupils I had stipulated for were found and awaiting me."[15] In another instance, Elizabeth Randles, a child piano prodigy in the early 1800s, settled in Liverpool from 1820 at least partly because she was "strongly urged by a select number of families at Liverpool, they engaging to find her as many pupils as she might feel disposed to accept."[16]

Teachers who could command the going rate or more and who had sufficient numbers of pupils could become very wealthy. Provincial organists who taught both piano and voice and who had enough pupils in the vicinity could earn one to two thousand pounds a year. In London, potential earnings were even greater. According to an observer of 1857, "A respectable London professor of the pianoforte will make from £400 to £800. Several, however, occupying a high position must realise by teaching alone at least £2,000."[17] And in 1849 S. S. Wesley reported that

the London professor, if *eminent*, obtains far more than this [£2,000]. He makes a fortune in not many years. And there are many mere teachers in London, men of simple industry, who work like moles, whose names are never heard, but who teach from six in the morning to ten at night throughout a life, and acquire great fortunes.[18]

Although such opportunities led most musicians to rely on teaching for part of their income, there were also possible disadvantages to this form of musical employment, not the least of which was competition for pupils. One way to attract pupils was success as a public performer. It was even more valuable, however, to have upper-class clients who would spread the word among their friends. G. G. Ferrari, for example, an Italian musician who had been working in Paris, left France in the 1790s and arrived in London "highly recommended to some of the first noblemen's and gentlemen's families, as well as to several foreign ambassadors, by whom he was constantly well received and employed for musical tuition, particularly in singing."[19] Such advantages were most easily obtained by concert soloists and chamber musicians, those who had studied at the Royal Academy of Music, or those who otherwise had good social or professional connections.

Another unpredictable aspect of teaching was the variation in the number of pupils. Private pupils could discontinue their lessons at any time, or fail to pay their fees. In 1827, John Mahon stated: "Pupils, I have not any[,] two or three called on me and took 9 or 10 Lessons each, but never paid me. This week a person call'd on me to take some Lessons on the Violin, and I made him pay me a Pound."[20]

In addition to the unreliability of individual students, the teacher was vulnerable to larger economic fluctuations, as well as to more subtle social obstacles. The cellist H. J. Banister addressed the first of these problems:

Music being classed among the luxuries of life, is, of course, among the first things set aside in seasons of pressure. Those who derive their income solely, or chiefly from teaching, have had sad confirmatory evidence of the truth of this. I have known instances in which the produce of teaching has varied, within a period of two years, as one to five.[21]

In addition, there were subtle social obstacles and ambiguities for the teacher who was invited into the student's home, usually to teach a girl. The enthusiasm for music lessons was largely fueled by families whose limited musical aspirations were often a source of frustration to the music teacher. In 1829, Thomas Danvers Worgan, a depressed and bitter music theorist and composer, lamented this state of affairs:

If those who turn their eyes towards the profession are unable to discover the intellectual dignity of the art in its teachers, the reason of this is on the surface. Music languishes and degenerates under the misgovernment of unintellectual fashion. The exclusive demand for practical tuition is imperious and irresistible.

Musical education is wholly effeminate, and the teacher of music sinks into the manufacturer of a female ornament.[22]

Furthermore, national differences could play a role as well as distinctions of class and gender between patron and teacher. While most teachers were native musicians, there was considerable demand for foreign, especially Italian, music teachers at least during the last decades of the eighteenth century. As Richard Leppert explains, "The practice of music teaching produced an immensely complicated and conflicted discourse centering largely on threats to a daughter's virtue, and hence her father's authority, by a social inferior who commonly was also a foreigner."[23] The ambiguities of musicians' social and professional status "constituted a social threat by its very inexactness."[24] The music teacher, perhaps as much as stage singers, needed to assuage the concerns of patrons about class, nationality, and gender. It is not surprising that many families avoided as many of these difficulties as possible by hiring women music teachers.

Despite these drawbacks, teaching offered another significant advantage – its respectability. Although many music teachers were not wealthy, they were protected from the low social status of orchestral instrumentalists and stage singers. As one observer pointed out in 1818, "of all classes of musicians, the teachers are the most respectable ... their moral character, their manners, and their general attainments, have kept more than usual pace with the advances of the science to which they devote themselves."[25] Although there were many impoverished music teachers with low social and professional status, the most fully and prestigiously employed teachers occupied the new high-status secular branch of the profession, along with concert singers and solo and chamber instrumentalists, fulfilling musicians' highest social and professional aspirations.

Composers

Very few of the 1,344 musicians in the catalogue who composed music worked solely as composers at any point in their careers. Composers of church music were frequently church or cathedral organists, while theatre composers tended to be stage singers or orchestral instrumentalists. Solo works were often composed by instrumentalists and teachers. Even those few musicians who were known primarily as composers were concurrently employed as church organists, instrumentalists, conductors, or teachers. One author wrote in 1857 that there were only eleven composers, "i.e., persons living by that art only," in the 1851 census, but that he had "heard this fact denied by members of the musical profession, asserting that no person is now subsisting on the profits of composition solely."[26]

Table 19. *Numbers of musicians in various branches of composition*
n = 1,344

	Male	Female	Total
Religious			
liturgical	244	—	244
"sacred"	119	10	129
both	112	3	115
Secular: "art"			
instrumental, orchestral	150	9	159
vocal (including glees)	259	10	269
both of the above	41	1	42
solo fantasias, virtuoso showpieces	39	2	41
Secular: popular			
stage and pleasure garden music	66	6	72
popular songs	252	32	284
"domestic" music	211	13	224
educational music	33	1	34
instruction books	257	15	272
Miscellaneous			
dance music	87	—	87
military music	7	—	7

Table 19 shows the numbers of musicians who composed works in various musical categories and contexts. Some of the categories are less tidy than others, but they reflect the range of compositional activities. Composers of religious music wrote for the Anglican service (see chapter 5), or sacred music such as psalm and hymn tunes, cantatas, and oratorios. Oratorios were frequently composed by musicians who were not otherwise church musicians, so the composers in the religious music category are more varied in background than those who wrote music primarily for the church service. "Art music" was directed at professional musicians, at well-trained amateurs and connoisseurs who attended concerts and bought printed music, as well as at some audience members who patronized music as a social statement. The "art music" genres include orchestral works as well as works for smaller ensembles. The designation "popular" in table 19 indicates music written for the consumer: theatre and pleasure garden audiences, and potential purchasers of music and educational materials.

The evolution of composers' careers was complex, and reflected differences in educational background, sources of income, and aspirations – social, economic, and artistic. Unlike church musicians, secular composers had no established educational institutions (before 1822), no steady engagements such as organist posts, and no established career patterns. Hence, religious and secular composing were not often combined in one career. Similarly, composers who specialized in popular works for the domestic market were not the same musicians who composed symphonies. On the other hand, some musicians wrote in several categories. Virtuoso instrumentalists, for example, might compose a wide range of works for their own instruments, from instruction books and easy educational pieces to solo fantasias and concertos. The same patterns are true for the relatively few women composers in the catalogue; they are represented in all areas except liturgical, dance, and military music.[27]

As long as the church- and university-linked branch of the musical profession retained its elite status, church composers enjoyed a relatively secure social and professional position. They also had a means of financial support that enabled them to devote their energies to composition. However, the declining real wages of organists and the poor performance standards in some cathedrals led many church musicians to turn to more remunerative activities. In the second half of the eighteenth century there still seem to have been vestiges of the professional esteem that had been associated with the church- and university-linked composer. But in time the gap widened between the status once accorded to this educational route and the realities of composing for the market. By the early nineteenth century, composers expressed much bitterness and frustration about their social, economic, and professional status. Their artistic role was – or was supposed to be – exalted. They saw themselves as highly educated and talented individuals who should occupy a privileged, if not revered, place in society. On the other hand, they were denied economic rewards in favor of composers of lighter works for the amateur market, and they enjoyed little or no social or professional esteem. As a result many chose to compose songs, "domestic" music, and educational pieces for the publishers of sheet music, while relatively few chose to pursue the "higher" forms of instrumental music or music for the church.

British composers of this period seem to have felt confused and frustrated by the absence of economic rewards for serious artistic effort and by the prejudices of the public. Roger Fiske notes the deluge of foreign competition, intensifying in the 1790s and continuing into the early 1800s, and credits this with the apparent failure of music to parallel the contemporaneous sea-change in literature and art: "no comparable figure emerged in the realm of music, and this national failure is hard to account for. Perhaps an excess of competition was the main reason. Our novelists and poets did not have to worry about foreign rivals and our painters were almost as fortunate, but our composers and instrumentalists had the whole of Western Europe to contend with, and they lost heart."[28]

Foreign competition was certainly important, but larger social and cultural values about music played at least as significant a role. Even more than the instrumentalists, composers seem to have experienced a period of decline, or "artistic depression," by the 1820s. In 1822, one observer insisted that the economic hierarchy of the profession was upside down. He felt that the ranking should start with the composer, descend to the teachers, and then to the performer, whereas in fact

I would ask anyone in the slightest degree acquainted with the present state of musical affairs in this country if the above-mentioned order of remuneration be not entirely reversed? if the performer, particularly when a foreigner, be not exorbitantly rewarded? if the fashionable master meet not with the next degree of encouragement? and if the poor composer, particularly when an Englishman, be not degraded to a mere pimp, employed to cater for a vitiated taste, by spinning waltzes, quadrilles, and paltry ballads? nay, even the favoured foreigner must submit to this humiliating drudgery.[29]

There are many other such passages in the writings of musicians of this period. In 1827, F. W. Horncastle commented:

[O]ur young professors who have passed a probationary education [as choristers] ... are reduced to the necessity in almost eighty out of a hundred instances, of subduing their talent for composition (if they have any)... The consequence of all this is, that many of these young persons when their voices are again usable, become teachers of singing, others of piano, harp and many other instruments, many take organs in parochial churches, while not a few find it their interest to write Quadrilles, Marches, Songs, and Rondos for warehouses. This is indeed sorry work for many of them.[30]

Contemporary sources credited economic hardships and lack of encouragement with the all-too-frequent choice by musicians either to renounce the struggle for artistic achievement in favor of lighter forms of composition, or to abandon composing altogether for more lucrative work. In 1823, one observer asked: "Situated as he [the composer] is, should we not have the greatest cause for astonishment were we not to find him yielding to 'imperious circumstances'; sinking calmly into the humble character of a teacher, consenting to be respectable and happy, rather than great?"[31] Of course teachers were "humble" only in terms of artistic achievement; they could attain a social and, possibly, economic status for which most composers could not even hope.

Twenty years later, the outlook for composers remained dreary. H. J. Banister attested that composers depended "on the drudgery of teaching, on the chance work of orchestral engagements, or on the hackney labour of writing for the shops."[32] And in 1829, T. D. Worgan complained, "In a worldly point of view ... the composer kicks the beam. Living, he is a drudge, an underling, a caterer for the music shops, a ladder for the vocal and instrumental performer, an obscene scribbler, or a pander to a corrupt taste."[33]

These comments did not derive solely from the admittedly poor economic outlook of composers, but also from their failure to achieve social and professional rewards commensurate with their perceptions of the difficulty and importance of their work. Musicians in general, and composers in particular, knew the rigors of their training and their work, and they were demoralized by the indifference of patrons and audiences. S. S. Wesley expressed this problem explicitly in his writings on church musicians and composers. In 1849 he wrote, "Before our Palestrinas can find a home at Cathedrals, the difficulties of musical composition must be appreciated, and our artists allowed to rank with men of true eminence in other walks of life."[34] This goal was not to be achieved, at least for most native composers, until much later in the nineteenth century.

Art music composers

The manuscript and published music of eighteenth- and nineteenth-century Britain reveals continuous compositional activity, despite the absence of the highest creative achievements during these years.[35] Native composers whose names recur frequently in eighteenth-century accounts virtually always had a variety of musical occupations. The few whose careers focused primarily or solely on composition tended to be the most illustrious foreign musicians, such as J. C. Bach and Joseph Haydn. Even C. F. Abel, who composed a number of symphonies and concertos, was also a concert impresario and performer.

Some of the greatest creative ferment among late-eighteenth-century native musicians seems to have been in glee composition and songs and concertos for the pleasure gardens.[36] These genres were followed in the nineteenth century by the madrigal revival and partsongs for Victorian choral societies. Another important native phenomenon was the emergence, around the turn of the century, of what has been termed the London piano school. Based on the work of foreign musicians who had settled in London (Clementi, Dussek, and later Kalkbrenner and Moscheles) it was continued by native musicians such as J. B. Cramer, Cipriani Potter, and Samuel Wesley.[37] The greatest national pride in musical composition, however, remained in the music for the Anglican Church and in the oratorio tradition begun by Handel. Oratorio writing was largely limited to native composers (with the exception of Spohr and Mendelssohn in the 1840s), but no English composer emerged as a viable successor to Handel.[38]

In the first half of the nineteenth century, the most serious composers also wrote orchestral and occasional chamber works, but they were at a distinct disadvantage financially and professionally. Publishers were rarely interested in serious works, even for small ensembles. There were few opportunities for performances of large-scale works, and concerts devoted to chamber music did not begin until the 1830s.[39] Reviewers sometimes sided with market forces over artistic goals, as when Ferdinand Ries, a well-known German pianist and composer living in England, received the following review of his new piano works in 1823:

Mr. Ries has been educated in the school of Beethoven, and, like his gifted master, abandons himself too much to the ambition of being *new*; hence it is, that his pianoforte works, with all their accuracy, are sometimes deficient in elegance and grace: while, actuated by this feeling, he forgets that the *ladies*, who constitute a majority of the patrons to whom he must appeal, are won by the most gentle and persuasive means, and turn with repugnance from mere judgment or ungarnished erudition. In studying to be *classical*, Mr. Ries has renounced the attributes of *fashion*, and been frequently mortified by seeing his austere and laborious effusions rejected for works of inferior skill, which came recommended, however, by traits of ease and animation, highly gratifying to the amateur. Society abounds in examples of a similar sort, and the preference enjoyed by every *companionable* man, over him who brings nothing into play but his profound knowledge and abstruse research, indicates with great precision the fortunes that are frequently experienced in music.[40]

The author appears to be sanctioning the "dictates of fashion," including the power of female and amateur patrons over musical values – an attitude that native musicians often bemoaned.[41] The reference to social parallels, such as preference for "companionable" rather than learned company, may suggest a degree of xenophobia in this instance, with the learned German composer being reprimanded for forgetting the gender and class values of his British audience.

The composer who wrote serious works for large ensembles hoped at best only to hear the works performed. There were very few concert institutions, professional musicians, or listeners who were willing to assist in the performance of new works, particularly if they were written by English composers. Even when a new English work was selected, the quality of the performance often left much to be desired, partly because of the attitudes of the players, but mainly because of the lack of adequate rehearsal time. The expense of paying for one meeting of an entire orchestra made rehearsals prohibitively expensive. In 1823, one writer argued that this expense

precludes the aspiring composer from the smallest portion of that aid which is, nevertheless, essential to him – unless he happen to receive it as a favour. And when this is the case, how is his music performed! What haste! What inaccuracy! What a scrambling to get to the end! Then what a shutting up of fiddle cases! What a pocketing of flutes and clarionets, and a running off in all directions! . . . The leader is in a hurry; the conductor is in a hurry; the singers, if they deign to attend, are in a very great hurry. In short, every one is in a hurry, but the poor author; who, in this general hurry, discovers a sad presage of the imperfect performance of his music and its probable failure.[42]

The same source reported that new works were often performed publicly with only one rehearsal, or without any rehearsal at all.[43] This is supported by the account records of the Philharmonic Society, which indicates that during most seasons, there were approximately equal numbers of re-hearsals and performances (usually nine rehearsals and eight concerts per season).[44] Although the prestige of the Philharmonic Society and its pro-fessional members seems to have been great among English and foreign musicians, there are hints that the absence of adequate rehearsal time was noticed. In 1848, for example, Frédéric Chopin "refused an invitation to play at the Philharmonic Society on the grounds that 'they have only one rehearsal – a public one.'"[45]

Early in the nineteenth century, there was no shortage of compelling reasons for English composers to refrain from indulging their higher artistic aspirations: serious creative work was time-consuming and dis-tracted composers from the more lucrative forms of commercial composi-tion. In 1835, Edward Loder, a gifted and prolific composer, "was driven by poverty to contract an artistically disastrous agreement with his pub-lisher, D'Almaine & Co., to produce a new song ... *every week*; conse-quently his best work lies buried under a heap of commercially-orientated trivialities."[46] If a composer did find time to write, the cost of having the score and parts copied, the odds against its being performed at all (not to mention adequately), the unlikelihood of success, and the absence of any financial or other type of reward were sufficiently discouraging. It is perhaps surprising that any musicians continued to write symphonies, oratorios, and chamber works at all. By 1820, one writer was exclaiming in despair that "the higher departments, oratorio, ecclesiastical and dramatic composition, are fading away, while the increasing multitude (*mob* we had almost written) of divertimentos and such things, present little of perma-nent character."[47]

By the middle of the century, there were signs of renewed seriousness in musical composition – perhaps an early foreshadowing of the "renais-sance" of a few decades later. New orchestral, piano, and chamber works began to appear. A RAM-trained generation of composers and pianists, including William Sterndale Bennett, George Macfarren, and others, pur-sued composition as a central aspect of their careers. Nicholas Temperley notes that this generation, particularly among the piano composers, was "*consciously* preserving a tradition of refinement and artistic integrity against commercial pressures. Unlike their predecessors, the new school of composers disdained to write popular piano music, turning to other activities such as teaching, journalism, and administration as means of livelihood.''[48]

Theatre composers

In the eighteenth century no theatre specialized in English operas; the focus of opera in London was the Italian Opera, and with very few exceptions (notably Stephen Storace) Italian composers and singers reigned there.[49] Still, there was scope for composers at the patent theatres (which employed at least a few professional singers) and the pleasure gardens.[50] Seventy-two musicians in the catalogue composed songs and other pieces for these venues.

In the early nineteenth century English opera continued largely under the leadership of Henry Bishop, until the 1830s, when a sea-change in the conditions for English opera altered the scope and character of theatre composers' careers. The first generation of RAM-trained professionals were transforming the London musical scene, and native opera was fueled by emerging Romantic nationalism (and in particular the success of Weber's operas at Covent Garden in the preceding decade). There was a renewed determination to compete with foreign musicians by creating English musical institutions (such as the founding of the English Opera in 1834), and a number of composers (including John Barnett, Edward Loder, and M. W. Balfe) came forward to write theatre music.[51] The enthusiastic patronage of Prince Albert after 1840 also seems to have played a significant role in overcoming British prejudices against the theatre.[52]

Still, the financial risks of composing for the theatres remained daunting and frustrating to many composers. Composers for the stage could submit their works to theatres on a free-lance basis, in which case there was little or no payment from the theatre itself, even if the piece was a great success. English composers generally had no share in the profits, unlike Continental composers, who seem to have been paid a percentage of the nightly receipts.[53] One extreme example was that of the successful theatrical composer William Vincent Wallace, "who had got rid of *Lurline* for half a guinea, [and] had the chagrin of seeing the management net £62,000."[54] The composer's main financial incentive was the hope that one or more of the songs performed at a theatre or pleasure garden would become a popular hit and be purchased by a publisher.

Theatres, at least, hired musicians as full-time composers or music directors. Henry Rowley Bishop, who worked in both capacities at the Covent Garden and Drury Lane Theatres, had a five-year contract as the music director of Covent Garden from 1818 to 1823,[55] and in 1823 reportedly earned about £1,000, although it is not clear how much of this sum came from the theatre and how much from publishers.[56] At Drury Lane the following year (1824), he earned £20 a week as music director and composer.[57] Such theatre jobs for composers required more arranging and adapting than original composition, however, especially in these years, when English operas were often patchwork affairs consisting of music by numerous composers. Bishop represents the most financially successful of the composers who wrote music for the theatres. Montague Corri (born in Edinburgh of an Italian musical family) offers a glimpse of a less exalted career in this branch of the profession. After an early accident which ended his work as a pianist (*circa* 1810), "composition and the arrangement of instrumental music, both for theatres and military bands, became his only means of support."[58] In 1813, he also worked as a free-lance music copyist for the Philharmonic Society, earning £44 17s 6d for the year[59] – good wages for the most routine and least creative of the skills necessary to a composer, yet undoubtedly a more reliable source of income than original composition.

Composers of theatre music, like other musicians, supplemented their income in various ways. Thomas Arne, perhaps the leading composer of English opera in the second half of the eighteenth century, also taught singing. He wrote many new works as vehicles with which to introduce his most talented pupils. Samuel Arnold, a prolific composer in many genres, combined opera composition with the most prestigious church positions at the Chapel Royal and Westminster Abbey. (The combination of church and theatre employment had become much less usual by the nineteenth century.) The best known of the nineteenth-century English opera composers tended to support themselves by teaching (John Barnett), conducting (Edward Loder, M. W. Balfe), performing (Balfe), or composing in other genres such as popular songs and arranging (Loder, M. V. Wallace).

Employment of this sort, which burdened one with many tasks other than composition, was undoubtedly frustrating to the composers, particularly in light of the domination of the theatres by foreign composers and foreign tastes. In 1833, the theatre composer G. H. B. Rodwell reported that "no English composer can now get an engagement at either of our great theatres but as an adapter of foreign music."[60] Henry Bishop, who produced original compositions for the theatre, felt compelled to cater to the foreign tastes of his audiences. As he wrote in 1840,

I have been a slavish servant to the Public; and too often when I have turned each way their weathercock Taste pointed, they have turned round on me, and up-braided me for not remaining where I was! Had the Public remained truly and loyally *English*, I would have remained so too! but I had my bread to get, and was obliged to watch their caprices, and give them an *exotic fragrance* (if I could not give them the plant) when I found they were tired of, and neglecting the native production.[61]

These complaints reflect the troubled relationship of musicians like Bishop with their patrons, but they also illustrate the theatre composer's relative lack of freedom. The founding of the English Opera in 1834, and the composition of entire operas by individual composers, was in part designed to address such problems.

Information on the earnings of theatre composers is sparse. In 1762, when Arne received £60 for *Artaxerxes*, it was "considered to be a ruinous sum."[62] But William Shield received £400 for one or two operas in the late eighteenth century, and John Braham, a successful stage singer, was paid £1,000 for one opera and £1,100 for another in the early 1800s. Bishop seems to have earned more than anyone else, with about £1,000 a year in the 1820s. Composers whose primary career was singing (such as John Braham and Michael Kelly) used their theatrical experience and connections to sell their dramatic music and get it performed. Nevertheless, foreign competition remained an obstacle, as in most areas of the profession. In 1833 Rodwell complained bitterly that when a foreign composer

is engaged by the management of an English theatre, instead of the offer to bring out his opera for *nothing*, he is offered £800 or £1000 to compose one, and is to receive the money whether the piece succeed or fail!! and to have his own time allowed him to complete the work!!! Weber had £1000 for *Oberon*, and took upwards of a year to compose it. Bishop was allowed *three weeks* to compose, in its original shape of three acts, the opera of *Clari*. Mr. Barnett, in putting music to *A Bold Stroke for a Wife*, was so pressed that he was compelled to work three days and nights without intermission, in order that he might complete the work in the given time, and was allowed ONE rehearsal, and did not receive one farthing for his work from the lessee!![63]

While Rodwell's intense xenophobia makes him a biased witness, it is clear that the economic rewards and professional reputation of musicians who wrote music for the theatre were extremely vulnerable to prejudices about the relative merits of English and Continental musicians and to shifting musical fashions. Even during the resurgence of English Romantic opera from the 1830s, composers and theatre impresarios took great risks to produce such works.

Composers of domestic music and instructional works

Four hundred and twenty-seven musicians (forty of them women) in the catalogue wrote for the popular sheet-music market or composed instructional works for the domestic market. For the most part these were pieces pleasing to the amateur ear, not difficult to play, and meant to be performed at home on readily available instruments (usually piano, but also flute, harp, or guitar). During the second half of the eighteenth century many serious composers wrote works specifically for the domestic setting.[64] By the early nineteenth century, increased demand by amateurs and students seems to have increased the division among art and commercial composition. At least the conflicts experienced by composers between artistic aspirations and market demands received more comment: "After a few trials, the major part of our writers abandon all thoughts of pursuing the higher species of composition, and take themselves to the more humble, but far more profitable employment of manufacturing for 'Messieurs les Marchands de Musique.'"[65]

Of all categories of composing, domestic music had the highest proportion of women.[66] One of the best known popular composers at the time was Mrs. Charles Barnard (1824–69), known to her audiences as "Claribel." During her life she published at least forty-five songs as well as vocal duets, trios, quartets, and piano pieces.[67] The titles of her songs reveal maudlin, trite subject matter, which seems to have been a key factor in her success: "The wide-spread popularity of the majority of the songs above noted, was primarily due to the homely events which they were intended to illustrate, and the pretty and extremely vocal melodies to which they were set."[68] While a few of the women who wrote popular songs and piano pieces also composed art music and sometimes had performing careers, the lighter forms of songs and "domestic" music for women had the advantage that they did not require a great deal of theoretical training and could be written in the home. As a result, several of the women in this category had no connection with professional musical life other than writing these pieces.

Publishers probably made most of their profits in the market for popular sheet music. It seems that the composer received a fixed price for each piece, and that the publisher took the risk or reward depending on its success. G. F. A. Wendeborn reported in 1785 that "those who compose such music find it very profitable, if their compositions meet with success. Not a great many sheets of new music are bought for half a guinea, and the composer is frequently very well paid for his copy."[69] It was apparently not uncommon for publishers to purchase songs for £50 each.[70] Another source estimated in 1822 that ten to thirty guineas per piece was not unusual,[71] although other accounts report much lower fees. G. H. B. Rodwell reported that the prices for original works were very low: "For *Cherry Ripe*, one of the most popular melodies, not only in this country but on the Continent also, Mr. Horn … received TEN POUNDS; and Mr. Barnett, for the *Light Guitar*, the prodigious sum of TWO GUINEAS!!!"[72] Yet the music publishing firm run by Muzio Clementi seems to have "paid as much as fifty guineas for a musical composition without words, and more than one hundred for one with words."[73]

The possibility of lucrative sales in the booming consumer culture of the time enticed many to produce light works for this market. In 1820, the editor of one musical journal commented on the challenge of reviewing the number of such pieces being submitted, referring to

the flood of compositions that was, within half a century, to deluge the land, wave after wave, and with almost as little distinction as there is to be found between the billows as they roll to land ... for sonatas and songs and divertimentos and duettinos flit by us in a succession so rapid ... at present we are alike puzzled to give either order or variety to our subjects.[74]

The number and the superficiality of such pieces led to many such comments on the sad state of the art: "what a figure we make, as manufacturers of divertimentos, &c. &c. &c. for the piano forte, harp, and flute! It is all true ... and may contribute much to the advantage of individuals, and of the music sellers ... [but] the great interests of the art are neglected."[75] The healthy market for amateur music-making inspired publication of educational pieces, instruction books, and arrangements of old or new works which had already been published. Music journals noted how easy or difficult the pieces were in their reviews, and occasionally commented on the trend toward undemanding works. Several piano pieces by T. A. Rawlings[76] were reviewed by the *Harmonicon* in 1823, with the comment that "in the present day we are sorry to find that ease is a better recommendation of new compositions than science; ... most composers now are endeavouring to simplify their writings, in order to procure a sale for them."[77] When a Mrs. Miles, who had a socially exclusive clientele of piano students, published an easy arrangement of an Italian theme, the reviewers remarked that "this lesson does not aim either at difficulty or great novelty; it is easy of acquirement, elegant, and tasteful, and therefore likely to be popular and in request."[78]

A companion to this trend was the proliferation of instruction books and primers, mainly on instrumental technique but also in music theory and harmony. Two hundred and seventy-two musicians in the catalogue, including fifteen women, produced books of this sort during this period. Although some of these primers were serious pedagogical works written by theorists or experienced teachers, many others were aimed exclusively at amateurs. The clearest indication of this is the authorship by one person of instruction books for a wide variety of instruments, or for an instrument on which the author did not actually perform. C. F. Eley, a German musician who played the cello in London theatres and concert orchestras from the 1790s through the 1830s, as well as the clarinet in a military band, produced a bassoon "tutor."[79] Other musicians seem to have written instruction books almost as a primary career. Charles Hancock published three "preceptors" in 1845–46, one each for accordion, flute, and violin.[80] And James P. Haskins published instruction books for the concertina, piano, voice, and "Modern Cornopean" (cornet) in the 1850s.[81]

Another trend that was supported by the market for sheet music was editing, arranging, or adapting other composers' works – well-known selections from operas, or current popular tunes – and in some cases compositions were pirated outright. One musician complained that after receiving £50 for a song

I soon discover many who are *kindly* willing to share the larger portion of the profit, to which I must certainly consider myself as fairly entitled; my song is immediately printed and published by others, and I have the mortification of seeing it exposed for sale at three-pence, and thumbed copies for two-pence half penny, on almost every old book-stand in the courts and alleys of the metropolis.[82]

The sense of compositional entrepreneurship driven by market demand – to the detriment of musical values – is reflected in contemporary images of musical manufacturing. An article entitled "English Manufacturing," written by "One of the Labouring Classes," addressed this issue in 1826:

[I]t is in music . . . that the manufacturing system now shines upon us with so much glory. Open the catalogues of our first houses – of Clementi, Goulding, and Chappell, for example – and what will you find there? original works? nonsense! The drudgery of invention we have left to the "old ones." They toiled, and sweated for our advantage; and it is with the capital which they have left us, that we now cut such a figure. Thus A takes the fashionable melody, or an air composed some sixty or an hundred years ago, which he arranges for the piano forte or harp; B arranges it for the harp and piano forte; C puts a flute accompaniment to A's arrangement, D confers the same favour on B – substituting the violoncello, or horn, for the flute; then comes E who rearranges the whole for "two performers," and E is followed by F who deranges it for the use of "one." In this way we might go through the alphabet – and what an admirable system it is! All are gratified – names find their way to title pages, which could not have got there by any other method, and the public pays for all.[83]

Another observer wondered why this system had developed, with fantasias and variations on borrowed themes "augmenting in number every day . . . From what has this *furor mutandi* arisen? Or may it not be fairly traced to those musicians of the third and fourth classes in which London abounds? People who find it much easier to produce variations than compose a sonata."[84] Certainly this explanation must have applied to many of these composers, but the temptation to churn out as many works as possible for the publishers must have been strong, particularly given the dim prospects of achieving performance or publication, let alone money or fame, in the realm of serious church, theatre, or orchestral composition.

Entrepreneurs

As Reginald Nettel observed, "the borderline between music as a profession and music as a business had in our most successful men ceased to exist."[85] It was only a short leap from writing instruction books and easy works for amateurs to music selling or publishing, concert management, and even the instrument trade, and a number of musicians in the eighteenth and early nineteenth centuries established shops or warehouses for the sale of musical instruments and sheet music.[86] Far from such options being alternatives chosen by unsuccessful performers, it was often the most successful musicians who could amass the capital to establish a music shop. Sometimes they also published music, although other musicians founded firms specifically for music publishing.[87] The catalogue includes 116 music sellers and/or publishers, 63 musical instrument makers, and 5 instrument dealers who were also professional musicians.

Teaching, composing, and the sale of musical goods lay along a continuum, with the higher artistic aspirations of some composers suspended in the larger milieu of subsistence and entrepreneurship. Nettel identifies this entrepreneurial spirit with the shift from traditional patronage to a more equal relationship with patrons: "The wealthy middle classes offered better prospects of a livelihood to musicians than aristocratic support, and it was natural for musicians to win recognition of social equality with the middle classes by the exercise of industry and a good head for business."[88]

Such ventures were not without risk, however. J. L. Dussek, one of the leading pianists and teachers in London throughout the 1790s, launched a music shop in partnership with fellow musician Domenico Corri. When the shop failed in 1800, Dussek fled the country to avoid debtors' prison, and continued his career in Hamburg. As McKendrick explains in relation to small enterprises of all sorts during these years, "spectacular success for the few must be measured against relative failure of the many, and complete collapse of an uncomfortably large number of business enterprises."[89] A number of musicians who risked ventures such as concert series and theatres ultimately faced bankruptcy and sometimes imprisonment (see chapter 9).

The date of most of these establishments – in the late eighteenth or early nineteenth century – supports Perkin's assertion that the professional middle-class ideal was initially "intertwined" with the entrepreneurial ideal.[90] But it also reflects the limited window of time during which musicians could realistically aspire to middle-class status. As Perkin argues, these two ideals diverged toward the mid-nineteenth century; accordingly, musicians who aspired to the gentility of high-status professional careers were less likely to focus their energies in warehouses and trading establishments than a Clementi, Dussek, Cramer, or Novello. Enterprising professional musicians in the mid- to late nineteenth century were more likely to found concert series, obtain a position at the Royal Academy of Music, or write music journalism and books – all more consistent with a middle-class professional ideal.

Musicians' concerns with social status, foreign competition, and cultural perceptions were accompanied by the persistent threat of financial hardship. The constant preoccupation with mere subsistence was a grave deterrent to professional aspirations, for it distracted musicians from collective efforts that might have helped them achieve professional autonomy, and it prevented many musicians from attaining even the trappings of middle-class respectability and social status.

The financial insecurities of musicians were not unique. They were shared by most artisans and many of the professions in eighteenth- and nineteenth-century Britain. These social strata, like the laboring classes, were vulnerable to shifts in market demand and to larger economic forces, such as income levels and fluctuations in currency and prices. After many decades of relative price stability, the cost of consumer goods began to rise gradually but steadily from around 1750; the pattern of gradual change ended with the dramatic inflation of the war years 1790–1815, estimated by some historians as between 65 and 85 percent. After the war, prices fell quickly (25 to 35 percent) for a few years, then more slowly (10 to 20 percent) from the early 1820s until the middle of the century.[1]

Income levels ranged widely among the middle ranks. Although the survey of social structure and income by the mid-eighteenth-century social observer Joseph Massie was perhaps too indebted to Gregory King's comparable study of 1688, it does provide a glimpse of the economic landscape.[2] His occupational categories in the middle ranks (including some clergy, lawyers, "persons professing the liberal Arts," civil servants, and military officers) earned annual incomes ranging from £50 to £100. The "liberal Arts" category, which is the only one that could have included musicians, indicates £60 annual income. But this figure is exactly the same as that of the 1688 survey; and based on wage information for musicians, it probably underestimates the incomes of established musicians (and other professionals) by 1760.

Applications to the Royal Society of Musicians provide a useful guide to what was considered a minimum income for an established professional

musician. New members in the 1780s claimed annual earnings of close to
£150. After that decade, however, £200 seems to have become the minimum income for a successful and respectable member of the profession.
This is supported by Colquhoun's estimated average income for musicians
in 1806 (£150),[3] and by much of the evidence about musicians' earnings.
An income on this level placed musicians well above moderately skilled
artisans or laborers, and, at least according to Colquhoun, put them on the
same footing as shopkeepers. It probably also ranked them with the most
successful of the highly skilled artisans in luxury trades, such as musical
instrument makers, jewellers, watchmakers, and fashionable hairdressers.
But certainly they had not attained the economic level of many members of
the established professions such as law and medicine.

Such occupations were hit doubly hard by the inflation of the war years.
Nominal wages remained stable but their value fell precipitously; at the
same time, musical impresarios and consumers alike were more cautious
with their money. Hence the noticeable decline of concert life in the early
years of the nineteenth century. Earnings that had been sufficient for
established musicians until about 1800 were less likely to keep them afloat
financially during the war years. In subsequent decades, the minimum
income required to achieve middle-class social and professional status
probably rose even further (see below).

The range of musicians' earnings

Although the hope of financial gain motivated some musicians at the
outset of their careers, professional musicians' lifetime earnings varied
greatly, and few were able to acquire wealth. The economic gradations
among musicians fall into six general categories: (1) salaries of £1,000 or
more; (2) salaries of £200–£1,000; (3) combined earnings of £200–£1,000;
(4) "average" earnings of approximately £200; (5) below £200 but not
destitute; and (6) destitute.

Only nineteen musicians from the catalogue are known to have earned
£1,000 or more in any one year of their careers. Sixteen, seven of them
Italians, were stage singers, although the tally of well-paid Italian singers
would be higher if the catalogue included those musicians who worked in
England only for a few seasons.[4] Non-singers in this category included
Henry Rowley Bishop (1786–1855), the successful theatre composer;
Giacobo Bassevi Cervetto (1682–1783), an Italian Jew who performed as a
cellist, gave private lessons and sold musical instruments, leaving £20,000
when he died;[5] John Festing (?–1757), a German oboist and flute teacher
who saved £8,000 from his teaching;[6] and Robert Janes (1806–66), a
cathedral organist with a vast teaching practice.[7] There were undoubtedly

a few other musicians with comparable earnings, particularly private teachers with wealthy clients, but such earnings remained exceptional in the music profession.

Just below this level of earnings, there are approximately twenty musicians in the catalogue who earned between £200 and £1,000 a year at some point in their careers. (Three of these musicians earned over £2,000 in some years, so they are also included in the highest-paid group: Henry Bishop, Manuel Garcia, a stage singer, and Harriett Waylett, a stage and concert singer.) Seven of this group were stage singers – either very successful English singers or secondary Italian singers at the King's Theatre who earned between £500 and £800 a year. Five musicians achieved comparable earnings by composing: Thomas Arne, Francesco Bianchi, Henry R. Bishop, William Shield, and Stephen Storace, all of whom wrote music for the theatres.[8] Five others were orchestral players, usually leaders: Wilhelm Cramer, Michael Rophino Lacy, James Sanderson, and G. B. Viotti. Occasionally players on other orchestral instruments earned more than £200 a year, the most famous of whom was the double bass player Domenico Dragonetti.[9] A couple of organists earned salaries of more than £200, although this was rare. In addition, this category probably included several private teachers whose earnings ranged from £200 to £1,000 a year at various points in their careers.

So far, this income category has referred primarily to those musicians who received a specific salary of more than £200. Yet there were many who earned this amount by combining a variety of musical occupations. The viola player Joseph Major, for example, reported in 1794 that he was "organist of Knightsbridge Chaple [*sic*], has Two Schools, and other Business that has brought him in above Two Hundred Pounds Per Annum for the last Two Years and is Still Increasing."[10] Another viola player, Nicholas Rolfe, who also gave piano lessons, reported a very satisfactory state of business in 1812: "his connections and business as a Piano Forte Master are of the first respectability including two Schools – and his Income arising from his professional exertions has (on the average) for the last three years, exceeded Three Hundred Guineas per annum."[11]

Before 1780, an income ranging from £100 to £200 a year seems to have indicated a flourishing career. Frederick James Messing, for example, made a detailed statement of his professional activities, claiming that his earnings had been £65 13s 6d (1770), £79 14s (1780), and £123 16s 7d (1781).[12] This was derived partly from performing on the violin, viola, cello, and guitar, but mainly from his work as a teacher and a music copyist. He applied for membership of the Royal Society of Musicians in 1781 or 1782, which suggests that only by that date did his earnings both recommend him as a member of the profession and enable him to pay the premiums. In 1781, another musician, John Francis Wood, applied to the same society, declaring that his professional engagements consisted of "Three Schools and private teaching bringing him in upwards of One Hundred and Fifty Pounds per Annum."[13] After 1780, however, £200 seems to have been the minimum income that could indicate a successful and respectable member of the profession, and by the 1830s that figure was probably closer to £300.[14]

But many professional musicians never achieved this economic level. Church organists earned between £20 and £50 a year. Most of them only achieved a more respectable income by teaching or additional performing. Although the most successful singers far surpassed the £200 annual income level, a great many singers did not. More importantly, even those who earned the highest salaries often fell far short of a minimal income at other points in their careers. Instrumentalists in general had to struggle hard to achieve an annual income of £200. Even the first-chair players in the leading orchestras required additional engagements to achieve such a sum, and the lower-ranking players were not likely to earn that much even with supplementary income.

Destitution

The amounts earned by musicians in a single year are less useful in assessing the economic realities of their careers than their lifetime earnings. Indeed, a long-term view of musicians' earnings makes it clear that their chances of avoiding destitution were very slim, and that *even the most successful musicians* could and frequently did find themselves completely destitute at some point, usually at the end of their careers. This was no secret to observers of the British musical scene. A German observer of London life in the 1790s wrote:

It might be supposed that, in England, people in a musical line, if they are eminent in their profession, have an opportunity of acquiring some fortune, or at least a sufficient income to live upon, but the case is generally the reverse. Several of the principal German and Italian musicians in London, I have known to live in a most deranged state of their finances; they were involved in debt, and died wretchedly poor.[15]

In 1821, a native observer commented:

The few only arrive at the perfection which leads to the eminence that elevates them to view... The million sink and are little seen or known, and they who reach the summit, struggle for it through such sorrow, privation and labour, as but for *the enthusiasm and force of talent* which distinguish them from the rest, would depress and destroy them as those evils do depress and destroy the others.[16]

Table 20. *RSM premiums, 1822*

Age	Premium (guineas)	Age	Premium (guineas)	Age	Premium (guineas)
22	1 Guinea	28	$10\frac{1}{2}$	34	26
23	2	29	12	35	28
24	3	30	$13\frac{1}{2}$	36	30
25	4	31	15	37	48
26	5	32	22	38	51
27	9	33	24	39	54

For each year beyond the age of 40, the premium was an additional 3 guineas.

How many are "the few" and "the million"? How many musicians found themselves in the dire circumstances described above?

One indication of the threat of impoverishment among musicians is the number and importance of institutions founded to assist musicians in financial distress. The largest and most prestigious of these institutions was the Royal Society of Musicians.[17] Founded in 1738, the RSM combined the functions of a friendly society, burial club, and professional organization. Each member paid a premium when he joined and every year subsequently, based on his age. Table 20 lists the premiums for members without children (each child cost two guineas extra) who joined in 1822.[18] The Society was restricted to males despite growing pressure from women musicians in the 1830s; women were finally admitted to partial membership in 1866.[19] In order to receive any aid from the Society, one had to prove absolute destitution. Other benefits, which were provided after the member's death (again, only if the survivors were destitute), included funeral expenses, aid to the widow and her family, and apprenticeship premiums for the children.

Because of the widespread need for assistance to musicians, and the growing cost and exclusiveness of the RSM, several other benefit societies were founded during this period: the New Musical Fund (1791–1850s), the Choral Fund (1791–at least 1845), the Choir Benevolent Fund, the Harmonic Brothers, the General Theatrical Fund (1838?), the Royal Society of Female Musicians (1839–66), and benefit funds for employees at specific theatres.[20] They seem to have operated on principles similar to those of the RSM. Members paid annual dues, in return for which they could expect some financial assistance for themselves or for their families. Not surprisingly, given the insecurity of musical careers, such organizations found themselves faced with staggering claims. Only the RSM, with its head start in attracting wealthy patrons and accumulating capital – combined with an extraordinary unwillingness to part with its funds – survived.

The catalogue provides only a partial view of the scope of destitution among professional musicians. It includes 161 impoverished musicians, most of whom were members of the RSM. In other words, 15 percent of the 696 RSM members during this period became destitute at some point. This tally does not include musicians who were relatively impoverished, or who refrained from appealing to the RSM even in destitution, after which the RSM was called upon to pay for their funerals and support their families. Nor does it include the countless others – not members of the RSM – who never attained the status to leave records of their destitution. Since so many RSM members became impoverished, after enjoying at least some measure of professional success and even fame, it is reasonable to estimate that an even larger proportion of professional musicians ended their careers no better and in many cases worse off financially than when they started.

That destitution was widespread in the musical profession is demonstrated by case after case of successful, seemingly well-established musicians whose situations were dramatically reversed by circumstances beyond their control. In 1824, Antonio Sapio, the London-born son of an Italian stage singer, was reported to be "unquestionably the most promising tenor singer that has for many years appeared in this metropolis."[21] Yet after an active singing career in the 1820s, he died in 1851 "completely destitute, having occupied a garret in Queen Street, Edgeware Road, under conditions of great distress, some time previous to his death."[22] Cecilia Davies, who was famous as an opera singer in Italy as well as in London during the late eighteenth century, was impoverished by the 1830s. A musical journal reported,

This celebrated cantatrice ... is still alive; but in very indigent circumstances, bed-ridden, almost blind, and upwards of fourscore years of age. She was held in great estimation, some sixty years ago, in Italy, and was prima donna at several theatres in that country as well as at the King's Theatre; ... [she is now] supported solely by a pension of £25 per annum from the National Benevolent Institution, casual donations from the Royal Society of Musicians and a few charitable institutions.[23]

In 1839, the musical press also noted the destitution of the singer Mme. Sala, and the RSM's occasional donations to assist her.[24] Another illustrious singer, Mrs. Salmon (once one of the most highly paid musicians), lived in poverty from the mid-1820s until her death in 1849, despite appeals in the press and even a benefit concert to help her in 1840.[25] An anonymous and undoubtedly less illustrious singer was observed in a low-life London tavern: "An Italian air was screamed and quivered by an elderly female, who once strutted upon the stage, but who was now half bent with care, want, and blue ruin [gin]."[26]

The career of John Purkis further illustrates the wide economic fluctuations of musical careers. A keyboard player, particularly as a church organist, he was blind from the age of one, although he regained partial vision at about the age of thirty after two operations. He was well known as an excellent organist, and by his early twenties had two important posts – St. Clement Danes and St. Olave, Southwark – as well as teaching a large number of pupils. The following biographical sketch, written in 1825, presents Purkis as the exemplar of contemporary beliefs about hard work, dedication, and the benefits that would inevitably follow:

This outline of the rise and progress of a genius bred and born in the centre of our metropolis, and who has raised himself, under the most extraordinary circumstances and disadvantages, from a middle state of society to the applause and patronage of the first personages of the country, and all by an indefatigable zeal and devotedness to the study of his profession, will, we trust, hold out encouragement to every young British artist. For let it not be said in this age, that native talent does not meet with encouragement; it is sure to meet with it when its merits are once brought into view and action, and especially when genius is accompanied by industry and private worth.[27]

But by 1847 Purkis was no longer enjoying the rewards of hard work and dedication. He reported to the RSM that he was suffering from a variety of physical ailments and had experienced "many heavy losses in his profession and unforeseen misfortunes." His savings were reduced to £2 to £3 cash. He still earned money from one organist post and from teaching; the total amounted to £70 a year, but that was far from sufficient to support him and his wife. After he died in 1849 his wife remained a claimant on the Society for two more years, after which she also died, the RSM paying for her burial.[28]

What led to the destitution of so many professional musicians? Job insecurity and unemployment, low earnings, illness, and old age all played a part. There were moreover few alternatives for musicians who confronted these hardships. Instrumentalists could try to make up for the loss of positions in theatre orchestras by seeking more pupils, competing for organist posts, and copying music. If they were fortunate enough to belong to a benefit society, they could apply for help, although the sums granted were generally quite small. James Simpson, for example, apparently an orchestral player, wrote to the RSM in 1796 that he was "deprived of his only Winters engagement the Italian Opera, in consequence of which, he is reduced to Extreme distress – the only support he has had for some time past has arisen from the sale of a few necessaries which are now Exausted [sic]."[29] The benefit funds were doled out parsimoniously, however, and the

Society did not generally consider unemployment sufficient grounds for an appeal. In 1814, the RSM argued that lack of work alone did not make a musician eligible for aid, no matter how destitute; only illness and old age qualified. The Governors of the RSM pointed out to one unemployed musician that the fund "was established for the relief of the aged and infirm, and not those whose only plea is want of business, as it is impossible for the fund to answer the numerous demands which would infallibly take place, if that were allowed."[30] The RSM's general level of response was characteristic of an age in which individuals were considered solely responsible for the success or failure of their careers, with intemperance or imprudent management the most likely explanations for failure.

Neither, apparently, did the RSM help musicians who found themselves in debt, as a few of their members, as well as other musicians during this period, landed in debtors' prison.[31] One of them, Parke, principal oboist at Drury Lane and Vauxhall Gardens for several decades, is well known to music historians for his *Musical Memoirs*, published in 1830. He was arrested for debt and taken to Marshalsea Prison in 1823 at the age of sixty-one,[32] from where he wrote to the RSM appealing for medicine and food:

Having been arrested and brought to this place ... with only one pound in my pocket (seven shillings and sixpence of which was immediately paid for fees) I have had no other means of subsisting myself, my Wife, and five young children but the remains of that and the County allowance, three and sixpence per week. I have not receiv'd a shilling from the Theatre although two nights pay are due to me. I therefore am depriv'd of the common comforts of life, proper food, fire and candle, added to which I am labouring under a billious attack, and am totally without the means of procuring either medicine or medical assistance ... I must remain here five or six weeks in order to take the benefit of the Insolvent Act, and as I trust that I have been "more sinn'd against, than having sinn'd" I feel no doubt of an honourable acquittal.[33]

Parke was not imprisoned for very long, in contrast to another musician, also a member of the RSM, Charles Jane Ashley. A successful cellist, secretary to the RSM, member of the Philharmonic Society and part of a prominent family of musicians, he was held for debt in King's Bench prison for almost sixteen years and released in 1834 at the age of sixty-one.[34] When he was released, he wrote the following letter to the RSM in which he described his attempts to reestablish himself in the profession:

I was released from the King's Bench ... and engaged at the Victoria Theatre: I devoted a portion of my salary to the discharge of some debts incurred necessarily during my long captivity, and which I should have been enabled to accomplish, had not the Manager Mr. Glossop decamped and left me Two Months in arrear. I then went to the Queens and from thence to the Adelphi and adopted the same course, and should [had] my health and strength continued have surmounted all my troubles and have been contented and happy. But I was taken from my Bed when ill for an old Debt to the County Prison, where I remained three weeks by which I lost my engagement, but this was of little moment, for being seized with a most virulent Bilious Fever, it has left me in such a very debilitated state, that for the present I could not I fear undertake any situation whatever.[35]

Astonishingly, Ashley did recover and establish himself professionally; when he died in 1843, he was the proprietor of the Tivoli Gardens in Margate.[36]

Illness, with the accompanying loss of income, and sometimes of jobs and pupils, presented a major challenge for musicians. The cellist H. J. Banister pointed out how much more devastating illness could be for musicians than for some other occupations:

[The musician's] gains, large or small, are derived from *personal labour* exclusively; a fit of illness dries up all his resources. A master artisan profits by the labour of his underlings; … the profits and resources of a tradesman or merchant remain untouched in a multitude of cases, although he may be laid low by sickness.[37]

The files of the RSM contain numerous instances that support Banister's view. In 1781, John Bassett, an orchestral player during the winter season at Drury Lane, wrote that he was "through Violent Illness, Unable to retain an engagement for the Summer Season, on which He much depended." Edmund Denman, who had enjoyed a long career as an orchestral and military performer on the bassoon, clarinet, and French horn, found himself impoverished in 1822 at the age of sixty when he was "afflicted with loss of hearing, and shortness of breath, which compels him to relinquish his professional engagements." The violinist, Charles Evans, became severely ill in 1821, at sixty-three years of age; his medical problems were numerous, including some paralysis of his hands. Nevertheless, he attempted to continue to play the organ at a church when he could get up, although several of his fingers were not working. He wrote to the RSM: "how I am to go on God knows – as I have lost the only thing of consequence (the Ladies school) the Governess having engaged another Master in consequence of my frequent Illnesses."[38]

The records reveal how little money musicians were able to save. When Walter Henry Maddock, an orchestral string player and piano teacher in London, became too sick to work in 1826, his total assets were "30 Pounds in the Southwark Savings Bank." Thomas Paul Chipp, who played several orchestral instruments, had an organist post and private teaching, but had only £2 in a savings bank and less than £5 cash when he applied for aid to the RSM at the age of seventy-three in 1866. When Edmund Bryan Harper died in 1869 after a relatively high-status career beginning with training at the Royal Academy of Music followed by private employment with the Marquis of Downshire, he left his widow an annual pension of £25 from his former employer, an insurance policy worth £100, and a few belongings including music books, valued at under £10. Henry Westrop, an organist whose daughter took over his job when he became too ill to work, left only £3 cash, some furniture, and debts totaling £40. And in 1875, Maria Louisa Peile, whose sight was failing and who could no longer work, had only £25 in the Post Office Savings Bank and "a little furniture and musical instruments value under £50."[39]

Clearly, then, musicians were not in a good position to provide for old age. John Davy, a fairly successful composer of stage music, died in 1824 at the age of sixty-three "in extreme indigence, having outlived all his kindred."[40] In the same year, Edward Jones, who had been a member of the RSM since 1778, applied for assistance, "being seventy-two years old, infirm, and totally unable to maintain himself, by his professional pursuits."[41] In 1823, a sixty-seven-year-old orchestral string player, George Veale, reported that "being as he supposes on account of his age (for he can derive no other cause) deprived of every engagement, that he held in public orchestras, and other business he used to have ... [he] has fifty pounds a Yr encumbered with many debts."[42]

Some musicians retired with pensions. A few cathedral organists and military musicians received a small annual payment when they retired. When James Rufus Tutton's widow sought assistance from the RSM, she was required to prove that her late husband had not received a military pension. The colonel of the Horse Guards wrote on her behalf, explaining that "Mr. James Rufus Tutton, late Band Master of the Royal Horse Guards – was not awarded any Pension on his Discharge from the Regiment, in consequence of his never having been enlisted, or attested."[43] But musicians who had held regular posts under royal patronage sometimes received pensions. The same Tutton had received an annuity of £40 from the Lord Chamberlain's office as one of Her Majesty's Household Trumpeters,[44] and some members of the Chapel Royal, at least early in the eighteenth century, received pensions. Noble patrons occasionally provided a modest level of retirement payments, but such arrangements were rare.

Conclusion

As noted in preceding chapters, professional musicians were well aware of the economic distress and failure of numerous colleagues. H. J. Banister summed up the depressing outlook for orchestral players when he wrote that the absence of all hope of permanent employment, of any thing like a certain income, operates as a great discouragement to instrumental performers. "What is the use of practising?" is a common saying among them. Were the question answered; it must be thus: "To obtain a pittance in the prime of life; and endure neglect, dependence, or probably destitution, in old age."[45]

He went on to note:

I should be sorry to put on paper the facts concerning individuals of high professional merit ... that afford doleful confirmation of the truth of the above statement. Suffice it to say, there are many of the class named, who may fairly look with envy upon the circumstances of a junior clerk in his first year of service, a petty shopman or journeyman mechanic. Yet how small the preparation in one case, compared with the other![46]

Such perceptions were not restricted to the later years of this period. Samuel Wesley, who was employed as an organist, a composer, and a teacher, and was thought of as "the greatest organist of his time,"[47] wrote in 1806:

I have every day more and more cause to curse the day that ever my poor father suffered *musick* to be my profession. In this country experience continually shows that only impudent and ignorant wretches make any considerable emolument by it excepting a few singers ... but the whole is a degrading business to any man of spirit or any abilities... If I had now three or four hundred pounds at my command, I would not hesitate to purchase a large share in a gin shop.[48]

It is not clear what "impudent and ignorant wretches" he was referring to. Aside from singers, only some popular composers and fashionable teachers made fortunes as professional musicians.

Music rarely proved to be the source of wealth that some musicians seem to have hoped for in the early years of their careers. In relatively few cases was it a vehicle for upward social mobility or financial gain. While it could provide a living in musicians' best years, it often failed to enable them to provide for old age or to pass on any earnings or advantages to their children. Musicians, who struggled against social and cultural prejudices as well as financial insecurity, were at a distinct disadvantage in their attempts to achieve the trappings of middle-class social status and respectability, the appearance and independence of a profession, or the luxury of adjusting their priorities to focus on artistic values rather than economic survival.

Musicians' progress toward the status and autonomy of a middle-class profession was hindered from the outset by financial hardships, absence of professional control over training or entrance to the profession, and social and cultural prejudices. Financial struggles were tempered slightly by benefit societies, which offered limited protection against destitution, but only some musicians could afford membership. Proposals by musicians to establish schools and licensing procedures met with little support or success; and the only school founded during these years, the Royal Academy of Music, was an aristocratic project from the start. The last-named obstacle – social and cultural prejudices – may have proved the most difficult. Persistent beliefs that musicians were linked with low social origins, immorality, femininity, and foreignness appear as recurring themes. In response, musicians launched a war of words in pamphlets, books, and the musical press, sometimes offering ideological critiques of patrons, managers, and even society at large, but with little effect.

Achieving professional status requires a unified effort and collective solutions to licensing, education, employment, earnings, and public perceptions. As described in the preceding chapters, however, patronage systems as well as foreign competition prevented musicians from gaining control over the market for music. Professional status was even more unlikely given cultural beliefs that persistently challenged music's social value and musicians' respectability. In response, musicians were divided, and the profession itself increasingly fragmented. We see a profession struggling against forces beyond its control, and one in which collective solutions never overcame the allure of individual ambitions and traditional patronage relationships.

The eighteenth century

In the eighteenth century, proposed reforms of the profession and the state of music in general centered mainly on two problems: the decline of church music and the competition from foreign musicians. The former was merely decried; the latter inspired a few proposals for training institutions (see chapter 4). Status was still determined primarily by association with the traditional church and university career path, and by employment by aristocratic or royal patrons. The only existing musicians' association that might have taken on the functions of a truly professional organization was the Royal Society of Musicians (founded in 1738), but the RSM remained too narrowly identified with charity to represent the status of a middle-class profession. Numerous other benefit societies for musicians appeared in the 1790s and later; these commanded smaller financial resources than the older society, lacked the recognition conferred on the RSM by its royal charter, and like the RSM remained primarily charitable relief organizations for destitute musicians.

In the 1790s, a decade of pervasive political and social upheaval, new currents appeared. The short-lived Society of Musical Graduates (see chapter 4) circled around notions of establishing professional control, but represented only a tiny, elite corner of the profession and lacked any clear sense of mission. At the other end of the spectrum, though, it was not unusual for members of aspiring professions – particularly those with ties to the urban artisanate to which many musicians belonged – to be in sympathy with radical, democratic political philosophies and more revolutionary solutions to the problems of social and economic status. The eminent surgeon Sir Astley Cooper, for example, who in the early 1790s was just establishing his career,

believed strongly that scientific knowledge was the only proper basis for the professional standing he claimed, with its associated social standing. It is consistent with this outlook that in 1792 he should have gone to Paris to see what was happening, and that he should have become known for a democrat at a time when most upper-class Englishmen thought of democracy as a brand of treason.[1]

Similarly, Robert Robson cites an attorney who was secretary of the radical democratic organization known as the London Corresponding Society, and another (probably an apprentice) who was removed from London by his father when he appeared to have been influenced by the same society.[2] According to Robson, such radicalism was not typical among attorneys, who were generally both conservative and patriotic.[3] But radicalism was in the air, especially in the 1790s, and it appealed to members of aspiring professions, especially before they achieved their goal of attaining unequivocal middle-class economic and social status.

Consistent with musicians' dual identities as literate urban artisans and aspiring professionals, there is evidence that some musicians of the 1790s and early 1800s shared radicals' democratic ideals. Samuel Webbe Sr. (1740–1816) was an organist, singer, teacher, music copyist, and composer.

Employed as the chapel-master of the Portuguese Chapel, London, from the 1770s, he was best known as a glee composer, and from 1794 was secretary to the Noblemen and Gentlemen's Catch Club, an aristocratic singing-club. His son, Samuel Webbe Jr. (*circa* 1770–1843) was also an organist and a singer, and one of the founding members of the Philharmonic Society.[4] Both belonged to the RSM. Even with this range of professional and patronage connections, both, according to the radical tailor Francis Place, were associated with the democratic ideals and activities of the London Corresponding Society. Place also wrote that when he was studying French by reading Helvétius, Rousseau, and Voltaire, "I never wanted books and could generally borrow those I most desired to peruse. I borrowed French books from two members of the Society, a Mr. Webbe, was one, his father and I believe he himself – was a musician, a musical composer as I heard."[5] Their political activities were also noted by Samuel Wesley in a letter to Vincent Novello in 1813: "Tomorrow Evening … we are likely to have the Point argued in a true parliamentary Manner by our Friend Sam Webbe, who you know has been a celebrated Man in Matters of political Discussion, which in the Reign of Tom Paine he carried so far, that he narrowly escaped, himself, from *being carried* into Quarters at least as uncomfortable as those of the Messieurs Hunt" (referring to Leigh Hunt and his brother, who were imprisoned for two years for their newspaper's libel on the Prince Regent in 1812).[6]

Such political associations confirm the view of musicians as urban artisans who might be more in sympathy with democratic ideals, at least during the radical 1790s. It would, however, be misleading to suggest that many musicians were candidates for revolutionary action in this period. As was true for other literate artisans, the pursuit of upwardly mobile solutions to the social and economic pressures of the times diluted the democratic impulses of the 1790s.

Since musicians were unlikely to gain control over education or licensing, some attempted to increase patronage and employment by founding concert series and concert institutions. Many important concert series, especially in the 1780s and 1790s, were initiated and run by professional musicians; famous examples include the Bach/Abel, Salomon, and Professional Concerts, and there were many others. Such institutions of course depended on aristocratic subscribers, but they remained in professional control. The reshuffling of audiences and consequent preference for private concerts in the early decades of the nineteenth century led to a period of decline in opportunities for large-scale professional patronage of this sort. When new professional concert series began to emerge in the 1840s, their tone and mission had changed to suit the social and musical values of the time (see below).

The early nineteenth century

Musicians sometimes founded institutions specifically designed to express and support professional values. The most important was the Philharmonic Society, founded in 1813. The ideals of the Philharmonic Society were a far cry from those of an aspiring profession, however. The rules and regulations established in its first years illustrate an uneasy synthesis of professional and artisanal ideals; they suggest sympathy with radical democratic principles and a consequent ambivalence about self-regulation based on professional criteria. For example, the Society, which was managed by a committee of professionals, began with the extraordinary policy that there would be no ranking of players in the orchestra; parts would be distributed on a rotating basis.[7] In addition, the founders expected the orchestral instrumentalists (including the founders) to play for free.[8] This decision was ostensibly to ensure the survival of the new concert series by limiting costs, and to demonstrate the pure and professional ideals by which the institution was driven. The latter rationale implied at least a nod toward professional ideals, and several of the other rules reflected typical preoccupations with propriety and decorum: members were not to use the Society's name to further personal ambitions, and breaches of respectable behavior were met with ferocious condemnation.[9] Still, the decision that musicians should play without payment sanctioned an all-too-common expectation of musicians, and reflected the continuing weakness of the profession. As Percy Young wrote in the 1960s, "the idea that musicians should be prepared to work for nothing is a principle in English society not even yet quite buried."[10] The persistence of this principle in the early nineteenth century and its institutionalization by the members of the Philharmonic Society illustrate how far musicians were from understanding the requirements of professional status or autonomy.

Some of the numerous proposals for the reform of musical education contained incipient bids for professional control, but such efforts came to nothing. Although the establishment of the Royal Academy of Music in 1822 under aristocratic control dealt a blow to professional autonomy, it did inspire one musician to suggest extending the RAM's educational role to include licensing and increased control over professional standards. J. P. Burrowes, a composer and member of the Philharmonic Society, suggested that professional musicians, including RAM graduates, should be licensed or certified by fellow musicians. He "argued with considerable force . . . for the necessity of the erection of a board of examination, similar to that in the College of Surgeons, to certify the capacity of all musicians who might choose to present themselves. He proposed to extend such certifications to all the existing members of the profession who might solicit such a distinction."[11] The reference to the College of Surgeons confirms that Burrowes was thinking along the same lines as other emerging professions of the time. He insisted that certification should also be required of musicians who had studied at the RAM, arguing that "such means and such means only will give the academy its due weight and ascendancy."[12] In other words, a few wealthy and influential aristocratic patrons could found a musical academy, but only professionals themselves could certify that the results were acceptable.

Ultimately, however, this assertion of power by a professional musician in 1822 was unrealistic. He was undoubtedly correct to insist that professionals were better equipped than most patrons to judge colleagues' musical abilities. Success in musical careers was not based solely on musical skills, however, but was still determined by musicians' ability to obtain patronage – often from individuals whose musical choices sometimes depended on social as much as musical criteria.

Competing visions

Musicians' equivocal social and occupational identities inspired a variety of interpretations and recommendations, illustrating the volatility and lack of consensus within the profession. The following passage, from a musical periodical in 1824, contains a vehement middle-class critique of declining tastes and levels of education among aristocratic patrons. In a thinly veiled threat, the author urges music teachers to remind their aristocratic pupils of the necessity of maintaining a high level of taste if they are to retain influence as leaders of culture:

They [music teachers] should inculcate the necessity of high attainment to those whose *honour* as it were is concerned – they should demonstrate the certainty of contempt into which apathy and mediocrity lead – they should point out the fatal results which must attend the aristocracy, if they voluntarily bring themselves to so low an estimation, for it is by attainment chiefly that wealth can demonstrate its advantages.[13]

The same author went on to note that the education and the concerns that should characterize the highest classes were increasingly being taken over by less wealthy but otherwise better qualified groups. Ultimately, "the highest class becomes the most despicable and the most despised, and power of all sorts is transferred. That the society of England has of late been rapidly hastening to such a division, is I fear but too obvious."[14]

Although the prospect of middle-class political and cultural ascendancy was real enough, musicians were not yet in a position to threaten their patrons in this way. Even in negotiating terms of employment with other musicians, their potential for collective action was weak. This is demonstrated by the labor disagreement which occurred in 1828 between orchestral musicians and the King's Theatre management.[15] When the music director, the French harpist N. Bochsa, attempted to impose an unprecedented and harsh contract on the members of the orchestra, sixteen of them "seceded" from the orchestra. In part, the musicians objected to the new contract because it was a formal, written agreement that attempted to regulate their professional activities to an unprecedented extent:

The performers are at *all* times to be at the disposal of the manager, if required, (the performances of the Philharmonic Society and King's Concert excepted) and no other engagement to be accepted, without the express sanction of the manager, who is to consider "how far such indulgence may interfere with the business of the theatre, or how far it may tend to injure its interests."[16]

In addition, a new requirement was instituted concerning the number of performances and the pay, as follows: "Fifty operas to be given at the *usual* salaries. An unspecified number to be given on *half* salaries and three to be performed *gratis*."[17] Payments were to be made monthly instead of by the week, and the management reserved the right to enforce penalties and expulsions for infringements of the rules, especially absenteeism.

The musicians were outraged. The practice of taking other engagements on opera nights was considered both a financial necessity and a professional privilege. Furthermore, while some of them may have agreed to play without pay when a joint venture with colleagues was involved, these particular musicians were unwilling to do so for the Italian Opera. In a pamphlet written by the sixteen "seceders," they protested:

To play on any occasion for *half price* carries with it a degree of degradation, not only inimical to our feelings as men, but also (and surely it may be said without arrogance) unjust to our reputation as professors. What man of respectable feelings and decent circumstances would subscribe to laws that should leave him, for the time being, scarcely anything of personal liberty? to engage at a morning concert is forbidden, because an operatic rehearsal may be called; to engage at an evening concert is prohibited, because an extra opera may, by chance seem a safe speculation.[18]

There is little evidence as to how the dispute was resolved. Some suspected that the contract was intended to force the musicians to resign, so that they might be replaced with more malleable foreign performers. But there is no evidence that this took place.

It is noteworthy that the editor of the journal that helped to publicize the case insisted on the common interest of the two parties, commenting that the musicians had behaved "like the professors of a liberal art negociating with a person whose views, circumstances, and interests, were all drawn from the same common source with their own."[19] Although this was potentially a bitter dispute between parties with clearly conflicting interests, it was important to this editor, and to the musicians themselves, to assert that as professionals their interests were compatible with those of the management. The claim of professional status and independence is here. What is missing is the reality, the "comparative aloofness from the struggle for income"[20] that was essential for the established professional.

The mid-nineteenth century

A few years later, musicians launched another concert institution characterized by what was perhaps misguided egalitarianism. The Society of British Musicians was founded in 1834 to provide a showcase for native composers and performers and to assist them in their competition with foreign musicians. The strength of its claims to public patronage was weakened by the uneven quality and interest of the new works presented. An article in the *Musical Examiner* in 1843 criticized the managers' lack of discrimination between good and bad works:

[I]t is a mistake altogether ... to suppose that music and musicians, in this country, are to be benefited by indiscriminate encouragement. According to these well-intentioned but erroneously judging professors, it is the interest of the "Society of British Musicians" to publish to the world, without distinction, the works of all the members, be they meritorious or otherwise: this is called, *giving every one a chance* – one of the stupidest sophistries ever invented ... Mr. Willy (the Director) then, would have the "Society of British Musicians" consist of a thousand members, one and all of whom ... must be acknowledged men of ability and receive as much promotion ... as the most gifted musicians who adorn its ranks.[21]

Such responses to the threat posed by foreign musicians weakened musicians' willingness to establish professional institutions that would regulate entrance to and advancement in the profession, a crucial step in the attainment of professional autonomy and status. In this sense, the inclination of native musicians to support democratic, egalitarian organizations was a major handicap.

Throughout these ideological shifts and institutional experiments, musicians continued to face cultural prejudices and fears about music and musicians. In the 1820s, one writer complained of the prejudice "that the love or the practice of what they had been taught to esteem a frivolous pursuit, cannot consist with other attainments."[22] Another stated, "The defects of character which have hitherto depressed the practical musician in the public opinion, have been a laxity of morals and the want of literary attainment."[23] One musician regretted that "a sweeping anathema so often condemns the whole class of musicians for the striking immorality of the few."[24] And when H. J. Banister remarked in 1843 that there had been "a steady, favourable, progression in the general character, as well as professional attainments" of musicians,[25] he was merely trying to convince the public that it should not judge all musicians by the occasional gap they might encounter between social and musical attainments. As he explained, "Musical professors are gathered from *every* grade in society; and some there are, of high talent, whose conversation and manners are sources of painful regret or jesting to their patrons and admirers."[26] The failure of musicians to achieve even minimal social control over the membership of their profession ensured the persistence of such perceptions.

After the founding of the Society of British Musicians, egalitarian ideals seem to have disappeared from the solutions proposed by musicians. In 1833 the theatre composer G. H. B. Rodwell decided to combat the advantages foreign performers and composers enjoyed in their dealings with patrons and also with theatre managers. In his view, the nation's reputation was at stake. He decided to sidestep both the aristocracy and the public by appealing directly to the King. He was not the first musician to suggest making such an appeal. In 1822 a musical journalist had proposed that

considering the prejudices of the *fashionable world* in favor of foreign music and musicians, the patronage and cordial support of some one, whose influence might excite the attention, and whose liberality might draw forth the pecuniary aid of the wealthy, must be obtained. Where shall we look for such a one, but to the "Throne" itself.[27]

The author went on to suggest that a group of eminent musicians meet to consider what was the best way to enlist royal assistance for musicians – exactly what Rodwell did ten years later.

Rodwell's proposal was extremely specific, and the group of eminent musicians he chose to represent the cause was the Royal Society of Musicians, at one of whose meetings he read his address, later published as a pamphlet. First he described the plight of native musicians, specifically English dramatic composers:

Those theatres to which he [the English composer] might naturally look and hope for some little encouragement – namely, Drury Lane and Covent Garden, and the misnamed English Opera House – have for some years past closed their doors against native talent, being entirely devoted as regards the operatic department, to foreign music, and latterly, to foreign singers also.[28]

He pointed out how much more generously music was supported in France and elsewhere. Finally, he proposed that the King grant to the "Musicians of Great Britain" a patent for a "New Grand National Opera." The King would also, presumably, finance the early stages of the institution. The

Directors of the Opera would receive fixed salaries plus an undetermined percentage of the profits. The authors and composers would divide among themselves 12 percent of the gross nightly receipts. Rodwell did not detail expenses such as the wages of actors, singers, and orchestral musicians, or the expenses for sets, costumes, and music. He assumed, however, that there would be profits left over, and these were to be divided between the Royal Society of Musicians, the New Musical Fund, the Choral Fund, and the Royal Academy of Music by a complicated system based on the number of claimants (or students) each institution supported. Furthermore, there would be two benefit concerts a year, the proceeds of which were to go into an Accumulating Fund for the support of the Opera.

Intended to sidestep the prejudices of aristocratic patrons, the plan was limited by its naiveté, its ignorance of the interests and limitations of the institutions upon which it depended, and its unrealistic appraisal of theatre finances. The Royal Academy of Music seems incongruous as a beneficiary of the opera's profits, while the inclusion of the three benefit societies turns a supposedly artistic project into a charitable venture. Rodwell's plan was even more deeply flawed, however, by its obsession with foreign competition. The successful competition of foreign musicians was indeed a highly visible and depressing feature of the musical scene. But just as important were the perhaps less overt but pervasive fears and prejudices about music as an activity inconsistent with middle-class values and the concomitant questions that always surrounded musicians' social status and respectability. As will be shown, only solutions that both offered uncompromising respectability and involved joining forces with foreign musicians were likely to succeed.

The cellist H. J. Banister, unlike Rodwell, tended to view musicians' problems primarily in terms of social status, giving much less emphasis to professional autonomy. In 1843 he published a pamphlet entitled *Domestic Music for the Wealthy; or, A Plea for the Art and its Professors*. By that time, rank and file orchestral musicians were unaccustomed to personal aristocratic patronage, and Banister proposed that aristocrats should support musicians as if this were a novel and original idea: "their doing so would exhibit a new feature in social economy, beneficial to the art, advantageous to all parties concerned, and, therefore, much to be desired."[29] He suggested several options varying in size, grandeur, and expense. It is noteworthy that all of them included attitudes of extreme deference from musicians to their patrons, as well as a willingness to perform with amateurs. In fact, the promise that amateurs could play with professionals was one of the enticements offered to patrons for the most ambitious scheme, suitable for only the wealthiest aristocrats: a chamber band of twenty to twenty-five orchestral musicians, the cost of which was estimated to be £3,000 a year.[30] Another plan Banister suggested was that a group of aristocrats or other wealthy patrons share the cost of putting together a fine orchestra. He argued that if the best professionals were hired, the venture might even prove to be a good investment:

[I]t is more than possible a band *well chosen*, numerous, effective, and *laboriously trained*, might be a good speculation on the part of a proprietary body, who should undertake their constant employment for public performances. Were the thing well done, every item of detail fully carried out, competition, perhaps, would be impossible.[31]

In general, however, Banister preferred the image of aristocrats expecting only a musical return on their investments.

For the aristocratic patron who was not willing or able to pay £3,000 a year, Banister suggested a smaller ensemble for performance and instruction, costing between £250 and £500 a year. He particularly liked the idea of an aristocratic family hiring one musician to supervise all of their musical needs: a "musician-in-ordinary" who would instruct family members during the day and perform for them in the evening. He argued that in a family with many daughters, the engagement of numerous teachers could be very expensive, but "an engagement might be with a professor for two or three hours' service per day, at a salary of from £80 to £130 per year, which should be far more efficient and less costly than the present system."[32]

Banister's fantasy of the household musician and the wealthy family necessitated that he address recurring themes of musicians' relatively low social status and lack of social graces or wider educational attainments. He emphasized how important it was to remove these personal shortcomings in order to deserve and attain an acceptable social and professional position:

An hour each evening is appropriated to the professor's performance. He enters, and mixes unconstrainedly with a circle of which, by adoption, he has become a member. He has had the sense, since the first establishment of his connection with the family, to improve his general attainments by diligent self-culture; for, being a man of sensibility, a consciousness of inferiority had originally made him sad, uneasy, and awkward. That day is departed; he has won general esteem by his good conduct and understanding; and, for his professional attainments and services, is looked up to as a patient instructor, the skilful illustrator, and the source of continual gratification to all.[33]

Note the emphasis on individual, as opposed to collective, mobility in this proposal. The goals of professional autonomy and independence are completely absent here, replaced by dependence on an anachronistic and idealized personal patronage relationship. Written in 1843, this passage illustrates the persistence of social over professional aspirations for many musicians.

In contrast to the anachronistic ideals of Banister's proposal, John Ella's concert series, the Musical Union, relied on the social and professional status of a few elite musicians and cultivated patrons.[34] Ella was a respected violinist at institutions including the King's Theatre, the Philharmonic Society, and the Concert of Ancient Music through the 1820s and 1830s, and he joined the RSM in 1825. The Musical Union, which he founded in 1845, was modeled in part on the small string quartet concerts that had begun a few years earlier (see chapter 7). Managed by well-respected native musicians, these small concerts had been highly distinguished musical, if not social, events. Ella, who was both extremely self-confident and socially ambitious, added social exclusiveness to the musical pretensions of the earlier chamber music concerts in his plans for the Musical Union, which was essentially a club. Tickets were not sold publicly; only members and their families could attend. The Committee consisted of wealthy patrons, many of them aristocratic, led by the Duke of Cambridge as President, and the Earl of Westmorland as Vice-President. Audiences were aristocratic and upper-middle-class. Even critics were excluded with the exception of "gentlemen of musical literary attainments, known to the Committee or Director."[35] Carefully selected professional musicians had the opportunity to hobnob with such elite audiences by receiving complimentary tickets.[36]

Ella's requirements for the Director of such a society were expressed very clearly. It was necessary for the Director to possess both broad cultural attainments and social skills, all of which Ella believed to be rare in professional musicians:

It is often the bane of amateur societies to be subject to the control and dictum of an officious member, whose musical qualifications in nowise render him a proper person for the assumed dictatorial capacity: or, it frequently happens that accident brings into the employ of a society of amateurs one of those mere practical and executive professional fiddlers, whose ignorance and whose notions of art are only on a level with the vulgarity of their manners.[37]

Not surprisingly, Ella shared the beliefs of those professional musicians who viewed the status of the "mere fiddler" with dismay, and insisted that musicians should be more broadly educated.[38] He clearly viewed himself as the ideal Director of concerts given by elite professionals for elite amateurs, i.e. one who combined both musical and social skills.

The success of the Musical Union was due to several important social, artistic, and professional policies. First, it welcomed wealthy, preferably aristocratic patrons as fellow connoisseurs of fine music. Second, it rejected public audiences and public taste by aiming for a small, dedicated audience who would listen to less familiar, less accessible chamber works. And finally, it buttressed these policies by inviting only the most able and best-known performers. The last policy brought Ella into direct conflict with his British colleagues because it renounced all pretense to egalitarianism and welcomed foreign musicians as fellow elite professionals.

Of course, the egalitarianism that characterized the early years of the Philharmonic Society had disappeared long before this. The Philharmonic Society had become the scene of factions and professional infighting during the 1830s and 1840s, particularly over the issue of foreign competition. Professional xenophobia had progressed to the point where some foreign guest artists were not welcomed as soloists at the Philharmonic concerts.[39] Ella reported that the pianist, Leopold de Meyer, for example, was not "allowed" to play at the Philharmonic concerts, although he was featured in the Musical Union concerts. It was apparently this issue that led Ella and other orchestra members to resign or to be expelled from the Philharmonic Society. As a result, the first program of the Musical Union included the following scathing attack on the Philharmonic's reigning factions and prejudices:

[T]hose members possessing the least talent and acquirement in their art, but endowed with the most cunning in worldly matters, attempted to conceal their incapacity and weakness by their connection with the society; veiled by its reputation and power, they assumed a most insufferable consequence and importance; by these parties have men of superior talent and abilities been subjected to insult and degradation at the ballot ... while others, matchless alone in stupidity and ignorance, have been triumphantly elected; ... to such an extent have the Philharmonic conferred their favours upon dulness, to the exclusion of all that is good, great, or excellent, that the society is becoming a worthless vessel manned with decrepid mariners, and o'erloaded with useless ballast.[40]

Ella made such a point of rejecting the xenophobia of his colleagues as to tally the numbers of foreign and native musicians who performed during the first season of the Musical Union, with the following results: "12 English, 7 French, 6 German, 3 Italians, 2 Belgians, 1 Spaniard." He was eager to point out that this result was the random outcome of a policy of choosing the best – English musicians such as the pianists Lucy Anderson and William Sterndale Bennett, and foreigners including the French violinists Prosper P. C. Sainton and Henri Vieuxtemps. The policies of the Musical Union to welcome foreigners and to make clear distinctions of professional ability were counter to the policies of the leading native musical cliques at that time.

One might expect Rodwell, Banister, and Ella to have identified with a highly professional ideal for musicians. As it was, while Rodwell was concerned with professional status and independence, he focused primarily on foreign competition, and appealed too narrowly to royal patronage as a way of sidestepping aristocratic indifference. By contrast, H. J. Banister is a perfect example of the persistent idealization of traditional patronage relationships. His astonishingly deferential tone and aspirations completely ignored ideals of professional autonomy and self-regulation. Ella's experiment offered a third model. The Musical Union relied on the collaboration of the most successful foreign and native musicians, and managed to combine elite colleagues and wealthy, cultured patrons. Such concerts were a solution only for the elite few among musicians, however, and accomplished little for the collective upward mobility or growing professional independence of musicians as a group.

Although not founded to remedy the status of music and the profession, one organization offers another perspective on the strategies employed by musicians to rally patronage and support. In 1839 the singer and composer Elizabeth Masson attempted to gain admittance to the hitherto all-male RSM. Although the RSM had enjoyed the gratuitous performance of women musicians at its annual benefit concerts for decades, it refused to consider revising its laws in order to admit women. In response Masson founded one of the earliest of a growing number of organizations for working women in Victorian England, the Royal Society of Female Musicians. She prepared a circular that stated clearly the intention to run an organization parallel to the RSM in purpose and design. The circular was signed by eighteen professional women musicians, sent to one hundred others, and published in the weekly *Musical World*. Masson acted swiftly to gain the highest patrons for the society, and to initiate annual benefit concerts to raise funds. In September of that year, she solicited help from Queen Victoria, who within a week agreed to become the Society's patroness and contributed twenty guineas, with a subsequent promise of ten guineas to be donated annually. Noble patrons followed suit. During the next twenty-six years the Society included many of the leading female musicians of the day, and through its annual concerts established a visible and elite presence on the musical scene. The concerts generally included foreign and native musicians, and appear to have been fashionable, and financially successful, ventures. In 1866, the substantial wealth amassed by the Society was welcomed, along with its members, into the RSM.[41]

The RSFM might seem to have little in common with Ella's Musical Union. The concerts occurred only once a year and were benefits to support a charitable cause. Certainly the focus on protecting destitute musicians constituted one of the long-standing challenges to both the perception and the reality of middle-class professional status for musicians. The concert programs did not have the high-brow, "connoisseurs-only" stamp of Ella's concerts. But there are some common elements, namely the cultivation of patrons from the highest social levels, and the collaboration of elite foreign and native performers. The founders of the RSFM gravitated to this successful formula around the same time as some of the early quartet concert series, and several years before the founding of the Musical Union. It is clear that, outside the mainstream of the predominantly male musical profession, the RSFM offered an ingenious combination of charitable mission and professional savvy.

Conclusion

The dramatic social and economic changes of the late eighteenth and early nineteenth centuries were a crucible for professional aspirations and opportunities. In many cases new or recast professions emerged with higher status and greater autonomy. But musicians in the years from 1750 to 1850 did not achieve the autonomy or the collective mobility necessary for professional status. By the mid-nineteenth century, the music profession had emerged in fragments, albeit larger and more clearly discernible fragments than had been evident in the eighteenth century. Those parts of the profession that benefited from these changes – teachers, organists, some instrumentalists and chamber musicians – jealously guarded their own status and respectability from the members whose education, character, manners, or economic status continued to uphold less desirable stereotypes of musicians (such as the "mere fiddler"). Other musicians – orchestral instrumentalists, theatre musicians – continued to inhabit a "profession of artisans."

Furthermore, the essential social value of music had not been established, and the moral character of musicians remained suspect. As W. J. Reader explains, "It was evident that some actors, some artists, some authors, and some musicians were educated, cultured men (and women), and it was well known that they were welcomed, even sought after, in the best society. It was equally well known that the majority were not."[42] This appraisal is fully supported by the description of the musical profession given in H. Byerley Thomson's 1857 guide to the professions. Although he recognized the important distinctions between the social origins, education and professional status of theoretical musicians on the one hand, and performers such as theatre musicians on the other,[43] he also recognized the degree to which this very diversity in the profession kept it from achieving a middle-class social and professional status:

Of all terms indicative of a profession, that of music is, perhaps, the most undefined and vague. We are told of one that he is in the church, the law, or in medicine, and we immediately assign to him a certain position in the social scale. Not so, however, with the musician. He may be, for aught we know, an itinerant fiddler, and of the lowest grade of society; or a man of the highest attainments, moving in the most exclusive circles, and occupying an exalted position in the literary world.[44]

He explained that the professional disadvantages caused by the social diversity of the profession were due to the profession's inability to regulate its membership, reinforcing a vicious circle that was the major obstacle to any aspiring profession. Thomson also believed, however, that as long as music was considered to be of minor or nonexistent social value, the social and professional status desired by musicians would remain elusive:

Undefined indeed, is the status of the musician; nor can this be a matter of much surprise, since, unlike the professions above named, that of music is altogether unprotected. Its portals are open to all who choose to enter. And thus it must continue to be, until this beautiful science and art (for it is both) shall cease to be regarded as a mere accomplishment, and until it shall be replaced in the position it once occupied, both in this country and on the continent... As yet, however, the musician, in the minds of many, scarcely ranks above an ordinary artizan, even let him be ever so talented, or his character ever so irreproachable.[45]

Attorneys struggled for many decades to overcome similar prejudices, ultimately abandoning the name "attorney" altogether because of its association with low social origins and unscrupulous ethics. Musicians, however, remained more morally suspect than attorneys, at least in part because of their association with entertainment, tavern singing-clubs, and theatrical lowlife. Despite the essential place that music held in the performance of the Anglican cathedral service, the decline of that role and the growth of secular musical activities supported the notion that music was, at best, merely a form of entertainment.

Paradoxically, at least as an amateur pursuit especially for the working classes, music became increasingly associated with morality.[46] Considered a preferred alternative to other less savory recreations, music seemed to offer solutions to larger social concerns. *Music and Morals* by the Reverend Hugh Haweis is the best known expression of this attitude, but the theme recurred in other writings as well. Large choral societies, the brass-band movement, and efforts to improve musical education all illustrate this shift.[47] As a professional pursuit for middle-class men, however, the old suspicions lingered.[48]

In sum, musicians' hopes of achieving middle-class professional status were thwarted by the day-to-day realities of economic survival, the competition of foreign musicians, and the persistence of damaging cultural perceptions. The persistence of economic insecurity in musical careers meant that achievement of middle-class status at one point in a musician's career was little guarantee of retaining that status or attaining longer-term social mobility. The wide range of career patterns ("mere fiddlers" vs. "musical graduates," church musicians vs. theatre players) meant that some musicians would always fall short of the social qualifications for membership of the middle class. The prevalence and success of foreign musicians perhaps received the most attention in contemporary writings. Although Rodwell and other musicians thought that patriotic resistance to the affinity of patrons for foreign musicians was the answer, such resistance was never successful.

Perhaps the most serious obstacle to the achievement of unequivocal professional status, although the least understood and discussed at the time, was the long-standing association of music with femininity. This association was reinforced by the role of music as an amateur accomplishment for women, and the presence of women within the profession itself. As has been shown, British society at the time was rife with anxieties about gender roles linked with social class, political power, and national identity. But unlike other aspiring professions (apothecaries, surgeons, engineers, attorneys), not to mention the traditional professions (law, medicine, and divinity), male musicians had to share their turf with women. Although the governors of the RSM had tried to maintain its manly, professional demeanor and exclusiveness by refusing Elizabeth Masson's request in 1839, they could not change the reality of their profession's more complex landscape. The ultimate failure of musicians to coalesce into a unified, autonomous profession was largely due to such issues.

The social, economic, and cultural pressures on musicians may have led them to focus more intently on social status and professional prestige than on musical aspirations. They were undoubtedly diverted by the cultural prejudices which questioned the respectability, masculinity, and even the Britishness of music and musicians. The achievement of professional status required a regular affirmation of larger cultural values, and a soothing of underlying anxieties about the stability of the political and social order, which depended in turn on preserving British mores, specifically in relation to gender roles and behavior. This complex of competing professional and cultural ideals and realities may help to explain the paradox presented by a century of British musical life, in which enthusiastic pursuit of music coexisted with a fragmented, often demoralized, and creatively depressed musical profession. A more confident generation of musicians would emerge only in the later Victorian age.

Epilogue

The second half of the nineteenth century saw real advances, although with increasing fragmentation of the profession. The respectability of careers in church music remained an advantage, although they never achieved the superior status they had once enjoyed relative to the rest of the profession. Foreign musicians continued to travel to Britain, particularly as instrumental and vocal soloists. Many organists and teachers chose to build practices in the provinces or abroad (particularly in America), where they appear to have enjoyed a prestige comparable to that of Continental musicians in Britain.

Although many musicians failed to attain a respectable social or financial status, some of the most virulent prejudices against their characters seem to have abated in the second half of the century. Reginald Nettel attributed this in part to the influence of Mendelssohn, who was idolized by the musical public for his personality as much as for his music.[1] Nettel also argued that the musical patronage exerted by the Prince Consort influenced "public opinion towards a more favourable acceptance of musicians in society."[2] A contemporary observer, Francis Hueffer, noted some status gains and similarly attributed them to royal influence. He reported in 1889 that the worst kinds of prejudice and ignorance about music had become less widespread than in earlier years:

This stolid obtuseness, formerly so common, can no longer be laid to the charge of intelligent Englishmen; and that this is so, and that musicians are no longer separated from the rest of society by the barriers which of old at fashionable parties took the tangible shape of a cord dividing the professionals from the rest of the company, is in no small measure due to the enlightened encouragement of art and artists by the reigning sovereign.[3]

Several new institutions for professional training sprang up in the next decades: Trinity College, founded in 1872 (initially to train choirmasters); the National Training School for Music, founded in 1873 (replaced by the Royal College of Music in 1882); and the Guildhall School of Music, founded in 1880.[4] These schools were professionally managed and provided increasingly important credentials, especially for teachers. The Royal College of Organists, founded in 1864, offered examinations and licensing for organists.[5] Secular performers – both foreign and native – remained more difficult to license.

The first organization of musicians with professional goals and characteristics (other than the schools) was the Society of Professional Musicians, founded in 1882. This organization began not in London but in Lancashire, where its influence spread for several years before an attempt was made to bring in London musicians. Its goals were

the union of the musical profession in a representative body; the provision of opportunities for the discussion of matters connected with the culture and practice of the art; the improvement of musical education; the organisation of musicians in a manner similar to that in which other learned professions were organised; and the obtaining of legal recognition by means of the registration of qualified teachers of music as a distinctive body.[6]

The membership grew to include groups in Yorkshire and the Midlands, and, in 1896, London musicians as well. In 1892 the Society was renamed the Incorporated Society of Musicians.

Two characteristics of this society illustrate the ongoing ambiguities of the professional status of musicians. The Incorporated Society, as a professional organization with powers of licensing and registration, was largely restricted to music teachers who continued to be more socially respectable than many performers. At the same time, the Society did not completely divorce itself from the charitable goals of earlier organizations. Many of the regional groups appear to have had Benevolent Funds for needy musicians, and in 1897 the Society took responsibility for an already established Orphanage for the Children of Musicians.

Another professional organization, the Union of Graduates in Music, was founded in 1893. It began at a meeting held at the Royal College of Organists with the objective of protecting "the interests of those who hold genuine musical degrees, and to counteract the influence of various schemers in different parts of the empire who supplied bogus 'degrees' for a slight pecuniary payment, making few or no inquiries into the capabilities of those who bought the distinction."[7] As was also true of the Incorporated Society of Musicians, the Union's role was greater for the teaching branch of the profession, where degrees had become widely accepted as credentials. While degrees certainly conferred status for performers, they were not essential for employment.

Although it could be argued that these developments are clear indications of an improvement in status for the profession as a whole, the advances were enjoyed for the most part by music teachers, whose status was raised considerably in this way. Performers, particularly orchestral instrumentalists and all musicians affiliated with theatres, continued to suffer from low wages and low social status. This is illustrated by the types of organizations they founded, as outlined in Charles Booth's *Life and Labour of the People in London* (1902–4). He pointed out that while successful soloists, or performers who were publicly recognized, were unlikely candidates for trade associations, "amongst those who are not so directly the objects of popular attention, there is a growing feeling in favour of united action."[8] He cited the Theatrical and Music Hall Operatives as the only actual trade union among this group, but also mentioned that

the Orchestral Association with 1,100 members, and the Theatrical Choristers' Association with 650 members, have much in common with ordinary trade societies. Though professedly established to take over the duties of agents without expense to members, to give legal aid, and for educational purposes, each of these institutions tries to establish a recognized minimum wage for their members, and so far they have been fairly successful.[9]

It is noteworthy that even in this stratum of the profession, musicians remained loath to give up what was for them a fiction of professional status and independence. In addition, there were numerous benefit societies for musical and theatrical performers. Booth listed the following: "the Royal General Theatrical Fund (1822); the Actors' Benevolent Fund (1882); the Music Hall Benevolent Fund (1888); the Music Hall Provident Sick Fund; the General Theatrical Operatives' Sick and Benevolent Society (1870); and the British and Foreign Musicians' Society (1822)."[10] He also noted that many of the theatres had their own sick clubs. The Royal Society of Musicians is absent from the list, probably because it had become relatively small and exclusive by this time. In sum, the lower-status orchestral and theatre musicians appear to a great extent to have been excluded from the more prestigious institutions, and were instead affiliated with benefit associations that increasingly resembled labor unions.

Although the growing status of teachers and some performers was real, the profession as a whole was held back by the uneven advances of different groups. Music did not attain clear recognition as a unified profession, and some of the old prejudices still surrounded the lower-status branches. In 1870, a guide to the professions for parents and their sons expressed predictable social and moral apprehensions about the arts in general. It completely omitted musicians, included only a brief section on painters, and said of aspiring writers: "Better, morally and physically, to live in any street but Grub street, which is overcrowded till there is hardly any breathing space, and where the conditions of tenancy are often incompatible with self-respect."[11] In 1880, T. H. S. Escott also noted the moral suspicions aroused by the world of the arts: "The keen-scented, eminently decorous British public perceives a certain aroma of social and moral laxity in the atmosphere of the studio, a kind of blended perfume of periodical impecuniosity and much tobacco-smoke."[12]

The first major study of the British professions, Carr-Saunders and Wilson's *The Professions* (1933), illustrates the long-standing misunderstandings about music as a profession. Musicians, authors, playwrights, and actors together take up only a page and a half of this book, and the brief space allotted to them contains some astonishingly inaccurate remarks, especially about music.[13] Carr-Saunders and Wilson did grant a kind of professional status to authors, composers, and playwrights, because they belonged to "the class of intellectual workers," although the fact that they employed "the aesthetic faculty" made them less professional. They admitted that this was true of architects as well, but they made the extraordinary claim that only architects – not authors, composers, or playwrights – "require ... an intellectual technique, which can be learnt and tested." They noted the wide range of abilities and status among musicians: "there are interpreters of great talent or even of genius, and at the other end of the scale there are performers in poorly paid orchestras." Despite the great talent of some performers, however, neither actors nor musical performers ranked as professionals, on the grounds that they did not require "any considerable formal training." They went on to note as exceptions the musicians who did receive extensive training and certification – teachers and organists (the traditionally more respectable branches of the profession). In sum, they expressed the belief that music was a profession only in a marginal sense. That such misconceptions of the nature of music as an art and as a profession could be contained in this major work is testimony to the negative perceptions that musicians continued to encounter.

Appendix

The social categories in table 21 (overleaf) are taken from Colquhoun's tables of national income distribution for 1806, and to a lesser extent from Perkin's adaptation of the same tables.[1] Colquhoun's categories were selected because they convey both occupational and social meanings and because they also provide income estimates. In order to use the occupations of musicians' relatives as an indication of musicians' social origins, the occupational names had to be interpreted with regard to social and economic level. In most cases it was not difficult to categorize the occupations, although there were some exceptions. For example, the description a "respectable cutlery manufacturer" suggests that the individual had both capital and employees, and so is listed with the manufacturers. Another, described simply as a "cutler," is less clear, and was classified as an artisan/laborer. The following table shows how each occupational name encountered in the primary sources as a description of the relative of a professional musician has been allocated to one of the Colquhoun/Perkin social and occupational categories.

Table 21. *Classification of occupations of musicians' relatives*

Colquhoun/Perkin categories	Annual income (£)	Occupational names
I. Aristocracy (nobles and other titled persons)	700–3,000	
II. Middle ranks		
1. Agriculture		
Farmers	120	farmer; dairyman
2. Industry and commerce		
Eminent merchants	2,600	merchant; rich tea merchant and M.P.; bank manager
Lesser merchants	800	wine merchant and dancing master; music publisher; wine merchant
Manufacturers	800	respectable cutlery manufacturer; plate-glass manufacturer; lace manufacturer
Shipbuilders	700	shipbuilder
Surveyors, engineers	200	builder and contractor; civil engineer; land and mine agent, and surveyor; harbour-master
Independent artisans[2]	150	eyeglass manufacturer and optician; gold and silver engraver; harp manufacturer
Shopkeepers, and tradesmen in goods	150	bookseller; butcher; butcher and grazier; confectioner; dealer in soda water; haberdasher and hosier; haberdasher; hosier and glover; grocer; grocer and tallow chandler; music seller; stationer; tavern-keeper and pugilist; tobacconist; wood dealer
Clerks, shopmen	75	accountant; clerk; salesman
3. Professions		
Civil offices (1)	800	alderman; British Consul at Venice; Clerk of the Papers to the House of Lords; excise officer; government official; government offical in a colony; Lieutenant-Colonel in East India service; Middlesex judge
Civil offices (2)	200	
Law	350	attorney; barrister; solicitor
Clergy[3]	120–500	clergyman
Education	150–600	dancing master; dancing master and wine merchant
Army and naval officers	139–149	army captain; army officer; Chelsea pensioner; colonel; general; naval officer; navy captain (royal yacht); quartermaster; sergeant; soldier
Medicine	260	barber-surgeon; doctor; physician; surgeon

Table 21. (*cont.*)

Colquhoun/Perkin categories	Annual income (£)	Occupational names
Visual arts	260	architect; architect and sculptor; marine painter; miniature painter; painter; portrait painter; sculptor
Literature and letters	260	dramatist; dramatist and actress; dramatist, actor and journalist; dramatist and poet; editor, journalist, and essayist; historian; librettist; novelist; poet; scientist; writer about music
Theatre[4]	200	actor or actress; actor/comedian; circus performer; concert impresario; musician; prompter at a theatre; theatre manager
III. Lower orders		
Artisans/laborers[5]	55	baker; blacksmith; bootmaker; bread and biscuit baker; bricklayer; builder; cabinet maker; cabriole chair and sofa manufacturer; carpenter; carpenter, joiner and undertaker; carver; carver and gilder; coach painter; cordwainer; cutler; dairyman; dressmaker; dressmaker and milliner; embroideress; engraver; engraver on metal; fringe maker; glass stainer; glazier; gold embroiderer; hairdresser and wig maker; hairdresser and perfumer; hosier; juvenile clothing maker; lace and fringe maker; mantua maker; mason; military cap maker; milliner; milliner and baby-linen maker; milliner, dress and corset maker; monumental mason; needlewoman; painter, plumber, and glazier; shoebinder; shoemaker; stonemason; tailor; tailor and draper; tailor's cutter; tin-plate worker; upholsterer
Seamen	38–40	seaman
Soldiers	29	soldier
Laborers[6]	31–40	artificial flower maker; calico glazier; coach driver; gardener; joiner; lighterman; mechanic; silk weaver; spinner in a cotton mill; waterman
Domestic servants		butler; female domestic; nursemaid; valet de chambre (Dresden)

INTRODUCTION

1 Classic studies include E. D. Mackerness, *A Social History of English Music* (London, 1964); Walter Woodfill, *Musicians in English Society from Elizabeth to Charles I* (Princeton, 1953); William Weber, *Music and the Middle Class: The Social Structure of Concert Life in London, Paris and Vienna* (New York, 1975); and the more general works by Henry Raynor, *A Social History of Music, from the Middle Ages to Beethoven* (New York, 1972) and *Music and Society since 1815* (New York 1976). The emphases in these works continue to be reflected in the British chapters in the important series *Man and Music* (known in the US as *Music and Society*), ed. Stanley Sadie. These chapters expand the social and institutional context for music well beyond patronage.

2 "The production of ideas, of conceptions, of consciousness, is at first directly interwoven with the material activity and the material intercourse of men, the language of real life." Karl Marx and Friedrich Engels, "The German Ideology," in Robert Tucker (ed.), *The Marx-Engels Reader* (New York, 1972), p. 118.

3 For a discussion of this historiographical tradition, see Peter Burke, *The French Historical Revolution: The Annales School, 1929–89* (Cambridge, 1990).

4 For the origins of this term, see the discussion in the *Musical Times*: Bernarr Rainbow, 106/1468 (June 1965), 446; Charles Cudworth, 106/1469 (July 1965), 524; Ernest Bradbury, 106/1472 (October 1965), 776–77.

5 For a useful historiographical survey of this question, see Nicholas Temperley, "Xenophilia in British Musical History," in Bennett Zon, ed., *Nineteenth-Century British Music Studies* (Aldershot, 1999), pp. 3–19.

6 For the evolution of the concept of *mentalités*, see Burke, *The French Historical Revolution*.

7 Lawrence Stone, "Prosopography," *Daedalus* 100 (1971), 46–79; a revised discussion of the technique can be found in his *The Past and the Present Revisited* (London, 1987), where he writes that "In the last forty years collective biography (as the modern historians call it), multiple career-line analysis (as the social scientists call it), or prosopography (as the ancient historians call it) has developed into one of the most valuable and most familiar techniques of the research historian" (p. 45). For an example of this technique applied to the history of science, see Arnold Thackray, "Natural Knowledge in Cultural

Context: The Manchester Model," *American Historical Review* 79 (1974), 672–709.

8 See Cyril Ehrlich, *The Music Profession in Britain since the Eighteenth Century: A Social History* (Oxford, 1985) and *First Philharmonic: A History of the Royal Philharmonic Society* (Oxford, 1995); Simon McVeigh, *Concert Life in London from Mozart to Haydn* (Cambridge, 1993); William Weber, *The Rise of Musical Classics in Eighteenth-Century England: A Study in Canon, Ritual, and Ideology* (Oxford, 1992); Zon, ed., *Nineteenth-Century British Music Studies*; and many other more specialized works.

9 Patrick Curry, "Towards a Post-Marxist Social History: Thompson, Clark and beyond," in Adrian Wilson, ed., *Rethinking Social History: English Society 1570–1920 and its Interpretation* (Manchester, 1993), pp. 158–200.

10 Peter Burke and Roy Porter, eds., *The Social History of Language* (Cambridge, 1987) and Penelope Corfield, ed., *Language, History and Class* (Oxford, 1991).

11 Adrian Wilson, "A Critical Portrait of Social History," in Wilson, ed., *Rethinking Social History*, pp. 21–23; Joan Wallach Scott, *Gender and the Politics of History* (New York, 1988); Juliet Gardiner, "What Is Women's History?" chapter 7 of Gardiner, ed., *What Is History Today?* (Atlantic Highlands, N.J., 1988).

12 While the history of *mentalités* had always incorporated the material conditions of life to some extent, later French historians such as Georges Duby and Michel Vovelle attempted specifically to integrate the approach with a Marxian concept of ideology, and with attention to social and economic contexts. Burke, *The French Historical Revolution*, p. 73.

13 Simon McVeigh notes the "sudden explosion of concert activity" in the early 1750s, although the full flowering of new tastes and institutions occurred in the early 1780s. *Concert Life,* pp. xiv, 7.

14 "Women and the Music Profession in Victorian England: The Royal Society of Female Musicians, 1839–1866," *Journal of Musicological Research* 18 (1999), 307–46.

1   THE SOCIAL AND PROFESSIONAL STATUS OF MUSICIANS IN THE EIGHTEENTH CENTURY

1 Penelope Corfield, "Class by Name and Number in Eighteenth-Century Britain," in Corfield, ed., *Language, History and Class*, pp. 101–30; M. L. Bush, ed., *Social Orders and Social Classes in Europe since 1500: Studies in Social Stratification* (London, 1992), especially Peter Burke, "The Language of Orders in Early Modern Europe," pp. 1–12, William Reddy, "The Concept of Class," pp. 13–25, and John Seed, "From 'Middling Sort' to Middle Class in Late Eigheenth- and Early Nineteenth-Century England," pp. 114–35; and Peter Earle, "The Middling Sort in London," in Jonathan Barry and Christopher Brooks, eds., *The Middling Sort of People: Culture, Society and Politics in England, 1550–1800* (New York, 1994), pp. 141–58.

2 Seed, "From 'Middling Sort' to Middle Class," p. 125.

3 R. S. Neale, "Class and Class Consciousness in Early Nineteenth-Century England: Three Classes or Five?," *Class and Ideology in the Nineteenth Century*

(London, 1972), pp. 15–40.

4 Seed, "From 'Middling Sort' to Middle Class," p. 127.

5 See also Ehrlich, *The Music Profession.*

6 Christopher Brooks, "Professions, Ideology and the Middling Sort in the Late Sixteenth and Early Seventeenth Centuries," in Barry and Brooks, eds., *The Middling Sort of People*, pp. 113–40; and Wilfred Prest, ed., *The Professions in Early Modern England* (London, 1987).

7 W. J. Reader, *Professional Men* (London, 1966), pp. 9–10.

8 Brooks, "Professions, Ideology and the Middling Sort," p. 119.

9 Reader, *Professional Men*, p. 21.

10 Penelope Corfield, *Power and the Professions in Britain, 1700–1850* (London, 1995); M. S. Larson, *The Rise of Professionalism: A Sociological Analysis* (Berkeley, 1977); Geoffrey Millerson, *The Qualifying Associations: A Study in Professionalization* (London, 1964); Howard M. Vollmer and Donald L. Mills, eds., *Professionalization* (Englewood Cliffs, N.J., 1966).

11 Larson, *The Rise of Professionalism*, see especially pp. xii, xvi–xvii, 14–15.

12 Prest, *The Professions in Early Modern England*, p. 83.

13 Robert Robson, *The Attorney in Eighteenth-Century England* (Cambridge, 1959), pp. 22–24.

14 Jeremy Black, ed., *Culture and Society in Britain, 1660–1800* (Manchester, 1997), p. 18.

15 Harold Perkin, *The Origins of Modern English Society, 1780–1880* (Toronto, 1972), pp. 270, 319–39.

16 Reader, *Professional Men*, p. 203.

17 *Ibid.*, p. 159.

18 See J. H. Plumb, "The Commercialization of Leisure," in Neil McKendrick, John Brewer, and J. H. Plumb, *The Birth of a Consumer Society: The Commercialization of Eighteenth-Century England* (Bloomington, Ind., 1982), pp. 265–85.

19 "Sketch of the State of Music in London," *QMMR* 11 (1821), 399.

20 Patrick Colquhoun, *A Treatise on Indigence* (London, 1806), pp. 23–24.

21 Reader, *Professional Men*, p. 164.

22 *Ibid.*, p. 165.

23 Pippa Drummond, "The Royal Society of Musicians in the Eighteenth Century," *Music and Letters* 59 (1978), 268–89; Betty Matthews, *The Royal Society of Musicians of Great Britain, List of Members 1738–1984* (London, 1985). A centuries-old guild organization had long since lost any real connection with professional musicians. See H. A. F. Crewdson, *A Short History of the Worshipful Company of Musicians* (London, 1971 [1950]) and Ehrlich, *The Music Profession*, pp. 26–27.

24 "The Royal Society of Musicians of Great Britain," leaflet, available from the RSM, based on an article in the *Musical Times* of April 1958. The leaflet was printed by Novello & Co.

25 See Corfield, *Power and the Professions in Britain*, pp. 184–85.

26 Kristina Straub, *Sexual Suspects: Eighteenth-Century Players and Sexual Ideology* (Princeton, 1992), pp. 90–91.

27 Timotheus, "Vocal Science – of the Chamber," *QMMR* 6 (1820), 131.

28 *Musical World*, April 11, 1839, 222.

29 Linda Colley, *Britons: Forging the Nation 1707–1837* (New Haven, 1992), pp. 248, 250.

30 See also Ehrlich, *The Music Profession*, pp. 16–19.

31 Lowell Lindgren, "Handel's London: Italian Musicians and Librettists," in Donald Burrows, ed., *The Cambridge Companion to Handel* (Cambridge, 1997), pp. 80–81.

32 Daniel Defoe, *Augusta Triumphans; or, The Way to Make London the Most Flourishing City in the Universe* (London, 1728), p. 17.

33 G. F. A. Wendeborn, *A View of England*, 2 vols. (London, 1791 [1785]), vol. II, p. 237.

34 M. d'Archenholz, *A Picture of England* (Dublin, 1791), p. 235, quoted in Percy Young, *A History of British Music* (London, 1967), p. 344.

35 *Dramatic Censor* 1811, 283.

36 Vetus, "On the Encouragement of English Musical Talent," *QMMR* 11 (1821), 282.

37 "Sketch of the State of Music in London," *QMMR* 14 (1822), 237.

38 George Herbert Bonaparte Rodwell, *A Letter to the Musicians of Great Britain* (London, 1833), p. 30.

39 "Sketch of the State of Music in London," *QMMR* 37 (1828), 95.

40 Black, ed., *Culture and Society in Britain*, pp. 12, 14, 16–18.

41 See also Simon McVeigh''s survey of eighteenth-century attitudes toward public concerts in *Concert Life*, pp. 64–67.

42 William Hayes, *Remarks on Mr. Avison''s Essay on Musical Expression. In a Letter from a Gentleman in London to his Friend in the Country* (London, 1753), p. 92.

43 John Potter, *Observations on the Present State of Music and Musicians* (London, 1762), p. 61.

44 *Ibid.*, pp. 65–66.

45 *Ibid.*, p. 61.

46 *Ibid.*, pp. 61–62.

47 *Ibid.*, p. 61.

48 *Ibid.*, pp. 69–70.

49 Wendeborn, *A View of England*, vol. II, p. 183.

50 "Letter on the Character of Musicians," *QMMR* 3 (1818), 289.

51 *Ibid.*, 290.

52 *Ibid.*, 285.

53 *Ibid.*, 291.

54 The centuries-old view of one gender, with men and women occupying different points along a biological and behavioral continuum, was replaced by a model of fundamental differences between masculine and feminine. In turn, homosexuality was reclassified from a practice to an identity. See Thomas Laqueur, *Making Sex: Body and Gender from the Greeks to Freud* (Cambridge, Mass., 1990); Michael McKeon, "Historicizing Patriarchy: The Emergence of Gender Differences in England, 1660–1760," *Eighteenth-Century Studies* 18 (1995), 295–322; Anthony Fletcher, *Gender, Sex, and Subordination in England, 1500–1800* (New Haven, 1995); Tim Hitchcock, *English Sexualities, 1700–1800*

(Basingstoke, 1997), "Redefining Sex in Eighteenth-Century England," *History Workshop Journal* 41 (1996), 73–90, and "Demography and the Culture of Sex," in Black, ed., *Culture and Society in Britain*, pp. 69–84. For some implications of these developments in the visual arts, see Gill Perry and Michael Rossington, eds., *Femininity and Masculinity in Eighteenth-Century Art and Culture* (Manchester, 1994).

55 Linda Phyllis Austern, "'Alluring the Auditorie to Effeminacie': Music and the Idea of the Feminine in Early Modern England," *Music and Letters* 74 (1993), 343. See also Austern's "'Forreine Conceites and Wandring Devises': The Exotic, the Erotic, and the Feminine," in Jonathan Bellman, ed., *The Exotic in Western Music* (Boston, 1998), pp. 26–42.

56 Austern, "'Alluring the Auditorie to Effeminacie,'" 349.

57 *Ibid.*, 350–51.

58 *Ibid.*, 352–53.

59 For similar issues experienced by actors during this period, see Straub, *Sexual Suspects*.

60 Thomas McGeary, "'Warbling Eunuchs': Opera, Gender, and Sexuality on the London Stage, 1705–1742," *Restoration and Eighteenth-Century Theatre Research* 2nd series 7 (1992), 1–22; and "Gendering Opera: Italian Opera as the Feminine Other in Britain, 1700–42," *Journal of Musicological Research* 14 (1994), 17–34.

61 Such associations in fact preceded the arrival of the Opera. See Paul Hammond, "Titus Oates and 'Sodomy,'" in Black, ed., *Culture and Society in Britain*, pp. 85–101.

62 Thomas Gilbert, *The World Unmask'd* (1738), cited in McGeary, "'Warbling Eunuchs,'" 15.

63 McGeary, "'Warbling Eunuchs,'" 16.

64 John Dennis, *Essay on the Operas after the Italian Manner* (1706), cited in McGeary, "'Warbling Eunuchs,'" 5.

65 See G. J. Barker-Benfield, *The Cult of Sensibility: Sex and Society in Eighteenth-Century Britain* (Chicago, 1992).

66 Richard Leppert, "Social Order and the Domestic Consumption of Music (The Politics of Sound in the Policing of Gender Construction)," in his *The Sight of Sound: Music, Representation, and the History of the Body* (Berkeley, 1993), p. 63.

67 *Ibid.*, p. 65.

68 See Richard Leppert, "The Female at Music: Praxis, Representation and the Problematic of Identity," in his *Music and Image: Domesticity, Ideology and Socio-Cultural Formation in Eighteenth-Century England* (Cambridge, 1993 [1988]), pp. 147–75.

69 See Richard Leppert, "The Male at Music: Praxis, Representation and the Problematic of Identity," in his *Music and Image*, pp. 107–46.

70 Vetus, "Music as a Pursuit for Men," *QMMR* 5 (1820), 7.

71 *Ibid.*, 7–14.

72 *Ibid.*, 7.

73 Richard Leppert, "Music, Socio-Politics, Ideologies of Male Sexuality and Power," in his *Music and Image*, p. 25.

74 Barker-Benfield, *The Cult of Sensibility*, p. 360.

75 While the separate spheres ideology was widespread, especially in the nineteenth century, important questions have been raised about its usefulness as a description of contemporary views and realities. See Amanda Vickery, "Golden Age to Separate Spheres? A Review of the Categories and Chronology of English Women's History," *Historical Journal* 36 (1993), 383–414; Lawrence E. Klein, "Gender and the Public/Private Distinction in the Eighteenth Century: Some Questions about Evidence and Analytic Procedure," *Eighteenth-Century Studies* 29 (1995), 97–109. And for a critique of the larger notion of public versus private in the eighteenth century, see Dena Goodman, "Public Sphere and Private Life: Toward a Synthesis of Current Historiographical Approaches to the Old Regime," *History and Theory* 31 (1992), 1–20.

76 Colley, *Britons*, p. 252.

77 Ehrlich, *The Music Profession*, p. 31.

78 Vetus, "Music as a Pursuit for Men," *QMMR* 5 (1820), 11.

79 David Kuchta, "The Making of the Self-Made Man: Class, Clothing, and English Masculinity, 1688–1832," in Victoria de Grazia, *The Sex of Things: Gender and Consumption in Historical Perspective* (Berkeley, 1996), pp. 54–78.

80 Catherine Hall, "Gender Divisions and Class Formation in the Birmingham Middle Class, 1780–1850," in her *White, Male and Middle-Class: Explorations in Feminism and History* (New York, 1992), p. 106.

81 R. Campbell, *The London Tradesman* (1747), cited in Ehrlich, *The Music Profession*, p. 9.

2 SOCIAL PROFILE

1 RSM, Members' Files.

2 See Ehrlich, *The Music Profession*, pp. 6–12.

3 Rev. William Walond Cazalet, *The History of the Royal Academy of Music*, (London, 1854), p. 317.

4 C. F. Abdy Williams, *A Short Historical Account of the Degrees in Music at Oxford and Cambridge, with a Chronological List of Graduates . . . from the Year 1463* (London and New York, 1894), pp. 87–88.

5 "Letter on the Character of Musicians," *QMMR* 3 (1818), 290.

6 John S. Bumpus, *Sir John Stevenson: A Biographical Sketch* (London, 1893), p. 1.

7 Michael Kelly, *Reminiscences* (London, 1975 [1826]), p. 3.

8 Vetus, "On Amateur and Professional Singers," *QMMR* 13 (1822), 1–2.

9 Sainsbury (1824), p. 199.

10 *Ibid.*, pp. 95–96.

11 Cazalet, *Royal Academy of Music*, p. 291.

12 Sainsbury (1824), p. 414.

13 Sainsbury (1825), vol. II, p. 425; Grove (1926), vol. IV, p. 278.

14 Grove (1879), vol. III, p. 139.

15 B&S, p. 12.

16 For the role of émigré musicians in Philadelphia, see Otto Albrecht, "Opera in Philadelphia, 1800–1830," *JAMS* 32 (1979), 499–515.

17 Roy Porter, *London: A Social History* (Cambridge, Mass., 1994), pp. 147–48.

18 Joseph Doane, ed., *A Musical Directory for the Year 1794* (London, 1794).

19 Porter, *London*, p. 99. See *Harris's List of Covent Garden Ladies; or, Man of Pleasure's Kalendar for the Year 1793* (Edinburgh, 1982 [1793]).
20 Porter, *London*, p. 102.
21 One hundred and twenty-seven musicians lived in an area bordered to the south by Oxford Street and High Holborn and to the north by the New Road: forty-five between Gray's Inn Road and Tottenham Court Road; forty from there west to Portland Place; and forty-two west of Portland Place (in Marylebone).
22 McVeigh, *Concert Life*, p. 202.
23 Simon McVeigh, "Felice Giardini: A Violinist in Late Eighteenth-Century London," *Music and Letters* 64 (1983), 162–72; and *The Violinist in London's Concert Life, 1750–1784: Felice Giardini and his Contemporaries* (New York, 1989).
24 Philharmonic Society, Foundation Book, BL, MS loan 48/1.
25 Fiona M. Palmer, *Domenico Dragonetti in England (1794–1846): The Career of a Double Bass Virtuoso* (Oxford, 1997), pp. 26–27, 257.
26 Charles Dickens, *Nicholas Nickleby* (New York, 1981 [1839]), p. 65.
27 Great Britain, Parliament (Commons), 1852–1853. LXXXVIII, I, "Population Tables, 1851," pp. 135–41, 384–95.
28 Census, Enumerators' Books, 1851, District: Westminster, Subdistrict: St. Anne's Soho, Public Record Office, London.
29 For the conditions of artisans at and below the level of many professional musicians, see M. Dorothy George, *London Life in the Eighteenth Century* (New York, 1965), especially chapter 4, "The People and the Trades of London."
30 Reddy, "The Concept of Class," p. 18.

3   PATRONAGE

1 Harold Perkin, *The Origins of Modern English Society, 1780–1880* (Toronto, 1972 [1969]), p. 49.
2 *Ibid.*, p. 224.
3 Donald Jay Grout, *A History of Western Music* (New York, 1973 [1960]), p. 450.
4 Rey Longyear, *Nineteenth-Century Romanticism in Music* (Englewood Cliffs, N.J., 1969), p. 209.
5 See William Weber, "London: A City of Unrivalled Riches," in Neal Zaslaw, ed., *The Classical Era: From the 1740s to the End of the Eighteenth Century*; part of the series *Man and Music* (London, 1989), pp. 293–302.
6 Raynor, *Music and Society since 1815*, p. 1.
7 Raynor, *A Social History of Music*, p. 351.
8 See Ralph P. Locke and Cyrilla Barr, eds., *Cultivating Music in America: Women Patrons and Activists since 1860* (Berkeley, 1997).
9 For earlier royal patronage of music , see Peggy Ellen Daub, "Music at the Court of George II (R. 1727–1760)," Ph.D. dissertation (Cornell University, 1985).
10 S. S. Wesley, *A Few Words on Cathedral Music and the Musical System of the Church, with a Plan of Reform* (London, 1849), p. 351.

11 McVeigh, *Concert Life*, pp. 49–52, based on contemporary sources; "Royal Patronage of Music," *QMMR* 2 (1818), 154–55.

12 "Royal Patronage of Music," *QMMR* 2 (1818), 154–55.

13 *Ibid.*

14 Kelly, *Reminiscences*, p. 154.

15 "Sketch of the State of Music in London," *QMMR* 14 (1822), 240.

16 Cazalet, *Royal Academy of Music*, p. 286.

17 Daniel Defoe, *A Tour through the Whole Island of Great Britain* (New York, 1971 [1724–26]), p. 342.

18 B&S, p. 279.

19 B&S, pp. 326, 98.

20 For the musicians listed in this paragraph see B&S, pp. 184 (Harper), 280 (Milgrove), 344 (Ridley), 377 (Sloman) and 382 (Smith); Sainsbury, vol. I, p. 334 (Hart); and RSM, Members' Files (Coote).

21 For the musicians listed in this paragraph see James Duff Brown, *Biographical Dictionary of Musicians, with a Bibliography of English Writings on Music* (London, 1886), p. 30 (Ashe); B&S, pp. 22 (Baker), 171 (Greatorex), 214 (Hyde), 241 (Lazarus) and 259 (Macfarlane); Sainsbury, vol. II, p. 537 (White); and RSM, Members' Files (Tibet).

22 Sainsbury, vol. II, p. 537.

23 See McVeigh, *Concert Life*.

24 "Sketch of the State of Music in London," *QMMR* 14 (1822), 241.

25 Jennifer Hall, "The Re-fashioning of Fashionable Society: Opera-going and Sociability in Britain, 1821–1861," Ph.D. dissertation (Yale University, 1996).

26 Weber, *The Rise of Musical Classics*.

27 McVeigh, *Concert Life*, pp. 23–24.

28 Young, *A History of British Music*, p. 342, quotation from BL, Egerton MS 2159, f. 57.

29 McVeigh, *Concert Life*, p. 12.

30 Hall, "The Re-fashioning of Fashionable Society."

31 McVeigh, *Concert Life*, p. 2.

32 *Ibid.*, p. 48.

33 *Ibid.*, p. 47.

34 "Sketch of the State of Music in London," *QMMR* 26 (1825), 209–10.

35 "Private Concerts," *QMMR* 27 (1825), 298.

36 "Sketch of the State of Music in London," *QMMR* 26 (1825), 210.

37 "Sketch," *QMMR* 11 (1821), 396.

38 "Sketch," *QMMR* 7 (1820), 375.

39 *Ibid.*

40 "Sketch," *QMMR* 26 (1825), 210.

41 "Sketch," *QMMR* 18 (1823), 251.

42 "Sketch," *QMMR* 11 (1821), 396.

43 *Ibid.*, 256.

44 "Sketch," *QMMR* 37 (1828), 96.

45 "Sketch," *QMMR* 14 (1822), 238–39.

46 Vetus, "On the Encouragement of English Musical Talent," *QMMR* 11 (1821), 276.

47 Honest Pride, "Pallix v. Scudamore," *QMMR* 16 (1822), 443–44.

48 *Ibid.*, 440.

49 McVeigh, *Concert Life*, p. 68.

50 William Weber, "The Muddle of the Middle Classes," *Nineteenth-Century Music* 3 (1979), 175–85.

51 McVeigh, *Concert Life*, pp. 11–13; Hall, "The Re-fashioning of Fashionable Society."

52 Bumpus, *Sir John Stevenson*, pp. 2–3.

53 McVeigh, *Concert Life*, pp. 32–35.

54 "The City Concerts," *QMMR* 9 (1821), 65–66.

55 *Ibid.*, 67.

56 Weber, *Music and the Middle Class*, p. 160.

57 *Ibid.*, p. 24.

58 William Weber, "Artisans in Concert Life in Mid-Nineteenth-Century London and Paris," *Journal of Contemporary History* 13 (1978), 253–67.

59 George Rowell, *The Victorian Theatre, 1792–1914* (Cambridge, 1978), p. 3; Marc Baer, *Theatre and Disorder in Late Georgian London* (Oxford, 1992).

60 W. T. Parke, *Musical Memoirs* (London, 1830), vol. II, p. 15.

61 *Ibid.*, pp. 14–15.

62 *Harmonicon* I (1823), 16.

63 Pro Veritate, "Antient and Modern Music Compared," *QMMR* 6 (1820), 146.

64 J. W. H., "On the General Superiority of Instrumentalists over Singers," *QMMR* 15 (1822), 280–81.

65 "Sketch of the State of Music in London," *QMMR* 39 (1828), 306.

66 "Sketch," *QMMR* 18 (1823), 249.

67 *QMMR* 11 (1821), 280.

68 *Musical Examiner* September 23, 1843, 349.

69 See McVeigh, *Concert Life*, pp. 185–87.

70 Daub, "Music at the Court of George II," pp. 180–82.

71 Grove (1926), vol. IV, p. 144.

72 The term was coined by Deborah Cherry, *Painting Women: Victorian Women Artists* (London, 1993).

73 John Ebers, *Seven Years of the King's Theatre* (London, 1828). See also contracts arranged by Henry Bishop (then music director at Covent Garden Theatre) in 1818: BL, Add. MS 29365, ff. 1–32.

74 George Hogarth, *Musical History, Biography, and Criticism: Being a General Survey of Music from the Earliest Period to the Present Time* (New York, 1848 [1838]), p. 128.

75 *Monthly Magazine of Music* I (1823), 31.

76 H. J. Banister, *Domestic Music for the Wealthy; or, A Plea for the Art and its Professors, in Eighteen Letters* (London, 1843), p. 35.

77 Thomas Danvers Worgan, *The Musical Reformer* (London, 1829), p. 39.

78 McVeigh, *Concert Life*, and "The Professional Concert and Rival Subscription Series in London, 1783–1793," *RMA Research Chronicle* 22 (1989), 1–135.

79 Ehrlich, *First Philharmonic*.

80 *QMMR* 11 (1821), 325.

81 Equalization, "Singers and Instrumentalists," *QMMR* 16 (1822), 433.

82 *QMMR* 4 (1818), 435.

83 "Sketch of the State of Music in London," *QMMR* 18 (1823), 245.

84 Wesley, *A Few Words on Cathedral Music*, p. 10.
85 *Ibid.*, pp. 11–12.
86 *Ibid.*, p. 36.
87 *QMMR* 4 (1818), 430.
88 "Letter on the Character of Musicians," *QMMR* 3 (1818), 288.
89 *Ibid.*, 286–87.

4 MUSICAL EDUCATION

1 For a comprehensive survey of musical practices in parish churches, see Nicholas Temperley, *The Music of the English Parish Church*, 2 vols. (Cambridge, 1979).
2 Maria Hackett, *Brief Account of Cathedral and Collegiate Schools, with an Abstract of their Statutes and Endowments* (London, 1824), p. iv.
3 *Ibid.*, p. 25. See also John Nichols, *Literary Anecdotes of the Eighteenth Century* (London, 1812–16), p. 359.
4 Hackett, *Brief Account*, p. 22.
5 *Ibid.*, p. 40.
6 Westminster Abbey, Chapter Minute Books, 1815.
7 Hackett, *Brief Account*, p. iv.
8 *Ibid.*, p. 42.
9 Edward Pine, *The Westminster Abbey Singers* (London, 1953), p. 138.
10 Hackett, *Brief Account*, p. 12.
11 *Ibid.*, p. 17.
12 F. W. H., "Plan for the Formation of an English Conservatorio," *QMMR* 14 (1822), 132–33.
13 S. S. Wesley, *Reply to the Inquiries of the Cathedral Commissioners, Relative to Improvement in the Music of Divine Worship in Cathedrals* (London, 1854), p. 13.
14 Hackett, *Brief Account*, p. 51.
15 *Ibid.*, pp. 32, 42.
16 *Ibid.*, p. 43. See also pp. 7, 32, 35, 44.
17 "The Concert of Antient Music," *QMMR* 1 (1818), 61.
18 James Edgar Sheppard, *Memorials of St. James's Palace*, 2 vols. (London, 1894), pp. 320–21. This passage was quoted by Sheppard, probably from the Lord Chamberlain's Papers.
19 Hackett, *Brief Account*, p. xli.
20 Williams, *A Short Historical Account*; John Caldwell, "Music in the Faculty of Arts," in James McConica, *The History of the University of Oxford*, vol. III, pp. 201–12.
21 H. Byerley Thomson, *The Choice of a Profession: A Concise Account and Comparative Review of the English Professions* (London, 1857), p. 312.
22 Banister, *Domestic Music for the Wealthy*, p. 20.
23 Williams, *A Short Historical Account*, p. 39.
24 B&S, p. 396; Grove (1926), vol. IV, p. 697.
25 The following account is from the manuscript notebook of J. W. Callcott, who kept a diary of the Society's meetings, BL, Add. MS 27693.
26 *Ibid.*, p. 21.

27 See Ehrlich, *The Music Profession*, pp. 7–9.

28 Sir John Hawkins, *A General History of the Science and Practice of Music* (London, 1875 [1776]), p. 481n.

29 Vetus, "On Amateur and Professional Singers," *QMMR* 13 (1822), 2–3.

30 O. Jocelyn Dunlop and R. D. Denman, *English Apprenticeship and Child Labour* (London, 1912), p. 134.

31 Vetus, "On Amateur and Professional Singers," *QMMR* 13 (1822), 2–3.

32 *QMMR* 4 (1818), 470.

33 "The Music at the Winter Theatres," *QMMR* 35 (1827), 351.

34 Sainsbury, vol. I, p. 376.

35 Vetus, "On Amateur and Professional Singers," *QMMR* 13 (1822), 2–3.

36 Cazalet, *Royal Academy of Music*, p. 13.

37 An Englishman, "Foreign Institutions and English Judgment," *QMMR* 32 (1826), 413.

38 McVeigh, *Concert Life*, p. 185.

39 Clara Kathleen Rogers, *Memories of a Musical Career* (Boston, 1919), p. 95.

40 *Musical World* July 19, 1838, 189.

41 "Foreign Institutions and English Judgment," 406.

42 For English military music and musicians see Henry George Farmer, *Handel's Kettledrums and Other Papers on Military Music* (London, 1950).

43 Sainsbury, vol. I, p. 258.

44 Larson, *The Rise of Professionalism*, p. 16.

45 Defoe, *Augusta Triumphans*, pp. 17–19.

46 *Ibid.*, p. 21.

47 Hayes, *Remarks on Mr. Avison's Essay*, pp. 85–86.

48 *Ibid.*, p. 86.

49 *Ibid.*, p. 87.

50 *Ibid.*, pp. 87–88.

51 "Letter on the Character of Musicians," *QMMR* 3 (1818), 291.

52 *Ibid.*, 290.

53 "Royal Academy of Music," *QMMR* 15 (1822), 370.

54 "Sketch of the State of Music in London," *QMMR* 30 (1826), 183.

55 *Dramatic Censor* 1811, 348.

56 *QMMR* 14 (1823), 129–33.

57 *Ibid.*, 133.

58 Royal Academy of Music, Archives, Box 1, File 1, 1822–23.

59 Cazalet, *Royal Academy of Music*, pp. 8–12.

60 Cazalet, *Royal Academy of Music*, p. 28.

61 *QMMR* 18 (1823), 274–75.

62 *Ibid.*, 336–37.

63 *Ibid.*, 348.

64 *Ibid.*, 337.

65 *Ibid.*, 338–39.

66 "Public Establishments for Music in London," *QMMR* 21 (1824), 82.

67 *Harmonicon* 1 (1823), 52.

68 Cazalet, *Royal Academy of Music*, pp. 295–96.

69 B&S, p. 342.

70 *Ibid.*, p. 409.

71 Report of the RAM Committee, *QMMR* 18 (1823), 269.

72 Cazalet, *Royal Academy of Music*, p. 336.

73 *Monthly Magazine of Music* 1 (1823), 27.

74 "The Royal Academy of Music," *QMMR* 26 (1825), 148.

75 "The Royal Academy of Music," *QMMR* 15 (1822), 391–96.

76 "Sketch of the State of Music in London," *QMMR* 18 (1823), 271.

77 F. Corder, *Royal Academy of Music Centenary Souvenir* (1922), cited in Ehrlich, *The Music Profession,* p. 81.

78 "The Royal Academy of Music," *QMMR* 26 (1825), 151.

79 H. C. Banister, *George Alexander Macfarren: His Life, Works, and Influence* (London, 1891 [1871]), p. 25.

80 "Letter from an Old Musician," *Harmonicon* 1 (1823), 21–22.

81 *Monthly Magazine of Music* 1 (1823), 29.

82 *Harmonicon* 1 (1823), 52.

83 Grove (1926), vol. 1, p. 345.

84 Ehrlich, *The Music Profession*, p. 79.

85 *Ibid.*, p. 80.

86 Royal Academy of Music, *A List of Pupils Received into the Academy*.

87 See my article, "Women and the Music Profession in Victorian England."

88 Ehrlich, *The Music Profession*, pp. 107–20, 126–39.

5 CHURCH MUSICIANS

1 Jeremy Gregory, "Christianity and Culture: Religion, the Arts and the Sciences in England, 1660–1800," in Black, ed., *Culture and Society in Britain*, pp. 102–23.

2 Walsh, John, Colin Haydon, and Stephen Taylor, eds., *The Church in England c. 1689–c. 1833: From Toleration to Tractarianism* (Oxford, 1989).

3 Hogarth, *Musical History, Biography, and Criticism*, p. 122. See also *QMMR* 21 (1824), 17–18.

4 "On the Present State of Church Music in England," *QMMR* 24 (1824), 459–60.

5 *Of the Use and Abuse of Music, Particularly the Music of the Choir, by a Friend of Church-Music* (n.p., 1753), p. 19.

6 *Ibid.*, pp. 20–21.

7 Richard Miller, *English, French, German and Italian Techniques of Singing: A Study in National Tonal Preferences and How They Relate to Functional Efficiency* (Metuchen, N.J., 1977).

8 Grove (1954), vol. II, p. 754.

9 Grove (1926), vol. II, p. 222.

10 Doane, ed., *A Musical Directory*, p. 211.

11 Calvert Johnson, *Organ Music by Women Composers before 1800* (Pullman, Wash., 1993), p. 3.

12 Sainsbury, vol. 1, p. 386 (mentioned in the entry for Benjamin Jacob, who umpired the competition).

13 Augusta A. Austen, Elizabeth Chamberlaine Von Hoff, and a Mrs. Pawsey. See Royal Academy of Music, *A List of Pupils Received into the Academy since its Foundation in 1822–3* (London, 1838), and *The Musical Directory, Register, and*

Almanack; and Royal Academy of Music Calendar for the Year 1855 (London, 1855).

14 Mary Cowden Clarke, *The Life and Labours of Vincent Novello, by his Daughter* (London, 1862), p. 4.

15 "Sketch of the State of Music in London," *QMMR* 7 (1820), 390–91.

16 See Watkins Shaw, *The Succession of Organists of the Chapel Royal and the Cathedrals of England and Wales from c. 1538* (Oxford, 1991).

17 Grove (1926), vol. II, p. 335, and vol. I, p. 778.

18 James T. Lightwood, *Samuel Wesley, Musician: The Story of his Life* (London, 1937), pp. 114–15.

19 B&S, p. 218.

20 RSM, Members' Files.

21 Doane, ed., *A Musical Directory*, p. 11.

22 Grove (1954), vol. I, p. 696.

23 John E. West, *Cathedral Organists, Past and Present* (London, 1899), p. 17.

24 RSM, Members' Files.

25 B&S, p. 442.

26 Clarke, *Novello*, pp. 6–8.

27 Young, *A History of British Music*, p. 456. Young quotes from the *Musical World*, February 17, 1837.

28 Sainsbury, vol. II, pp. 321–26.

29 Thomson, *The Choice of a Profession*, p. 318.

30 John Rouse Bloxam, *A Register of the Presidents, Fellows, Demies, Instructors in Grammar and in Music, Chaplains, Clerks, Choristers, and other Members of St. Mary Magdalen College in the University of Oxford, from the Foundation of the College to the Present Time*, 8 vols. (Oxford, 1853–58), vol. II, pp. cxcii, cciv, ccviii.

31 Joseph Pring, *Papers, Documents, Law Proceedings &c. &c. Respecting the Maintenance of the Choir at the Cathedral Church of Bangor* (Bangor, 1819), pp. viii, 23.

32 Wesley, *A Few Words on Cathedral Music*, p. 60.

33 Grove (1926), vol. I, p. 322.

34 Sainsbury, vol. II, pp. 321–22 (Purkis); RSM, members' files.

35 RSM, Members' Files.

36 West, *Cathedral Organists*, pp. 3, 69.

37 For a detailed account of one London organist's life, see Mark Argent, ed., *Recollections of R. J. S. Stevens, an Organist in Georgian London* (Carbondale, Ill., 1992).

38 "On the Present State of Church Music in England," *QMMR* 24 (1824), 463.

39 West, *Cathedral Organists*, p. 46.

40 Grove (1879), vol. IV, p. 378.

41 "On the Present State of Church Music in England," *QMMR* 24 (1824), 463.

42 Wesley, *A Few Words on Cathedral Music*, p. 60.

43 West, *Cathedral Organists*, p. 31.

44 RSM, Members' Files.

45 *Ibid.*

46 Grove (1879), vol. II, p. 48.

47 West, *Cathedral Organists,* p. 81.

48 Grove (1926), vol. v, pp. 426–27; West, *Cathedral Organists,* p. 2.

49 RSM, Members' Files.

50 *Ibid.*

51 West, *Cathedral Organists,* p. 33.

52 *Ibid.,* p. 68.

53 *Ibid.,* p. 49.

54 *Ibid.,* p. 14.

55 Thomson, *The Choice of a Profession,* p. 318.

56 Nicholas Temperley, "Music in Church," in H. Diack Johnstone and Roger Fiske, eds., *The Eighteenth Century,* vol. iv of *Music in Britain* (Oxford, 1990), p. 380.

57 B&S, p. 96.

58 Sainsbury, vol. ii, pp. 305, 115.

59 Wesley, *A Few Words on Cathedral Music,* p. 72.

60 John Hullah, *Music in the Parish Church* (London, 1856), pp. 23–24.

61 Bumpus, *Sir John Stevenson,* pp. 25–26.

62 *Ibid.,* p. 26.

63 "Royal Patronage of Music," *QMMR* 2 (1818), 156.

64 Westminster Abbey, Treasury Accounts, 1840. (A page summarizing changes in choir expenses since the 1790s.)

65 Westminster Abbey, Chapter Minute Books, December 29, 1819, p. 49.

66 *Ibid.,* March 6, 1838, p. 103.

67 RSM, Members' Files.

68 B&S, pp. 167–68, 256, 445.

69 "On the Present State of Music in England," *QMMR* 23 (1824), 284.

70 RSM, Members' Files.

71 Grove (1926), vol. iv, p. 211.

72 B&S, pp. 189–90; RSM, Members' Files.

73 "On the Present State of Music in England," *QMMR* 23 (1824), 283.

74 Pine, *The Westminster Abbey Singers,* p. 139.

75 Pring, *Papers, Documents, Law Proceedings,* pp. 28, 31.

76 "On the Present State of Church Music in England," *QMMR* 24 (1824), 458.

77 *Ibid.,* 461.

78 Wesley, *Reply to the Inquiries of the Cathedral Commissioners,* p. 7.

79 William Gardiner, *Music and Friends; or, Pleasant Recollections of a Dilettante,* (London, 1838–53), vol. i, pp. 282–83.

80 "On the Present State of Church Music in England," *QMMR* 24 (1824), 459.

81 Wesley, *A Few Words on Cathedral Music,* p. 57.

82 *Ibid.,* pp. 25–26.

83 Bernarr Rainbow, *The Choral Revival in the Anglican Church, 1839–1872* (New York, 1970).

84 See Temperley, "Music in Church," in Johnstone and Fiske, eds., *The Eighteenth Century,* pp. 357–96, and "Cathedral Music," in Nicholas Temperley, ed., *The Romantic Age, 1800–1914,* vol. v of *Music in Britain* (London, 1981), pp. 171–213; also William J. Gatens, *Victorian Cathedral Music in Theory and Practice* (Cambridge, 1986).

85 B&S, pp. 154, 359; Julie Anne Sadie and Rhian Samuel, eds., *The Norton/Grove Dictionary of Women Composers* (New York, 1995), pp. 180, 401–2.

86 B&S, p. 263; Sadie and Samuel, eds., *The Norton/Grove Dictionary of Women Composers*, pp. 298–99.

87 See Weber, *The Rise of Musical Classics*.

88 *Cathedral Music, Being a Collection in Score of the Most Valuable and Useful Compositions for that Service by the Several English Masters of the Seventeenth and Eighteenth Centuries, Selected by Samuel Arnold, Mus. Doc.*, 3 vols. (London, 1790).

89 Weber, *The Rise of Musical Classics*, pp. 190, 191.

90 Sainsbury, vol. II, pp. 478–79.

91 E. H. Fellowes, *English Cathedral Music* (London, 1969 [1941]), p. 9.

92 Wesley, *A Few Words on Cathedral Music*, p. 68.

93 "On the Present State of Church Music in England," *QMMR* 24 (1824), 457–58.

94 See chapter 10.

6   SECULAR MUSICIANS: SINGERS

1   The table omits street ballad-singers, who were numerous but rarely or never overlapped with professional categories, and music-hall singers, who became more important later in the century (the catalogue includes only one example, Robert "Harry" Clifton, B&S, pp. 93–94).

2   Brian W. Pritchard, "The Musical Festival and the Choral Society in England in the Eighteenth and Nineteenth Centuries: A Social History," Ph.D. dissertation (University of Birmingham, 1968).

3   McVeigh, *Concert Life*, pp. 191–92.

4   Judith Milhous and Robert T. Hume, "Opera Salaries in Eighteenth-Century London," *JAMS* 46 (1993), 44.

5   *Ibid.*

6   "Singers and Instrumentalists," *QMMR* 16 (1822), 428.

7   Sainsbury, vol. I, p. 375.

8   Young, *A History of British Music*, p. 428.

9   *Ibid.*, p. 429.

10 Philharmonic Society, Account Book, 1813–1866, BL, MS loan 48/9/1.

11 B&S, p. 235; RSM, Members' Files.

12 B&S, p. 16; Doane, ed., *A Musical Directory*, p. 3; RSM, Members' Files.

13 RSM, Members' Files.

14 B&S, p. 311.

15 *Ibid.*, p. 361.

16 For information about the Italian Opera including finances and the musicians employed there, see Ebers, *Seven Years of the King's Theatre*; Kelly, *Reminiscences*; the Earl of Mount Edgcumbe, *Musical Reminiscences, Containing an Account of the Italian Opera in England from 1773* (London, 1834); Daniel Nalbach, *The King's Theatre, 1704–1867* (London, 1972); Frederick C. Petty, *Italian Opera in London, 1760–1800* (Ann Arbor, 1980); and Curtis Price,

Judith Milhous, and Robert D. Hume, *Italian Opera in Late Eighteenth-Century London* (Oxford, 1995).

17 The managers, generally English non-musicians or Italian musicians, had a thankless job, owing to the scheming and temperamental singers as well as the perpetual insolvency of the theatre. See Kelly, *Reminiscences.*

18 Milhous and Hume, "Opera Salaries," 26–83.

19 *Ibid.*, 78; Price, Milhous, and Hume, *Italian Opera in Late Eighteenth-Century London*, pp. 132–34; Simon McVeigh, "The Benefit Concert in Nineteenth-Century London: From 'Tax on the Nobility' to 'Monstrous Nuisance,'" in Zon, ed., *Nineteenth-Century British Music Studies*, pp. 242–66.

20 *Ibid.*, p. 64.

21 *Ibid.*, pp. 67–68, 76.

22 Ebers, *Seven Years of the King's Theatre*, p. 250.

23 Milhous and Hume, "Opera Salaries," 60, 61.

24 Ebers, *Seven Years of the King's Theatre*, pp. 170–72, 201, 229.

25 "The Music at the Winter Theatres," *QMMR* 35 (1827), 351.

26 For further information on the patent theatres and their repertoires see Jane Girdham, *English Opera in Late Eighteenth-Century London: Stephen Storace at Drury Lane* (Oxford, 1997); Charles Beecher Hogan, *The London Stage, 1776–1800* (London, 1968); Allardyce Nicoll, *British Drama: An Historical Survey from the Beginnings to the Present Time* (New York, 1978 [1925]); John Sims Reeves, *Life and Recollections* (London, 1888); Rowell, *The Victorian Theatre*; George Winchester Stone, *The London Stage, 1747–1776* (London, 1968).

27 "Singers and Instrumentalists," *QMMR* 16 (1822), 425–26.

28 *Ibid.*

29 Grove (1879), vol. IV, p. 463.

30 B&S, p. 315.

31 Grove (1926), vol. I, p. 337.

32 *Ibid.*

33 "Sketch of the State of Music in London," *QMMR* 30 (1826), 175.

34 Grove (1926), vol. I, pp. 381–82.

35 B&S, p. 39.

36 "Sketch of the State of Music in London," *QMMR* 26 (1825), 192.

37 "Sketch of the State of Music in London," *QMMR* 37 (1828), 90.

38 Ebers, *Seven Years of the King's Theatre*, pp. 57–58.

39 *Ibid.*, p. 369.

40 RSM, Members' Files.

41 B&S, p. 115.

42 A book entitled *Memoirs of Mrs. Billington, from her Birth* (London, 1792) accused her of many scandalous acts. *An Answer to the Memoirs of Mrs. Billington* (London, 1792) defended her from these accusations.

43 Ebers, *Seven Years of the King's Theatre*, pp. 48–49.

44 McVeigh, *Concert Life*, p. 119, and see chapters 7–9.

45 For the eighteenth-century origins of such associations, see Richard Leppert, "Social Order and the Domestic Consumption of Music," in his *The Sight of Sound*, especially pp. 63–70.

46 Anglicus, "On the Differences Between Italian and English Manner in Singing," *QMMR* 16 (1822), 407.
47 *Ibid.*, 402.
48 *Ibid.*, 402–3.
49 McVeigh, *Concert Life*, pp. 144–48.
50 Anglicus, "On the Differences Between Italian and English Manner in Singing," 404.
51 *Ibid.*, 408.
52 Miller, *English, French, German and Italian Techniques of Singing*, pp. 148–49.
53 The correlations between singing styles and social and political structures have been explored by a number of ethnomusicologists. For a classic early study, see Alan Lomax, *Folk Song Style and Culture* (New Brunswick, N.J., 1978). See also John Shepherd, "Timbre and Gender," in his *Music as Social Text* (Cambridge, 1991), pp. 164–71; and Peter J. Martins, "Sound Structures and Musical Structures," in his *Sounds and Society: Themes in the Sociology of Music* (Manchester, 1995), pp. 126–66.
54 Elizabeth Hehr, "How the French Viewed the Differences between French and Italian Singing Styles of the Eighteenth Century," *International Review of the Aesthetics and Sociology of Music* 16 (1985), 73–85.
55 For further exploration of these themes, see Leslie C. Dunn and Nancy A. Jones, eds., *Embodied Voices: Representing Female Vocality in Western Culture* (Cambridge, 1994).
56 Sainsbury, vol. II, pp. 454–55.
57 *Ibid.*, p. 455.
58 *Musical Examiner* February 11, 1843, 101.

7   SECULAR MUSICIANS: INSTRUMENTALISTS

1 *QMMR* 16 (1822), 430.
2 *Musical Examiner* November 19, 1842, 9.
3 *QMMR* 2 (1818), 171.
4 The categories derive from repertoire, performance setting, and patronage. "Band" in contemporary usage denoted both wind bands and larger orchestras with wind and string instruments. Military and some royal bands were wind ensembles; other royal, theatre, and the Philharmonic "bands" were full-scale orchestras.
5 RSM, Members' Files.
6 *Ibid.*
7 BL, Add. MS 29365, ff. 1–32.
8 RSM, Members' Files.
9 See Palmer, *Domenico Dragonetti in England*.
10 Ehrlich, *First Philharmonic*, pp. 26–27.
11 McVeigh, *Concert Life*, p. 192.
12 Charles Hallé, *The Autobiography of Charles Hallé, with Correspondence and Diaries* (New York, 1973 [1896]), p. 123. Reginald Nettel, *The Orchestra in England: A Social History* (London, 1956 [1946]), p. 119.

13 *QMMR* 14 (1822), 155.
14 Nettel, *The Orchestra in England*, p. 119.
15 John Ella, *Record of the Musical Union* (London, 1845–52), 1845, p. 13.
16 For the Dando quartet, see Grove (1926), vol. I, pp. 660–61, and F. G. Edwards, *Programmes of Dando's Quartett Concerts, 1836–1859* (London, 1836, etc.). See also Ella, *Record of the Musical Union*, 1845, p. 13; and Christina Bashford, "Public Chamber-Music Concerts in London, 1835–50: Aspects of History, Repertory and Reception," Ph.D. dissertation (University of London, 1996).
17 See also chapter 10, and Bashford, "Public Chamber-Music Concerts."
18 "Sketch of the State of Music in London," *QMMR* 18 (1823), 252.
19 The "elder Sapio" was an Italian singer and teacher who taught singing in France (apparently to Marie Antoinette) before the French Revolution, then fled to England where he became a very successful singing teacher. He was the father of the singer Antonio Sapio (see p. 27 above). Sainsbury (1824), p. 414.
20 Parke, *Musical Memoirs*, vol. II, p. 9.
21 Honest Pride, "Pallix v. Scudamore," *QMMR* 16 (1822), 440.
22 Sainsbury, vol. I, p. 2.
23 Grove (1954), vol. IX, p. 235.
24 RSM, Members' Files.
25 *Ibid.*
26 *Ibid.*
27 McVeigh, "The Professional Concert," 1–135.
28 Nettel, *The Orchestra in England*, p. 69.
29 See George Hogarth, *The Philharmonic Society of London, from its Foundation, 1813, to its Fiftieth Year, 1862* (London, 1862) and Ehrlich, *First Philharmonic*.
30 This was the Little Theatre (not the King's Theatre) in the Haymarket. See Rowell, *The Victorian Theatre*, p. 8.
31 RSM, Members' Files.
32 *Ibid.*
33 *Ibid.*
34 Doane, ed., *A Musical Directory*, p. 50.
35 RSM, Members' Files.
36 *Ibid.*
37 *Ibid.*
38 *Ibid.*
39 *Dramatic Censor* 1811, 100.
40 Banister, *Domestic Music for the Wealthy*, p. 35.
41 *QMMR* 16 (1822), 428.
42 Milhous and Hume, "Opera Salaries," 57.
43 Banister, *Domestic Music for the Wealthy*, p. 35.
44 RSM, Members' Files.
45 *Ibid.*
46 See Adam Carse, *The Orchestra in the Eighteenth Century* (Cambridge, 1940), p. 11.
47 *QMMR* 34 (1827), 238.
48 Milhous and Hume, "Opera Salaries," 43.

49 "A Statement of Matters Relative to the King's Theatre," *QMMR* 2 (1818), 239–63.
50 Milhous and Hume, "Opera Salaries," 63.
51 William C. Smith, *The Italian Opera and Contemporary Ballet in London, 1789–1820* (London, 1955), p. 89.
52 Ebers, *Seven Years of the King's Theatre*, p. 43.
53 Milhous and Hume, "Opera Salaries," 61.
54 Smith, *The Italian Opera*, p. 89.
55 Ebers, *Seven Years of the King's Theatre*, p. 43.
56 BL, Add. MS 29365, ff. 1–32.
57 Philharmonic Society, Account Book, 1813–1866, BL, MS loan 48/9/1; see also Ehrlich, *First Philharmonic*, pp. 23–28.
58 *Ibid.*
59 Ehrlich, *First Philharmonic*, p. 23.
60 *Ibid.*, pp. 55–56.
61 RSM, Members' Files.
62 *Ibid.*
63 *Ibid.*
64 Banister, *Domestic Music for the Wealthy*, pp. 35–36.
65 RSM, Members' Files.
66 *Ibid.*
67 *Ibid.*
68 See also Laura Alyson McLamore, "Symphonic Conventions in London's Concert Rooms, circa 1755–1790," Ph.D. dissertation (University of California at Los Angeles, 1991), pp. 151–57, and Simon McVeigh, "The Benefit Concert in Nineteenth-Century London," in Zon, ed., *Nineteenth-Century British Music Studies*, pp. 242–66.
69 Ella, *Record of the Musical Union*, 1845, p. 23.
70 *Monthly Musical and Literary Magazine* 1 (1830), 19.
71 *QMMR* 18 (1823), 251.
72 *English Musical Gazette* July 1819, 120.
73 RSM, Members' Files.
74 *QMMR* 37 (1828), 89.
75 For further information on military music, see Daub, "Music at the Court of George II," chapter 6, "Military Musicians at Court"; Farmer, *Handel's Kettledrums*; and Robert A. Marr, *Music for the People: A Retrospect of the Glasgow International Exhibition, 1888, with an Account of the Rise of Choral Societies in Scotland* (Edinburgh and Glasgow, 1888).
76 Marr, *Music for the People*, p. 94.
77 *Ibid.* One such black "military bandsman" appears in a politically significant painting, Sir David Wilkie's *Chelsea Pensioners Reading the Gazette of the Battle of Waterloo*; see Colley, *Britons*, pp. 364–67.
78 Marr, *Music for the People*, p. 102.
79 *Ibid.*, pp. 88, 97.
80 RSM, Members' Files.
81 Doane, ed., *A Musical Directory*, p. 11.
82 RSM, Members' Files. (Covent Garden contracts, BL, Add. MS 29365, ff.

1–32.)
83 RSM, Members' Files.
84 Marr, *Music for the People*, p. 98.
85 *Ibid.*
86 RSM, Members' Files.
87 *Ibid.*
88 *Ibid.* (George Flower).

8   TEACHERS, COMPOSERS, AND ENTREPRENEURS

1 Great Britain, Parliament (Commons), 1844 [587], XXVII, I, "Occupation abstract, 1841," pp. 27–51. See also Ehrlich, *The Music Profession*, p. 235.
2 An Observer, "On the Present State of the English Musician," *QMMR* 20 (1823), 437.
3 Great Britain, Parliament (Commons), 1852–1853, LXXXVIII, I, "Population Tables, 1851," pp. 135–41, 381–85; 1863, LIII, I, "Population Tables, 1861," pp. 295–303, 399–412.
4 Royal Academy of Music, *A List of Pupils Received into the Academy*.
5 Ehrlich, *The Music Profession*, p. 19.
6 "Musical Tuition," *QMMR* 23 (1824), 308.
7 *Ibid.*, 307.
8 Sainsbury, vol. I, p. 97.
9 Wendeborn, *A View of England*, vol. II, p. 238.
10 Lightwood, *Samuel Wesley*, p. 114.
11 *QMMR* 14 (1822), 154.
12 Ella, *Record of the Musical Union*, 1848, p. 28.
13 *QMMR* 4 (1818), 435.
14 West, *Cathedral Organists*, p. 31.
15 Hallé, *Autobiography*, pp. 119–20.
16 Sainsbury (1824), p. 336.
17 Thomson, *The Choice of a Profession*, p. 318.
18 Wesley, *A Few Words on Cathedral Music*, p. 60.
19 Sainsbury, vol. I, p. 243.
20 RSM, Members' Files.
21 Banister, *Domestic Music for the Wealthy*, p. 35.
22 Worgan, *The Musical Reformer*, p. 37.
23 Leppert, "Social Order and the Domestic Consumption of Music," in his *The Sight of Sound*, p. 66.
24 Leppert, *Music and Image*, p. 58. See also his "Music Teachers of Upper-Class Amateur Musicians in Eighteenth-Century England," in Allan W. Atlas, ed., *Music in the Classic Period: Essays in Honor of Barry S. Brook* (New York, 1985), pp. 133–58.
25 "Letter on the Character of Musicians," *QMMR* 3 (1818), 286.
26 Thomson, *The Choice of a Profession*, p. 8.
27 See also Deborah Hayes, "Some Neglected Women Composers of the Eighteenth Century and their Music," *Current Musicology* 39 (1985), 42–65; Derek

Hyde, *New-Found Voices: Women in Nineteenth-Century English Music* (Ash, 1991); and Sadie and Samuel, eds., *The Norton/Grove Dictionary of Women Composers*.

28 Roger Fiske, "Concert Music II," in Johnstone and Fiske, eds., *The Eighteenth Century*, p. 260.

29 Nominis Umbra, "On the Just Objects of Music," *QMMR* 13 (1822), 17–18.

30 F. W. Horncastle, "School of Composition," *QMMR* 35 (1827), 305.

31 An Observer, "On the Present State of the English Musician," *QMMR* 20 (1823), 439.

32 Banister, *Domestic Music for the Wealthy*, p. 14.

33 Worgan, *The Musical Reformer*, p. 21.

34 Wesley, *A Few Words on Cathedral Music*, pp. 68–69.

35 For the music of British composers in this period, see Young, *A History of British Music*; Johnstone and Fiske, eds., *The Eighteenth Century*; Temperley, ed., *The Romantic Age*.

36 Michael Hurd, "Glees, Madrigals, and Partsongs," and Geoffrey Bush, "Songs," in Temperley, ed., *The Romantic Age*, pp. 242–87.

37 Nicholas Temperley, "Piano Music, 1800–1870," in his *The Romantic Age*, pp. 424–34.

38 Nigel Burton, "Oratorios and Cantatas," in Temperley, ed., *The Romantic Age*, pp. 214–41.

39 Percy Young, "Orchestral Music," and Geoffrey Bush, "Chamber Music," in Temperley, ed., *The Romantic Age*, pp. 358–99.

40 *Monthly Magazine of Music* 1 (1823), 14.

41 For issues of gendered music composition in Germany, with a number of parallels to Britain, see Matthew Head, "'If the Pretty Little Hand Won't Stretch': Music for the Fair Sex in Eighteenth-Century Germany," *JAMS* 52 (1999), 203–54.

42 An Observer, "On the Present State of the English Musician," *QMMR* 20 (1823), 433.

43 *Ibid.*, 434.

44 Philharmonic Society, Account Book, 1813–1866, BL, MS loan 48/9/1.

45 Young, *A History of British Music*, p. 435. Quoted from A. Hedley, *Selected Correspondence of Fryderyk Chopin* (London, 1962), pp. 315–16.

46 Bush, "Songs," in Temperley, ed., *The Romantic Age*, p. 273.

47 "Sketch of the State of Music in London," *QMMR* 7 (1820), 389–90.

48 Temperley, "Piano Music, 1800–1870," in his *The Romantic Age*, p. 414.

49 Jane Girdham, *English Opera in Late Eighteenth-Century London*.

50 Robert Hoskins, "Theatre Music II," in Johnstone and Fiske, eds., *The Eighteenth Century*, pp. 261–312.

51 See Nicholas Temperley, "Musical Nationalism in English Romantic Opera," in his *The Lost Chord: Essays on Victorian Music* (Bloomington, Ind., 1989), pp. 143–57; George Biddlecombe, *English Opera from 1834 to 1864, with Particular Reference to the Works of Michael Balfe* (New York, 1994).

52 Michael Hurd, "Opera, 1834–1865," in Temperley, ed., *The Romantic Age*, p. 308.

53 Rodwell, *A Letter to the Musicians*, p. 6.

54 Young, *A History of British Music*, p. 471.
55 Covent Garden contracts between orchestral musicians and H. R. Bishop: BL, Add. MS 29365, ff. 1–32.
56 *QMMR* 14 (1822), 154.
57 Bruce Carr, "Theatre Music, 1800–1834," in Temperley, ed., *The Romantic Age*, p. 291.
58 Sainsbury, vol. I, pp. 178–79.
59 Philharmonic Society, Account Book, 1813–1866, BL, MS loan 48/9/1.
60 Rodwell, *A Letter to the Musicians*, p. 4.
61 BL, Egerton MS 2159, f. 96.
62 *QMMR* 14 (1822), 154.
63 Rodwell, *A Letter to the Musicians*, p. 5.
64 Stanley Sadie, "Music in the Home II," in Johnstone and Fiske, eds., *The Eighteenth Century*, pp. 313–54.
65 An Observer, "On the Present State of the English Musician," *QMMR* 20 (1823), 434.
66 See Derek B. Scott, *The Singing Bourgeois: Songs of the Victorian Drawing Room and Parlour* (Milton Keynes, 1989), especially chapter 3, "The Rise of the Woman Ballad Composer"; also his "The Sexual Politics of Victorian Musical Aesthetics," *Journal of the Royal Musical Association* 119 (1994), 91–114.
67 B&S, p. 26.
68 Brown, *Biographical Dictionary*, p. 51.
69 Wendeborn, *A View of England*, vol. II, p. 240.
70 *QMMR* 10 (1821), 152.
71 *QMMR* 14 (1822), 154.
72 Rodwell, *A Letter to the Musicians*, p. 7.
73 *QMMR* 10 (1821), 152.
74 *QMMR* 7 (1820), 370.
75 An Observer, "On the Present State of Music in England," *QMMR* 23 (1824), 290.
76 Sainsbury, vol. II, pp. 339–40.
77 *Harmonicon* 3 (1823), 40.
78 *QMMR* 29 (1826), 104.
79 Sainsbury, vol. I, p. 229.
80 B&S, pp. 181–82.
81 *Ibid.*, p. 187.
82 *QMMR* 10 (1821), 152–53.
83 One of the Labouring Classes, "English Manufacturing," *QMMR* 31 (1826), 297.
84 *Monthly Magazine of Music* 1 (1823), 17.
85 Nettel, *The Orchestra in England*, p. 95.
86 See Plumb, "The Commercialization of Leisure," in McKendrick, Brewer, and Plumb, *The Birth of a Consumer Society*, pp. 265–85.
87 See Frank Kidson, *British Music Publishers, Printers and Engravers from Queen Elizabeth's Reign to George the Fourth's* (London, 1901); C. Humphries and W. C. Smith, *Music Publishing in the British Isles* (Oxford, 1970).
88 Nettel, *The Orchestra in England*, p. 95.

89 Neil McKendrick, "The Consumer Revolution of Eighteenth-Century England," in McKendrick, Brewer, and Plumb, *The Birth of a Consumer Society*, p. 32.
90 Perkin, *The Origins of Modern English Society*, p. 261.

9   THE FORTUNES OF MUSICIANS

1 These developments are summarized by M. J. Daunton, *Progress and Poverty: An Economic and Social History of Britain, 1700–1850* (Oxford, 1995), p. 433. See also B. R. Mitchell, *Abstract of British Historical Statistics* (Cambridge, 1962), pp. 328–62, and *British Historical Statistics* (Cambridge, 1988), pp. 719–21.
2 Peter Mathias, "The Social Structure in the Eighteenth Century: A Calculation by Joseph Massie," in his *The Transformation of England: Essays in the Economic and Social History of England in the Eighteenth Century* (New York, 1979), pp. 171–89.
3 Colquhoun, *A Treatise on Indigence*, pp. 23–24.
4 Examples include Mrs. Billington, John Braham, Angelica Catalani, Mrs. Salmon, Catherine "Kitty" Stephens, Anna Storace, Mary Ann Wilson, and others.
5 Grove (1926), vol. I, p. 493. RSM, Members' Files.
6 Grove (1926), vol. II, p. 27.
7 West, *Cathedral Organists*, p. 31.
8 For Bianchi, Shield and Storace, see "A Statement of Matters Relative to the King's Theatre," *QMMR* 2 (1818), 239–63.
9 Palmer, *Domenico Dragonetti in England*.
10 RSM, Members' Files.
11 *Ibid.*
12 *Ibid.*
13 *Ibid.*
14 J. A. Banks, *Prosperity and Parenthood: A Study of Family Planning among the Victorian Middle Classes* (London, 1954), p. 48.
15 Wendeborn, *A View of England*, p. 239.
16 Vetus, "On Amateur and Professional Singers," *QMMR* 13 (1821), 3.
17 For a complete list of members see Matthews, *The Royal Society of Musicians*.
18 See RSM, Minutes of the General Meetings, Annual Meeting, December 1822, p. 4.
19 See my article, "Women and the Music Profession in Victorian England."
20 For accounts of some of these benefit funds, see Grove (1879). See also the Royal Academy of Music, *The Musical Directory, Register, and Almanack; and Royal Academy of Music Calendar for the Years 1853–1862* (London, 1853–62). For the New Musical Fund, see Sir George Smart, *Programmes, Books of Words, etc., of the New Musical Fund Concerts in 1794, 1805, 1815–41*, 2 vols., London, 1794–1841.
21 Sainsbury (1824), pp. 414–15.
22 B&S, p. 363.
23 *Musical World* April 1, 1836, 47.

24 *Musical World* January 3, 1839, 30, and February 7, 1839, 91.

25 *Ibid.*, March 21, 1839, 186; *Athenaeum* 661 (June 27, 1840), 518; Grove (1926), vol. IV, p. 213.

26 *Sinks of London Laid Open: A Pocket Companion for the Uninitiated* (London, 1848), pp. 82–83.

27 Sainsbury, vol. II, p. 326.

28 RSM, Members' Files.

29 *Ibid.*

30 RSM, Minutes of the Governors' Meetings, 1823.

31 RSM members Charles Jane Ashley, Thomas Holmes, Willoughby Theobald Monzani, William Thomas Parke, and William Henry Ware. Another musician imprisoned for debt was François Lamotte (Sainsbury [1824], p. 38).

32 Marshalsea Prison, *Day Book of Commitments, 1822–1824*, Public Record Office, London, PRIS, 11: 7.

33 RSM, Members' Files.

34 *Ibid.*, and B&S, p. 16.

35 *Ibid.*

36 Brown, *Biographical Dictionary*, p. 30.

37 Banister, *Domestic Music for the Wealthy*, p. 30.

38 RSM, Members' Files.

39 *Ibid.*

40 B&S, p. 119.

41 RSM, Members' Files.

42 *Ibid.*

43 *Ibid.*

44 *Ibid.*

45 Banister, *Domestic Music for the Wealthy*, p. 20.

46 *Ibid.*, p. 31.

47 B&S, p. 440.

48 Lightwood, *Samuel Wesley*, p. 113.

10   THE STRUGGLE FOR SOCIAL AND PROFESSIONAL STATUS

1 Reader, *Professional Men*, pp. 49–50.

2 Robson, *The Attorney in Eighteenth-Century England*, pp. 153–54.

3 *Ibid.*, pp. 154ff.

4 Hogarth, *The Philharmonic Society*, p. 6.

5 Francis Place, *Autobiography*, ed. Mary Thale (Cambridge, 1972), p. 176.

6 Philip Olleson, ed., *The Letters of Samuel Wesley: Professional and Social Correspondence, 1797–1837* (Oxford, 2001), pp. 192–93. I am indebted to Philip Olleson for pointing out this confirmation of the Webbes' political activities. See also A. V. Beedell, *The Decline of the English Musician, 1788–1888* (Oxford, 1992), pp. 60–62.

7 Hogarth, *The Philharmonic Society*, p. 6.

8 *Ibid.*, p. 6; Percy Young, *The Concert Tradition, from the Middle Ages to the Twentieth Century* (New York, 1969 [1965]), p. 167.

9 Ehrlich, *First Philharmonic*, p. 8.
10 Young, *The Concert Tradition*, p. 170.
11 "Royal Academy of Music," *QMMR* 15 (1822), 397–98.
12 *Ibid.*, 398.
13 Spectator, "On the Influence of Manners Upon Art," *QMMR* 22 (1824), 182.
14 *Ibid.*
15 "The King's Theatre," *QMMR* 38 (1828), 261–68.
16 *Ibid.*, 261.
17 *Ibid.*
18 *Ibid.*, 262.
19 *Ibid.*, 268.
20 Perkin, *The Origins of Modern English Society*, p. 256.
21 *Musical Examiner* September 23, 1843, 350.
22 Spectator, "On the Attainments of Musicians," *QMMR* 8 (1820), 116.
23 "The Royal Academy of Music," *QMMR* 26 (1825), 148.
24 Equalization, "Singers and Instrumentalists," *QMMR* 16 (1822), 430–31.
25 Banister, *Domestic Music for the Wealthy*, p. 34.
26 *Ibid.*, pp. 40–41.
27 F. W. Horncastle, "Plan for the Formation of an English Conservatorio," *QMMR* 14 (1822), 129.
28 Rodwell, *A Letter to the Musicians*, p. 10.
29 Banister, *Domestic Music for the Wealthy*, p. 2.
30 *Ibid.*, pp. 2ff.
31 *Ibid.*, p. 25.
32 *Ibid.*, p. 26.
33 *Ibid.*, pp. 27–28.
34 For a comprehensive study of Ella's Musical Union as well as its chamber-music concert precursors, see Bashford, "Public Chamber-Music Concerts."
35 Ella, *Record of the Musical Union*, 1845, p. 8.
36 Christina Bashford, "Learning to Listen: Audiences for Chamber Music in Early-Victorian London," *Journal of Victorian Culture* 4 (1999), 32.
37 Ella, *Record of the Musical Union*, 1845, p. 14.
38 *Ibid.*, 1845, p. 7.
39 *Ibid.*, 1845, p. 48.
40 *Ibid.*, 1845, p. 7.
41 See my article, "Women and the Musical Profession in Victorian England."
42 Reader, *Professional Men*, p. 148.
43 Thomson, *The Choice of a Profession*, pp. 316–18.
44 *Ibid.*, p. 308.
45 *Ibid.*, pp. 308–9.
46 Dave Russell, *Popular Music in England, 1840–1914: A Social History* (Manchester, 1997 [1987]), especially chapter 2, "Music and Morals, 1840–1880," pp. 23–40. See also Donald Burrows, "Victorian England: An Age of Expansion," in Jim Samson, ed., *The Late Romantic Era: From the Mid-Nineteenth Century to World War I*, part of the series *Music and Society* (Englewood Cliffs, N.J., 1991), p. 285.
47 Trevor Herbert, "Victorian Brass Bands, Class, Taste, and Space," in Andrew

Leyshon, David Matless, and George Revill, eds., *The Place of Music* (New York, 1998), pp. 104–28.

48 For a discussion of the paradoxical attitudes toward music, see Robert Stradling and Meirion Hughes, *The English Musical Renaissance 1860–1940: Construction and Deconstruction* (London, 1993), pp. 11–13.

EPILOGUE

1 Nettel, *The Orchestra in England*, p. 122.

2 *Ibid.*, p. 123. See also Burrows, "Victorian England: An Age of Expansion," p. 267.

3 Francis Hueffer, *Half a Century of Music in England, 1837–1887: Essays towards a History* (London, 1889), p. 3.

4 Sadie, Stanley, ed., *The New Grove Dictionary of Music and Musicians* (London, 1980), vol. XI, pp. 212–13.

5 *Ibid.*, vol. XI, pp. 213–14.

6 *Ibid.*, vol. IX, p. 63.

7 Grove (1926), vol. V, p. 197.

8 Charles Booth, *Life and Labour of the People in London* (New York, 1970 [1902–4]), vol. IV, pp. 147–48.

9 *Ibid.*

10 *Ibid.*, p. 148.

11 Francis Davenant, *What Shall my Son Be? Hints to Parents on the Choice of a Profession or Trade; and Counsels to Young Men on their Entrance into Active Life* (London, 1870), p. 161.

12 T. H. S. Escott, *England: Its People, Polity and Pursuits*, 2 vols. (New York, 1880), p. 322.

13 A. M. Carr-Saunders and P. A. Wilson, *The Professions* (London, 1964 [1933]), pp. 271–72.

APPENDIX

1 Colquhoun, *A Treatise on Indigence*, pp. 23–24; Perkin, *The Origins of Modern English Society*, pp. 20–21.

2 This is my label for what Perkin's table refers to as "Tailors, etc." and Colquhoun's as "Persons employing capital as tailors, mantua-makers, milliners and in the manufacture of stuffs in wearing apparel." The category is expanded here to mean highly skilled artisans whose skills gave them a social and economic position comparable at least to that of shopkeepers. Colquhoun's term "persons employing capital" as well as its placement in the middle ranks indicates an occupational level above that of the "artisans/laborers" category.

3 For both the Clergy and Education categories, the examples of musicians' relatives were probably at the lower end of the income range.

4 Colquhoun's category is "Persons employed in theatrical pursuits and attached to theatres and concerts, as musicians, etc."

5 Colquhoun's category is "Artisans, handicrafts, mechanics and labourers employed in manufactures, buildings, and workers of every kind."

6 Colquhoun's income level of £31 is for "labouring people in husbandry, including earnings of females" and that of £40 for "labouring people in mines and canals." He does not, therefore, account for other types of wage labor, such as the lighterman and spinner included in this table.

Bibliography

MANUSCRIPT SOURCES

Bishop, Henry Rowley, contracts with orchestral musicians at Covent Garden Theatre, 1818 and 1819, BL, Add. MS 29365 ff. 1–32.
  letter from Bishop to Mackinlay, September 1, 1840, BL, Egerton MS 2159, f. 96.
Callcott, J. W., diary of meetings of the Society of Musical Graduates, BL, Add. MS 27693.
Census, Enumerators' Books, 1851, District: Westminster, Subdistrict: St. Anne's, Soho, Public Record Office, London.
Crotch, William, diaries and papers, Public Record Office, Norwich.
Marshalsea Prison, *Day Book of Commitments, 1822–1824*, Public Record Office, London, PRIS, 11:7.
Philharmonic Society, Account Book, 1813–1866, BL, MS loan 48/9/1.
  Foundation Book, BL, MS Loan 48/1.
Royal Academy of Music, Archives, 1822–1823.
Royal Society of Musicians, Members' Files.
  Minutes of the General Meetings, Minutes of the Governors' Meetings, and Miscellaneous Records.
Westminster Abbey, Chapter Minute Books, 1794–1819.
  Treasury Accounts, 1730–1840.

PERIODICALS

The Athenaeum, London, 1830–1921.
The Dramatic Censor; or, Critical and Biographical Illustration of the British Stage, London, 1811.
The English Musical Gazette; or, Monthly Intelligencer, London, January–July 1819.
The Harmonicon: A journal of music, London, 1823–33.
The Monthly Magazine of Music 1, London, 1823.
The Monthly Musical and Literary Magazine 1, London, 1830.
The Musical Companion, or Songster's Magazine, for the year 1777; Being a Select Collection of All the Newest Songs, That have been lately Sung at the Theatres Ranelagh, Vauxhall, and other Places of Public Entertainment, London, 1777.

The Musical Examiner: An impartial weekly record of music and musical events
1–112, London, 1842–44.
The Musical Herald: A weekly journal of music and musical literature, London,
1846–47.
The Musical Magazine 1–12, London, 1835.
The Musical Times and Singing Class Circular, London, 1844 to the present
(renamed *The Musical Times*).
The Musical World: A weekly record of musical science, literature, and intelligence,
London, 1836–91.
The Quarterly Musical Magazine and Review, London, 1818–28.
The Tonic Solfa Reporter and Magazine of Vocal Music for the People, London,
1851.

BOOKS, ARTICLES, AND DISSERTATIONS

Albrecht, Otto, "Opera in Philadelphia, 1800–1830," *JAMS* 32 (1979), 499–515.
Argent, Mark, ed., *Recollections of R. J. S. Stevens, an Organist in Georgian
London*, Carbondale, Ill., 1992.
Austern, Linda Phyllis, "'Alluring the Auditorie to Effeminacie': Music and the
Idea of the Feminine in Early Modern England," *Music and Letters* 74 (1993),
343–54.
    "'Forreine Conceites and Wandring Devises': The Exotic, the Erotic, and the
Feminine," in Jonathan Bellman, ed., *The Exotic in Western Music*, Boston,
1998.
Avison, Charles, *An Essay on Musical Expression*, 3rd ed., London, 1775 (1752).
    *Reply to the Author of Remarks on the Essay on Musical Expression in a Letter
from Mr. Avison, to his Friend in London*, printed in the 2nd ed. of the *Essay*,
London, 1753.
Baer, Marc, *Theatre and Disorder in Late Georgian London*, Oxford, 1992.
Baker, Michael, *The Rise of the Victorian Actor*, London, 1978.
Banister, H. C., *George Alexander Macfarren: His Life, Works, and Influence*,
London, 1891 (1871).
Banister, H. J., *Domestic Music for the Wealthy; or, A Plea for the Art and its
Professors, in Eighteen Letters*, London, 1843.
Banks, J. A., *Prosperity and Parenthood: A Study of Family Planning among the
Victorian Middle Classes*, London, 1954.
Barker-Benfield, G. J., *The Cult of Sensibility: Sex and Society in Eighteenth-
Century Britain*, Chicago, 1992.
Barry, Jonathan, and Christopher Brooks, eds., *The Middling Sort of People:
Culture, Society and Politics in England, 1550–1800*, New York, 1994.
Bashford, Christina, "Learning to Listen: Audiences for Chamber Music in Early-
Victorian London," *Journal of Victorian Culture* 4 (1999), 25–51.
    "Public Chamber-Music Concerts in London, 1835–50: Aspects of History,
Repertory and Reception," Ph.D. dissertation, University of London, 1996.
Baughan, Edward A., ed., *Sixty Years of Music: A Record of the Art in England
during the Victorian Era: Seventy Portraits of the Most Eminent Musicians*,
London, 1897.

Beedell, A. V., *The Decline of the English Musician, 1788–1888*, Oxford, 1992.

Biddlecombe, George, *English Opera from 1834 to 1864, with Particular Reference to the Works of Michael Balfe*, New York, 1994.

[Billington, Mrs.], *An Answer to the Memoirs of Mrs. Billington*, London, 1792.

Memoirs of Mrs. Billington, from her Birth, London, 1792.

Black, Jeremy, ed., *Culture and Society in Britain, 1660–1800*, Manchester, 1997.

Bloxam, John Rouse, *A Register of the Presidents, Fellows, Demies, Instructors in Grammar and in Music, Chaplains, Clerks, Choristers, and other Members of St. Mary Magdalen College in the University of Oxford, from the Foundation of the College to the Present Time*, 8 vols., Oxford, 1853–58.

Booth, Charles, *Life and Labour of the People in London*, New York, 1970 (1902–4).

Bowley, Arthur L., *Wages in the United Kingdom in the Nineteenth Century*, Cambridge, 1900.

Brewer, John, *The Pleasures of the Imagination: English Culture in the Eighteenth Century*, New York, 1997.

Briggs, Asa, and J. Saville, eds., *Essays in Labour History: In Memory of G. D. H. Cole*, London, 1990.

Brown, James Duff, *Biographical Dictionary of Musicians, with a Bibliography of English Writings on Music*, London, 1886.

Brown, James Duff, and Stephen S. Stratton, *British Musical Biography*, Birmingham, 1897.

Bumpus, John S., *The Organists and Composers of St. Paul's Cathedral*, London, 1891.

Sir John Stevenson: A Biographical Sketch, London, 1893.

Burchell, Jenny, *Polite or Commercial Concerts? Concert Management and Orchestral Repertoire in Edinburgh, Bath, Oxford, Manchester, and Newcastle, 1730–1799*, New York, 1996.

Burgh, Allatson, *Anecdotes of Music, Historical and Biographical*, 3 vols., London, 1814.

Burke, Peter, *The French Historical Revolution: The Annales School, 1929–89*, Cambridge, 1990.

Burke, Peter, and Roy Porter, eds., *The Social History of Language*, Cambridge, 1987.

Burney, Charles, *Music, Men and Manners in France and Italy, 1770*, London, 1969 (1771).

Burrows, Donald, "Victorian England: An Age of Expansion," in Jim Samson, ed., *The Late Romantic Era: From the Mid-Nineteenth Century to World War I*, part of the series *Music and Society*, Englewood Cliffs, N.J., 1991.

Busby, Thomas, *Concert-Room and Orchestra Anecdotes*, London, 1825.

Bush, M. L., ed., *Social Orders and Social Classes in Europe since 1500: Studies in Social Stratification*, London, 1992.

Caldwell, John, "Music in the Faculty of Arts," in James McConica, *The History of the University of Oxford*, vol. III, pp. 201–12.

Carr-Saunders, A. M., and P. A. Wilson, *The Professions*, London, 1964 (1933).

Carse, Adam von Ahn, *The Orchestra in the Eighteenth Century*, Cambridge, 1940.

Cazalet, Rev. William Walond, *The History of the Royal Academy of Music*,

London, 1854.

Cherry, Deborah, *Painting Women: Victorian Women Artists*, London, 1993.

Clarke, Mary Cowden, *The Life and Labours of Vincent Novello, by his Daughter*, London, 1862.

Colley, Linda, *Britons: Forging the Nation 1707–1837*, New Haven, 1992.

Colquhoun, Patrick, *A Treatise on Indigence*, London, 1806.

Corfield, Penelope, ed., *Language, History and Class*, Oxford, 1991.

Power and the Professions in Britain, 1700–1850, London, 1995.

Coward, Henry, *Reminiscences*, London, 1919.

Crewdson, H. A. F., *A Short History of the Worshipful Company of Musicians*, London, 1971 (1950).

Cummings, W. H., *Biographical Dictionary of Musicians*, London, 1892.

Daub, Peggy Ellen, "Music at the Court of George II (R. 1727–1760)," Ph.D. dissertation, Cornell University, 1985.

Daunton, M. J., *Progress and Poverty: An Economic and Social History of Britain, 1700–1850*, Oxford, 1995.

Davenant, Francis, *What Shall my Son Be? Hints to Parents on the Choice of a Profession or Trade; and Counsels to Young Men on their Entrance into Active Life*, London, 1870.

Defoe, Daniel, *Augusta Triumphans; or, The Way to Make London the Most Flourishing City in the Universe*, London, 1728.

A Tour through the Whole Island of Great Britain, New York, 1971 (1724–26).

Dent, Edward J., "Early Victorian Music," in G. M. Young, ed., *Early Victorian England, 1830–1865*, London, 1934.

Dibdin, Charles, *The Professional Life of Mr. Dibdin, Written by Himself*, London, 1803.

Dickens, Charles, *Nicholas Nickleby*, New York, 1981 (1839).

Doane, Joseph, ed., *A Musical Directory for the Year 1794*, London, 1794.

Drummond, Pippa, "The Royal Society of Musicians in the Eighteenth Century," *Music and Letters* 59 (1978), 268–89.

Dunlop, O. Jocelyn, and R. D. Denman, *English Apprenticeship and Child Labour*, London, 1912.

Dunn, Leslie C., and Nancy A. Jones, eds., *Embodied Voices: Representing Female Vocality in Western Culture*, Cambridge, 1994.

Ebers, John, *Seven Years of the King's Theatre*, London, 1828.

Edwards, F. G., *Programmes of Dando's Quartett Concerts ... 1836–1859*, London, 1836, etc.

Ehrlich, Cyril, *First Philharmonic: A History of the Royal Philharmonic Society*, Oxford, 1995.

The Music Profession in Britain since the Eighteenth Century: A Social History, Oxford, 1985.

Ehrlich, Cyril, and Dave Russell, "Victorian Music: A Perspective," *Journal of Victorian Culture* 3 (1998), 111–22.

Ella, John, *The First Annual Record of the Musical Winter Evenings, 1852, Containing the Analysis of Music Performed, and Miscellaneous Information on Art and Artists, etc.*, London, 1852.

Record of the Musical Union, London, 1845–52.

Escott, T. H. S., *England: Its People, Polity, and Pursuits*, 2 vols., New York, 1880.

Farmer, Henry George, *Handel's Kettledrums and Other Papers on Military Music*, London, 1950.

Fellowes, E. H., *English Cathedral Music*, London, 1969 (1941).

Fiske, Roger, *English Theatre Music in the Eighteenth Century*, London, 1973.

Fletcher, Anthony, *Gender, Sex, and Subordination in England, 1500–1800*, New Haven, 1995.

Fuller-Maitland, John Alexander, *English Music in the Nineteenth Century*, New York, 1902.

Gardiner, Juliet, ed., *What Is History Today?*, Atlantic Highland, N.J., 1988.

Gardiner, William, *Music and Friends; or, Pleasant Recollections of a Dilettante*, 2 vols., London, 1838–53.

Gatens, William J., *Victorian Cathedral Music in Theory and Practice*, Cambridge, 1986.

George, M. Dorothy, *London Life in the Eighteenth Century*, New York, 1965.

Gilboy, Elizabeth, *Wages in Eighteenth-Century England*, Cambridge, 1934.

Girdham, Jane, *English Opera in Late Eighteenth-Century London: Stephen Storace at Drury Lane*, Oxford, 1997.

Goodman, Dena, "Public Sphere and Private Life: Toward a Synthesis of Current Historiographical Approaches to the Old Regime," *History and Theory* 31 (1992), 1–20.

Great Britain, Parliament (Commons), 1844 [587], XXVII, I, "Occupation abstract, 1841," pp. 27–51; 1852–1853, LXXXVIII, I, "Population Tables, 1851," pp. 135–41, 381–95; 1863, LIII, I, "Population Tables, 1861," pp. 295–303, 399–412.

Grout, Donald Jay, *A History of Western Music*, New York, 1973 (1960).

Grove, Sir George, *Dictionary of Music and Musicians*, London, 1879 (and subsequent editions).

Hackett, Maria, *Brief Account of Cathedral and Collegiate Schools, with an Abstract of their Statutes and Endowments*, London, 1824.

A Series of Evidences Respecting the Ancient Foundation for the Education of the St. Paul's Choristers from the Twelfth to the Eighteenth Century, London, 1812.

Hadley, David, "British Musical Society in Early Nineteenth-Century England: Studies in the History of a Profession, 1800–1824," Ph.D. dissertation, Harvard University, 1972.

Hall, Catherine, "Gender Divisions and Class Formation in the Birmingham Middle Class, 1780–1850," in her *White, Male and Middle-Class: Explorations in Feminism and History*, New York, 1992.

Hall, Jennifer, "The Re-fashioning of Fashionable Society: Opera-going and Sociability in Britain, 1821–1861," Ph.D. dissertation, Yale University, 1996.

Hallé, Charles, *The Autobiography of Charles Hallé, with Correspondence and Diaries*, New York, 1973 (1896).

Harris's List of Covent Garden Ladies; or, Man of Pleasure's Kalendar for the Year 1793, Edinburgh, 1982 (1793).

Haweis, Rev. H. R., *Music and Morals*, London, 1871.

Hawkins, Sir John, *A General History of the Science and Practice of Music*,

London, 1875 (1776).

Hayes, Deborah, "Some Neglected Women Composers of the Eighteenth Century and their Music," *Current Musicology* 39 (1985), 42–65.

Hayes, William, *Remarks on Mr. Avison's Essay on Musical Expression. In a Letter from a Gentleman in London to his Friend in the Country*, London, 1753.

Head, Matthew, "'If the Pretty Little Hand Won't Stretch': Music for the Fair Sex in Eighteenth-Century Germany," *JAMS* 52 (1999), 203–54.

Hehr, Elizabeth, "How the French Viewed the Differences between French and Italian Singing Styles of the Eighteenth Century," *International Review of the Aesthetics and Sociology of Music* 16 (1985), 73–85.

Herbert, Trevor, "Victorian Brass Bands, Class, Taste, and Space," in Andrew Leyson, David Matless, and George Revill, eds., *The Place of Music*, New York, 1998.

Hitchcock, Tim, *English Sexualities, 1700–1800*, Basingstoke, 1997.

"Redefining Sex in Eighteenth-Century England," *History Workshop Journal* 41 (1996), 73–90.

Hobsbawm, Eric, *Labouring Men: Studies in the History of Labour*, London, 1964.

Hogan, Charles Beecher, *The London Stage, 1776–1800*, London, 1968.

Hogarth, George, *Musical History, Biography and Criticism: Being a General Survey of Music from the Earliest Period to the Present Time*, New York, 1848 (1838).

The Philharmonic Society of London, from its Foundation, 1813, to its Fiftieth Year, 1862, London, 1862.

Holmes, Edward, *A Ramble among the Musicians of Germany, by a Music Professor*, New York, 1969 (1828).

Hueffer, Francis, *Half a Century of Music in England, 1837–1887: Essays towards a History*, London, 1889.

Hullah, John, *A Course of Lectures on the Third or Transition Period of Music History, Delivered at the Royal Institution of Great Britain*, London, 1865.

Music in the Parish Church, London, 1856.

Humphries, C., and W. C. Smith, *Music Publishing in the British Isles*, Oxford, 1970.

Hunt, Leigh, ed., *Musical Evenings, or Selections, Vocal and Instrumental*, with an introduction by David R. Cheney, Columbia, Miss., 1964.

Hutchings, Arthur, *Church Music in the Nineteenth Century*, London, 1967.

Hyde, Derek, *New-Found Voices: Women in Nineteenth-Century English Music*, Ash, 1991.

Irving, Howard, *Ancients and Moderns: William Crotch and the Development of Classical Music*, Aldershot, 1999.

Jackson, William, *Observations on the Present State of Music in London*, London, 1791.

Jebb, John, *The Choral Service of the United Church of England and Ireland, being an Enquiry into the Liturgical System of the Cathedral and Collegiate Foundations of the Anglican Communion*, London, 1843.

Johnson, Calvert, *Organ Music by Women Composers before 1800*, Pullman, Wash., 1993.

Johnson, David, *Music and Society in Lowland Scotland*, London, 1972.

Johnstone, H. Diack, and Roger Fiske, eds., *The Eighteenth Century*, vol. IV of *Music in Britain*, Oxford, 1990.

Kelly, Michael, *Reminiscences*, London, 1975 (1826).

Kidson, Frank, *British Music Publishers, Printers and Engravers from Queen Elizabeth's Reign to George the Fourth's*, London, 1901.

Klein, Lawrence E., "Gender and the Public/Private Distinction in the Eighteenth Century: Some Questions about Evidence and Analytic Procedure," *Eighteenth-Century Studies* 29 (1995), 97–109.

Kuchta, David, "The Making of the Self-Made Man: Class, Clothing, and English Masculinity, 1688–1832," in Victoria de Grazia, *The Sex of Things: Gender and Consumption in Historical Perspective*, Berkeley, 1996.

Lang, Paul Henry, "The Composer," in J. L. Clifford, ed., *Man Versus Society in Eighteenth-Century Britain*, London, 1968.

Laqueur, Thomas, *Making Sex: Body and Gender from the Greeks to Freud*, Cambridge, Mass., 1990.

Larson, M. S., *The Rise of Professionalism: A Sociological Analysis*, Berkeley, 1977.

Leppert, Richard, *Music and Image: Domesticity, Ideology and Socio-Cultural Formation in Eighteenth-Century England*, Cambridge, 1993 (1988).

"Music Teachers of Upper-Class Amateur Musicians in Eighteenth-Century England," in Allan W. Atlas, ed., *Music in the Classic Period: Essays in Honor of Barry S. Brook*, New York, 1985.

The Sight of Sound: Music, Representation, and the History of the Body, Berkeley, 1993.

Lightwood, James T., *Samuel Wesley, Musician: The Story of his Life*, London, 1937.

Lindgren, Lowell, "Handel's London: Italian Musicians and Librettists," in Donald Burrows, ed., *The Cambridge Companion to Handel*, Cambridge, 1997.

Locke, Ralph P., and Cyrilla Barr, eds., *Cultivating Music in America: Women Patrons and Activists since 1860*, Berkeley, 1997.

Lomax, Alan, *Folk Song Style and Culture*, New Brunswick, N.J., 1978.

Longyear, Rey, *Nineteenth-Century Romanticism in Music*, Englewood Cliffs, N.J., 1969.

Lunn, Henry Charles, *Musings of a Musician: A Series of Popular Sketches, Illustrative of Musical Matters and Musical People*, 2nd ed., London, 1846.

Mackerness, E. D., *A Social History of English Music*, London, 1964.

Mapleson, J. H., *The Mapleson Memoirs, 1848–1888*, 2 vols., London, 1888.

Marr, Robert A., *Music for the People: A Retrospect of the Glasgow International Exhibition, 1888, with an Account of the Rise of Choral Societies in Scotland*, Edinburgh and Glasgow, 1888.

Martins, Peter J., "Sound Structures and Musical Structures," in his *Sounds and Society: Themes in the Sociology of Music*, Manchester, 1995.

Marx, Karl, and Friedrich Engels, "The German Ideology," in Robert Tucker, ed., *The Marx–Engels Reader*, New York, 1972.

Massip, Catherine, *La vie des musiciens de Paris au temps de Mazarin (1643–1661): essai d'étude sociale*, Paris, 1976.

Mathias, Peter, "The Social Structure in the Eighteenth Century: A Calculation by Joseph Massie," in his *The Transformation of England: Essays in the Economic and Social History of England in the Eighteenth Century*, New York, 1979.

Matthews, Betty, *The Royal Society of Musicians of Great Britain: List of Members 1738–1984*, London, 1985.

McGeary, Thomas, "Gendering Opera: Italian Opera as the Feminine Other in Britain, 1700–42," *Journal of Musicological Research* 14 (1994), 17–34.

"'Warbling Eunuchs': Opera, Gender, and Sexuality on the London Stage, 1705–1742," *Restoration and Eighteenth-Century Theatre Research* 2nd series 7 (1992), 1–22.

McKendrick, Neil, John Brewer, and J. H. Plumb, *The Birth of a Consumer Society: The Commercialization of Eighteenth-Century England*, Bloomington, Ind., 1982.

McKeon, Michael, "Historicizing Patriarchy: The Emergence of Gender Differences in England, 1660–1760," *Eighteenth-Century Studies* 18 (1995), 295–322.

McLamore, Laura Alyson, "Symphonic Conventions in London's Concert Rooms, circa 1755–1790," Ph.D. dissertation, University of California at Los Angeles, 1991.

McVeigh, Simon, *Concert Life in London from Mozart to Haydn*, Cambridge, 1993.

"Felice Giardini: A Violinist in Late Eighteenth-Century London," *Music and Letters* 64 (1983), 162–72.

"The Professional Concert and Rival Subscription Series in London, 1783–1793," *RMA Research Chronicle* 22 (1989), 1–135.

The Violinist in London's Concert Life, 1750–1784: Felice Giardini and his Contemporaries, New York, 1989.

Mee, John, *The Oldest Music Room in Europe: A Record of Eighteenth-Century Enterprise at Oxford*, London, 1911.

Mellers, Wilfrid, *Music and Society: England and the European Tradition*, London, 1946.

Milhous, Judith, and Robert T. Hume, "Opera Salaries in Eighteenth-Century London," *JAMS* 46 (1993), 26–83.

Miller, Edward, *Thoughts on the Present Performance of Psalmody in the Established Church of England*, London, 1791.

Miller, Richard, *English, French, German, and Italian Techniques of Singing: A Study in National Tonal Preferences and How They Relate to Functional Efficiency*, Metuchen, N.J., 1977.

Millerson, Geoffrey, *The Qualifying Associations: A Study in Professionalization*, London, 1964.

Mitchell, B. R., *Abstract of British Historical Statistics*, Cambridge, 1962.

British Historical Statistics, Cambridge, 1988.

Mount Edgcumbe, Earl of, *Musical Reminiscences, Containing an Account of the Italian Opera in England from 1773*, London, 1834.

Nalbach, Daniel, *The King's Theatre, 1704–1867*, London, 1972.

Neale, R. S., *Class and Ideology in the Nineteenth Century*, London, 1972.

Nettel, Reginald, "The Influence of the Industrial Revolution on English Music," *Proceedings of the Royal Musical Association* 72 (1945–46), 23–40.

Music in the Five Towns, 1840–1914: A Study of the Social Influence of Music in an Industrial District, London, 1944.

The Orchestra in England: A Social History, London, 1956 (1946).

Nichols, John, *Literary Anecdotes of the Eighteenth Century*, London, 1812–16.

Nicoll, Allardyce, *British Drama: An Historical Survey from the Beginnings to the Present Time*, New York, 1978 (1925).

"The Theatre," in G. M. Young, ed., *Early Victorian England, 1830–1865*, London, 1934.

Of the Use and Abuse of Music, Particularly the Music of the Choir, by a Friend of Church-Music, n.p., 1753.

Olleson, Philip, ed., *The Letters of Samuel Wesley: Professional and Social Correspondence, 1797–1837*, Oxford, 2001.

Palmer, Fiona M., *Domenico Dragonetti in England (1794–1846): The Career of a Double Bass Virtuoso*, Oxford, 1997.

Parke, W. T., *Musical Memoirs*, 2 vols., London, 1830.

Perkin, Harold, *The Origins of Modern English Society, 1780–1880*, Toronto, 1972 (1969).

Perry, Gill, and Michael Rossington, eds., *Femininity and Masculinity in Eighteenth-Century Art and Culture*, Manchester, 1994.

Peterson, M. Jeanne, *The Medical Profession in Mid-Victorian London*, Berkeley, 1978.

Petty, Frederick C., *Italian Opera in London, 1760–1800*, Ann Arbor, 1980.

Phillips, Henry, *Musical and Personal Recollections, during Half a Century*, London, 1864.

Pine, Edward, *The Westminster Abbey Singers*, London, 1953.

Place, Francis, *Autobiography*, ed. Mary Thale, Cambridge, 1972.

Porter, Roy, *London: A Social History*, Cambridge, Mass., 1994.

Potter, John, *Observations on the Present State of Music and Musicians*, London, 1762.

Prest, Wilfred, ed., *The Professions in Early Modern England*, London, 1987.

Price, Curtis, Judith Milhous, and Robert D. Hume, *Italian Opera in Late Eighteenth-Century London*, Oxford, 1995.

Pring, Joseph, *Papers, Documents, Law Proceedings &c. &c. Respecting the Maintenance of the Choir at the Cathedral Church of Bangor*, Bangor, 1819.

Pritchard, Brian W., "The Musical Festival and the Choral Society in England in the Eighteenth and Nineteenth Centuries: A Social History," Ph.D. dissertation, University of Birmingham, 1968.

Rainbow, Bernarr, *The Choral Revival in the Anglican Church, 1839–1872*, New York, 1970.

The Land without Music: Musical Education in England, 1800–1860, and its Continental Antecedents, London, 1967.

Raynor, Henry, *Music and Society since 1815*, New York, 1976.

A Social History of Music, from the Middle Ages to Beethoven, New York, 1972.

Reader, W. J., *Professional Men*, London, 1966.

Reeves, John Sims, *Life and Recollections*, London, 1888.

Relfe, J., *Remarks on the Present State of Musical Instruction; with the Prospects of an Improved Plan*, London, 1819.

Robins, Brian, ed., *The John Marsh Journals: The Life and Times of a Gentleman*

Composer (1752–1828), Stuyvesant, New York, 1998.

Robson, Robert, *The Attorney in Eighteenth-Century England*, Cambridge, 1959.

Rodwell, George Herbert Bonaparte, *A Letter to the Musicians of Great Britain*, London, 1833.

Rogers, Clara Kathleen, *Memories of a Musical Career*, Boston, 1919.

Rohr, Deborah, "Women and the Music Profession in Victorian England: The Royal Society of Female Musicians, 1839–1866," *Journal of Musicological Research* 18 (1999), 307–46.

Roper, E. Stanley, "The Chapels Royal," *Proceedings of the Royal Musical Association* 54 (1927–28), 19–33.

Routley, Eric, *The Musical Wesleys*, New York, 1968.

Rowell, George, *The Victorian Theatre, 1792–1914*, Cambridge, 1978.

Royal Academy of Music, *A List of Pupils Received into the Academy since its Foundation in 1822–3*, London, 1838.

The Musical Directory, Register, and Almanack; and Royal Academy of Music Calendar for the Years 1853–1862, London, 1853–62.

Russell, Dave, *Popular Music in England, 1840–1914: A Social History*, Manchester, 1997 (1987).

Sachs, Joel, "The End of the Oratorios," in Edmond Strainchamps and Maria Rika Maniates, eds., *Music and Civilization: Essays in Honor of Paul Henry Lang*, New York, 1984, pp. 168–82.

Kapellmeister Hummel in England and France, Detroit, 1977.

"London: The Professionalization of Music," in Alexander L. Ringer, ed., *The Early Romantic Era: Between Revolutions: 1789 and 1848*, part of the series *Music and Society*, Englewood Cliffs, N.J., 1991, pp. 201–35.

Sadie, Julie Anne, and Rhian Samuel, eds., *The Norton/Grove Dictionary of Women Composers*, New York, 1995.

Sadie, Stanley, ed., *The New Grove Dictionary of Music and Musicians*, 20 vols., London, 1980.

Sainsbury, John, *Dictionary of Musicians*, 2 vols., New York, 1966 (1825).

Scott, Derek B., "The Sexual Politics of Victorian Musical Aesthetics," *Journal of the Royal Musical Association* 119 (1994), 91–114.

The Singing Bourgeois: Songs of the Victorian Drawing Room and Parlour, Milton Keynes, 1989.

Scott, Joan Wallach, *Gender and the Politics of History*, New York, 1988.

Shaw, Watkins, *The Succession of Organists of the Chapel Royal and the Cathedrals of England and Wales from c. 1538*, Oxford, 1991.

Shepherd, John, "Timbre and Gender," in his *Music as Social Text*, Cambridge, 1991.

Sheppard, James Edgar, *Memorials of St. James's Palace,* 2 vols., London, 1894.

The Old Royal Palace of Whitehall, London, 1902.

Sinks of London Laid Open: A Pocket Companion for the Uninitiated, London, 1848.

Smart, Sir George, *Programmes, Books of Words, etc., of the New Musical Fund Concerts in 1794, 1805, 1815–41*, 2 vols., London, 1794–1841.

Smith, William C., *The Italian Opera and Contemporary Ballet in London, 1789–1820*, London, 1955.

Southgate, T. Lea, "Music at the Public Gardens of the Eighteenth Century," *Proceedings of the Royal Musical Association* 38 (1911–12), 141–59.

Stone, George Winchester, *The London Stage, 1747–1776*, London, 1968.

Stone, Lawrence, *The Past and the Present Revisited*, London, 1987.
  "Prosopography," *Daedalus* 100 (1971), 46–79.

Stradling, Robert, and Meirion Hughes, *The English Musical Renaissance 1860–1940: Construction and Deconstruction*, London, 1993.

Straub, Kristina, *Sexual Suspects: Eighteenth-Century Players and Sexual Ideology*, Princeton, 1992.

Temperley, Nicholas, "English Instrumental Music, 1800–1850," Ph.D. dissertation, University of Cambridge, 1959.
  "The English Romantic Opera," *Victorian Studies* 9 (1966), 293–301.
  Jonathan Gray and Church Music in York, 1770–1840, York, 1977.
  The Lost Chord: Essays on Victorian Music, Bloomington, Ind., 1989.
  The Music of the English Parish Church, 2 vols., Cambridge, 1979.
  ed., *The Romantic Age, 1800–1914*, vol. v of *Music in Britain*, London, 1981.

Thackray, Arnold, "Natural Knowledge in Cultural Context: The Manchester Model," *American Historical Review* 79 (1974), 672–709.

Thompson, E. P., *The Making of the English Working Class*, New York, 1963.

Thomson, H. Byerley, *The Choice of a Profession: A Concise Account and Comparative Review of the English Professions*, London, 1857.

Vickery, Amanda, "Golden Age to Separate Spheres? A Review of the Categories and Chronology of English Women's History," *Historical Journal* 36 (1993), 383–414.

Vollmer, Howard M., and Donald L. Mills, eds., *Professionalization*, Englewood Cliffs, N.J., 1966.

Walsh, John, Colin Haydon, and Stephen Taylor, eds., *The Church in England c. 1689–c. 1833: From Toleration to Tractarianism*, Oxford, 1989.

Weber, William, "Artisans in Concert Life in Mid-Nineteenth-Century London and Paris," *Journal of Contemporary History* 13 (1978), 253–67.
  "London: A City of Unrivalled Riches," in Neal Zaslaw, ed., *The Classical Era: From the 1740s to the End of the Eighteenth Century*, part of the series *Man and Music*, London, 1989, pp. 293–302.
  "The Muddle of the Middle Classes," *Nineteenth-Century Music* 3 (1979), 175–85.
  Music and the Middle Class: The Social Structure of Concert Life in London, Paris and Vienna, New York, 1975.
  The Rise of Musical Classics in Eighteenth-Century England: A Study in Canon, Ritual, and Ideology, Oxford, 1992.

Wendeborn, G. F. A., *A View of England*, 2 vols., London, 1791.

Wesley, S. S., *A Few Words on Cathedral Music and the Musical System of the Church, with a Plan of Reform*, London, 1849.
  Reply to the Inquiries of the Cathedral Commissioners, Relative to Improvement in the Music of Divine Worship in Cathedrals, London, 1854.

West, John E., *Cathedral Organists, Past and Present*, London, 1899.

Williams, C. F. Abdy, *A Short Historical Account of the Degrees in Music at Oxford and Cambridge, with a Chronological List of Graduates . . . from the Year 1463,*

London and New York, 1894.

Wilson, Adrian, ed., *Rethinking Social History: English Society 1570–1920 and its Interpretation*, Manchester, 1993.

Woodfill, Walter, *Musicians in English Society from Elizabeth to Charles I*, Princeton, 1953.

Wordsworth, Christopher, *Social Life at the English Universities in the Eighteenth Century*, Cambridge, 1874.

Worgan, Thomas Danvers, *The Musical Reformer*, London, 1829.

Young, Percy, *The Choral Tradition: An Historical and Analytical Survey from the Sixteenth Century to the Present Day*, New York, 1963.

The Concert Tradition, from the Middle Ages to the Twentieth Century, New York, 1969 (1965).

A History of British Music, London, 1967.

Zon, Bennett, ed., *Nineteenth-Century British Music Studies*, Aldershot, 1999.

Index